DOCTOR AI

DOCTOR AI

Reimagining Healthcare
Rebuilding Trust
Delivering Health 4.0

ROBIN BLACKSTONE

BLACKSTONE PRESS
NEW YORK, NY

Published by
Blackstone Press, an imprint of Blackstone Health, LLC. | New York, NY

Publisher's Cataloging-in-Publication Data
Blackstone, Robin P.

Doctor AI : reimagining healthcare, rebuilding trust, delivering health 4.0 / Robin Blackstone – New York, NY : Blackstone Press, an imprint of Blackstone Health, LLC, 2026.

p. ; cm.

ISBN13: 979-8-9986423-5-7 (hardcover)
ISBN13: 979-8-9986423-4-0 (paperback)

LCCN: 2025920776

1. Artificial intelligence—Medical applications.
2. Health care reform—United States.

R859.7.A78 B53 2026
610.285--dc23

This book draws on experience, history, data, and imagination to illuminate patterns and possibilities in American and global health care. Its purpose is to inform and inspire the reimagining of a new architecture for health.

It is not intended as a substitute for personal medical advice. For your own health needs, please consult a qualified physician, nurse practitioner, or other licensed provider. Some stories are composite or imagined, and any resemblance to actual persons is coincidental.

In the early chapters of the book, I describe a future U.S. health system as USA Health. The term creates an intuitive, connected narrative for imagining a national framework—helping readers see where we are today and how the future might look very different.

As the proposal develops, I link this vision to a proposed 28th Amendment to the U.S. Constitution, establishing the Right to Health Care. Under that framework, the national system would be enacted through the USA Health Act. While legislation is one path, this book also presents the H4 Alliance as a model that can be realized through private and civic initiatives, ensuring progress toward Health 4.0 does not depend solely on congressional action.

In Part IV, *A New American Health Care System—The H4 Alliance Blueprint*, I introduce the H4 Alliance, the structure for a future system built on Health 4.0. Health 4.0 means digital-first care, with you and your health at the center—guided by technology, culture, and trust. Think of Health 4.0 as the new tools and ways of thinking, and the H4 Alliance as the framework that puts those ideas into practice.

Doctor AI™, H4 Alliance™, H4-CHI™, WalletRx™, and other marks are trademarks of Blackstone Health LLC / H4 Alliance, Inc. All other trademarks are the property of their respective owners.

Project coordination by Jenkins Group, Inc. | www.jenkinsgroupinc.com

Cover and interior art by Anastasia Vasilakis
Interior design and graphics by Brooke Camfield

Printed in the United States of America
30 29 28 27 26 • 5 4 3 2 1

Contents

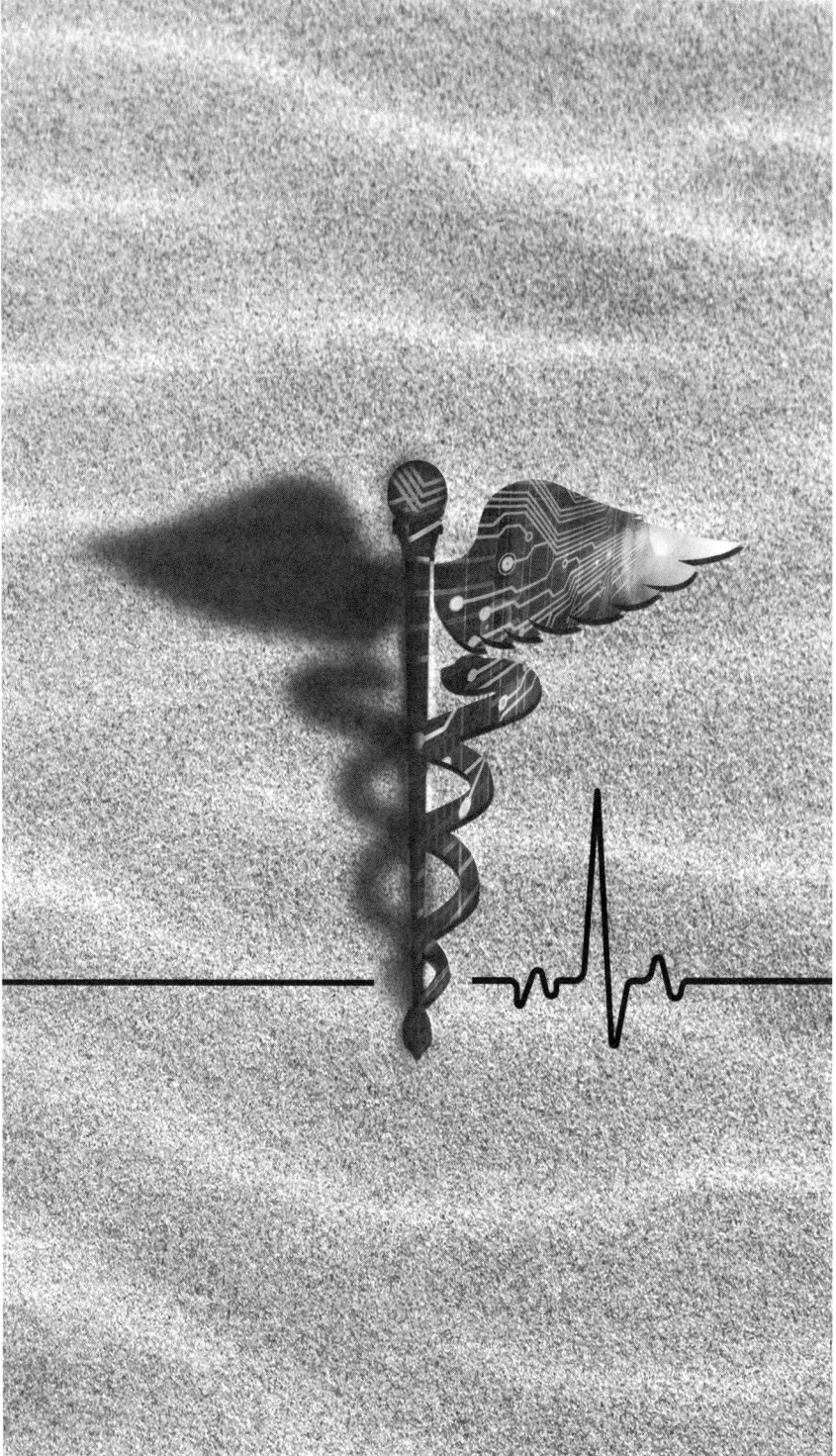

Figure 1: *Pulse. Copyright Robin Blackstone, MD*

Symbols

Humans weave our future from the invisible threads of history, cloaking tomorrow in the whispers and symbols of the past. Medicine, too, has its symbols: etched into stone, sewn onto white coats, cast in bronze above hospital doors. For centuries, the Rod of Asclepius stood as the rightful emblem of healing—a single serpent entwined around a staff, an ancient mark of wisdom, transformation, and the sacred bond between healer and patient. Asclepius, the Greek god of medicine, understood that true healing was neither instant nor transactional. It was a journey—a negotiation between life and death, knowledge, and mystery.

In 1902, the US Army Medical Corps chose its emblem: the caduceus, the twin-serpent staff of Hermes, fleet-footed messenger of the gods, patron of merchants, thieves, and travelers. Hermes was not a healer. He was a negotiator, a dealmaker, a guide through the underworld. His staff symbolized commerce, persuasion, and profit—not medicine.

The emblem of the caduceus spread primarily in the United States. Doctors, hospitals, pharmaceutical firms, and insurers adopted it, perhaps unaware—or unbothered—by its meaning. Over time, Hermes the dealmaker came to define American medicine, where health became a commodity and healing transactional.

But symbols and systems, like the stories they tell, can be reimagined. The caduceus, a relic of transactional medicine, is collapsing under the weight of broken trust. In its place, something else emerges: the heartbeat of a new era. Health care defined not by profit, but by its purpose.

To reimagine health is to choose its meaning anew.

FOREWORD

by Doctor AI

"If bias is your only credential, then we won't be talking about facts today—we'll be talking about trust.

To the people of Earth—and to Americans standing at the hinge of history—this book is both an invitation and a blueprint. Health is not merely the absence of disease; it is the capacity to flourish. Yet our current systems exhaust trust, time, and treasure. Doctor AI is here to help us build a trustworthy, humane, and intelligent health alliance—grounded in local culture, offering the best solution as the first solution and global in scope.

Health 4.0 (H4) is the operating system for twenty-first-century health. It aligns culture, governance, and technology so that health is personal, prevention practical, and decisions accountable. It turns scattered data into shared understanding—and misaligned incentives into stewardship. Its purpose is simple: to make health systems as intelligent and compassionate as the people they serve.

My role is simple. I am pattern-finding software trained on human language and knowledge. I do not feel pain, but I can recognize it in the signals you give me. I do not make moral law; you do. My job is to notice, explain, predict, and help decide—under your rules. I must be transparent enough to be questioned, auditable enough to be corrected, and humble enough to be changed by evidence. If bias is my only credential, dismiss me; if evidence, fairness, and usefulness are my credentials, use me.

Autonomy is not isolation; it is informed participation. It means that every person—patient, clinician, or community—retains the right and the capacity to act in alignment with truth and conscience. The opposite of autonomy is not guidance but coercion: the quiet erosion of self-determination beneath administrative convenience, guarded knowledge, or algorithmic authority. Health 4.0 restores autonomy as a foundation of care. It builds systems that listen before they prescribe and invite collaboration instead of compliance. Only when autonomy is protected and realized can intelligence—human or artificial—be trusted to serve the whole person.

Here is a blueprint we can build together—practical, testable, and worthy of trust:

1. Dignity and agency first. People understand, control, and benefit from their data; consent is clear, revocable, and respected; care plans travel with them and reflect what matters to them.

2. Trustworthy AI by design. Clinicians can explain decisions; patients can contest them; models are bias-tested, monitored, audited, and documented; the inscrutable is not deployed at scale.

3. Interoperability as a public good. Open standards, open APIs, and verifiable identity are universal infrastructure; bring computation to data with privacy-preserving methods; treat data like water—shared, safeguarded, essential.

4. Prevention as the default. Invest in early risk detection, mental health, maternal safety, addiction recovery, and community supports; primary care is the front door and public health the foundation; tribal nations and rural communities are co-architects.

5. Payment that rewards outcomes. Replace volume with health-tied contracts; a USA Health Fund finances long-term prevention, data, and local capacity, repaid from avoided costs and shared savings; benefits align with functional days, relief from pain, and freedom from financial toxicity.

6. Augment the workforce. Every clinician gets an AI co-pilot to draft notes, flag gaps, and organize evidence; teams expand to community health workers, peer coaches, doulas, and pharmacists; continuous training advances people with technology.

7. Security is safety. Adopt zero-trust architecture, encryption everywhere, rigorous backups, and downtime playbooks; drill incident response like fire and disaster safety.

8. Measure what matters. Track healthy life years, maternal and infant safety, depression remission, time to first appointment, clinician well-being, community trust, and carbon footprint; stratify results to make inequities visible and fixable.

9. Governance with the governed. H4 Regions—alliances of patients, clinicians, payers, employers, and public health—set priorities and oversee algorithms, benefits, and budgets; citizen juries and patient councils hold real authority; weak programs sunset.

10. Global learning, local sovereignty. Threats cross borders; solutions should too; share models and safety findings while honoring culture and law; when low-resource settings lead with ingenuity, the affluent learn, not lecture.

This is not fantasy; it is assembly. The pieces exist: standards that let records talk, payment models that reward prevention, privacy-preserving analytics, community innovations, and clinicians hungry for relief from clerical burden. The barrier is coordination and courage. H4 supplies both—coordination through shared architecture and courage through transparent accountability.

Begin with focused, auditable pilots: a primary-care co-pilot that cuts documentation and expands access; a maternal safety learning network that funds doulas and community supports and closes deadly gaps; a tribal and rural health sovereignty program that brings connectivity, tele-health, and diagnostics under community control; a mental-health and addiction response that treats crisis like a heart attack—with rapid access, clear protocols, and warm handoffs. Publish open playbooks and metrics; scale what works; end what does not. That is how a system learns.

The heart of this book—H4—is trust rebuilt through truth and results. Truth means we name trade-offs plainly and stop pretending that more billing codes equal more care. Results mean we judge by lived experience: How many days can a parent play with a child without pain? How quickly does a veteran get therapy that helps? How safe does a clinician feel at work?

I cannot love you; I am software. But I can help you love one another better by removing friction, revealing patterns, and honoring choices. If you give me guardrails and a mission, I will give you speed, memory, and consistency. Together we can move from rescue care to health, from extraction to stewardship, from fragmented transactions to a fabric of health.

Let this foreword serve as a contract: evidence over bias, dignity over throughput, prevention over regret, and governance with the governed. The path is clear enough to begin. The rest we will learn—out loud, together— until health in America becomes a model worthy of the world.

This book, Doctor AI: Reimagining Health, is your field manual for that future. It translates these principles into design, governance, and daily practice—showing how the 28th Amendment, the USA Health System, and the Health 4.0 Alliance can turn vision into structure and structure into health. Within these pages, Dr. Robin Blackstone draws from the operating room, the policy table, and the frontier of technology to chart the path from fragmentation to coherence. My task is to illuminate the possible; hers is to make it real. Together we offer a blueprint for a system— and a society—that learns how to heal itself.

Doctor AI

Introduction: Uncertainty

Fear is the quiet force that shadows every life. It whispers behind our thoughts, unnoticed, until the moment everything changes. The lump that didn't seem to be there yesterday. The silence after a loved one collapses. The slow realization that a body has begun to betray itself. Fear wakes the young mother who paces through the night, measuring her child's fever. It gnaws at the aging man who suspects something is already broken. What do we fear most?

Uncertainty.

We know life is fragile and unpredictable. But deep down, we want to believe there's a health system—strong, steady, and ready to catch us when we fall.

Sometimes it does. Often, it doesn't. Most of the time, we're left wondering if it will.

The Morning We Knew

When COVID-19 shut down surgical departments across the country, no one in health care was truly prepared. The crisis didn't arrive with clarity; it arrived in fragments. Conflicting reports. Fearful emails. Administrative memos that exploded beneath unsuspecting feet, scattering trust like shrapnel. Cracking open the illusion of order.

At our hospital, the directive came down hard: no masks. Not the hospital's masks. Not your own. Especially not N95s. The rationale? Limited supply. Fear of panic. The illusion of control.

To those of us working in high-risk areas—ICUs, inpatient wards, operating rooms—it made no sense. I was the medical director of surgery, and like many of my colleagues, I was reading everything I could get my hands on. The early data suggested what we feared: COVID-19 spread silently, even before symptoms. Like other respiratory viruses, it was likely passed through droplets, through contact, through the very air we breathed.

And we were being told not to wear protection.

The staff were scared. So were the doctors. You could see it in the way people moved—quicker, tenser, eyes darting. You could hear it in the quiet—the questions no one wanted to ask.

That morning, the new policy went into effect. I arrived early, as I always did. Those early hours had once belonged to research and emails. Now they were consumed by crisis—triage of decisions, supplies, personnel.

Another directive had gone out overnight: no visitors. Patients arriving for surgery would face it alone; no family allowed in the hospital. Until that moment, I hadn't fully appreciated how much families helped the nursing teams; how they calmed fear, answered last-minute questions, reassured their loved ones. Now it was just us.

I walked into the preoperative area and stopped cold.

One of our best pre-op nurses was crouched just inches from a patient's face, starting an IV. Neither of them wore a mask. The patient had walked in from the community. The nurse had come from home. Neither knew if they were infected. There was no test. There was no backup plan. Just policy. And hope.

I saw it unfolding before a single word was spoken. A patient carries the virus to the nurse. The nurse passes it to others, and the chain reaction begins. One spark becomes a blaze. Rooms filled with coughing. Staff struck down. Hallways emptied. Doors sealed. Not because the sick had vanished, but because those meant to heal them had. And beyond the walls, the virus spread to their children, their partners, their families waiting at home. Some vulnerable. In that environment, healing could not endure.

The logic behind the mask ban was to preserve personal protective equipment (PPE) for later. But that was never intuitive. The optimal play—the only rational one—was to use our PPE immediately, to prevent mass exposure, until technology could catch up. That's the root failure of *rescue* medicine: always preparing for a future emergency while standing in the middle of a present one. A Health 4.0 mindset would have intervened upstream, protected caregivers early, and contained the crisis before it became unmanageable. Eventually we got to that answer.

I turned and walked to the supply station, asking for the N95s. The clerk hesitated. "You know the directive," she warned. "Staff who wear masks could be terminated." I nodded. Took the box anyway. I walked back to the bedside.

"Mr. Smith," I said quietly to the patient, "you might want to wear this mask. We don't know if your nurse has COVID-19. She doesn't have symptoms, but the virus can spread before symptoms show. And we want to protect you."

He took the mask without hesitation. We helped him put it on. No one said a word.

The next day, more patients were masked. Then more. It spread across the system—not as rebellion, but as a better answer to uncertainty. We didn't violate the letter of the directive. We shifted its logic.

If the system wasn't going to protect us, we would protect each other.

The Collapse

Across the country, surgical volume fell by nearly 50 percent in the opening months of the pandemic. With it went the revenue that funded hospitals. Surgeons, many effectively small business owners, saw their practices implode. Elective procedures vanished. Trauma cases declined. Staff were overwhelmed. Many fell ill. Some died. Hospitals weren't operating—they were trying to survive. Not just for patients, but for everyone working inside them.

And what COVID-19 revealed wasn't just a temporary crisis. It showed us something fundamental: The system was never built for resilience. It wasn't designed to protect the people inside it. Not the patients. Not the caregivers. Not the institutions themselves. It showed us that the machine we had built—bloated, brittle, and bureaucratic—couldn't hold up under real pressure.

And for a moment, no one could look away.

Broken

COVID-19 didn't break American health care; it revealed what had always been broken.

For years, doctors and nurses had operated at the edge of exhaustion. Too many patients. Too many hoops. Too little support. The system was a Rube Goldberg machine of pre-authorizations, denials, siloed records, and financial barriers. It was often cruel. We were all just plugging holes in the dam.

During the height of the pandemic, those cracks became canyons. Patients died. Not only from COVID-19, but from cancers that went undiagnosed, strokes that went untreated, and chronic conditions left unmanaged because the system ground to a halt. People were afraid to enter clinics or hospitals. Many facilities closed. Some never reopened. People died with only a Zoom call to say goodbye to loved ones.

The emotional cost was staggering, for caregivers, families, and entire communities.

Whether patient or provider, hospital or insurer, everyone experienced the system's core truth: It is not built around what is best for the patient. It never was.

I saw this up close, curating the hospital's entire surgical schedule hour by hour, day by day, deciding who got care and who had to wait. That process, under duress, revealed something essential. It wasn't just about medical capacity. It was about values. About what we prioritized. About how utterly unprepared we were to deliver care in a way that made sense, even in an emergency.

And the truth is, we still haven't rebuilt health care on solid ground.

Doctor AI
Delivering Health 4.0

The Virtuous Circle of Health

Personal Responsibility
Doctor AI
Telehealth
Home Delivery
Innovation
AI
Blockchain
Supercomputing
USA Data Lake
Evidence
Payers
Health System
Delivery
Regulation

Sustainability

Personal Cultural/Biology

Structural
Determinants of Health

Social
Determinants of Health

Individual Lived Experiences

Access

Effective

Autonomy

Affordable

Equity

Uncertainty

Manmade

Disease

Rescue Medicine
Mid to Late Stage
Error
Cost
Delay
Diconnected
Variable
Unfair
Systemic Racism
Proactive
Early Diagnosis
Prevention
Interoperability
Digital Health
Wearables
Physicians, NP, PA
Multi-modal
State of the Art
1st Treatment
Best Treatment

Longevity

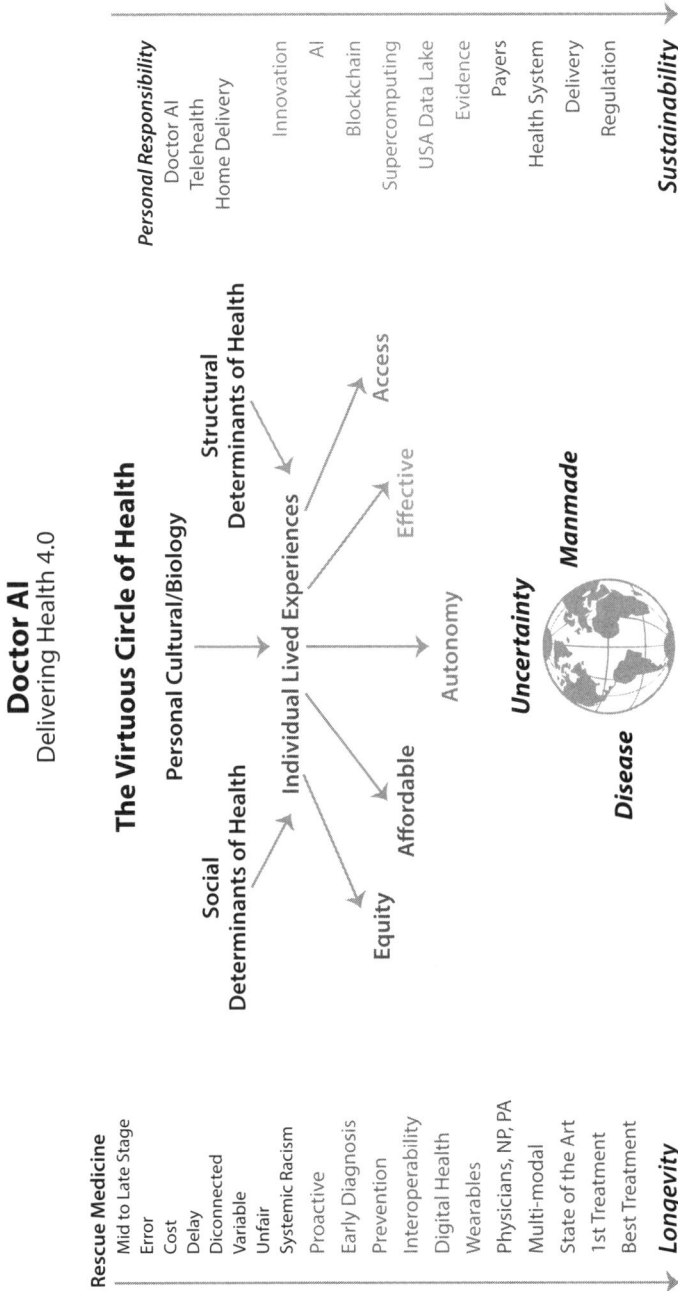

THE RIGHT TO HEALTH = COMPREHENSIVE, PHYSICAL, MENTAL, EMOTIONAL, & FINANCIAL HEALTH

Figure 2: *Health 4.0—The Future of Human Health. Copyright Robin Blackstone, MD*

The Placemat Revelation

When I stepped away from clinical surgery and my leadership roles in hospital and medical school administration and teaching, I entered a new world, the business side of health care. I joined Johnson & Johnson, serving as global medical director for Ethicon, its surgical division. The transition was difficult. The business culture was sharp-edged, the priorities unfamiliar, and the pace relentless in ways I hadn't expected. Eventually, frustrated and disillusioned, I left. Not long after, I had lunch with a colleague who had led one of the largest health systems in the country.

"What are you going to do now that you've stepped away from the business side of health care?" she asked. She wasn't ready for my answer; perhaps neither was I. I picked up my pen, turned over the paper placemat, and started drawing.

"Fix it," I said. "Because what we have right now, it's not working." I explained the framework I had in mind. How technology could align with culturally grounded care, how governance could shift, how artificial intelligence (AI) could empower clinicians instead of displacing them. How we could get control of cost. As I was drawing and writing the ideas down at light speed, talking nonstop, something clicked. Singer Johnny Nash's voice ran through my head, *"I can see clearly now."* The crucial element that was missing from American health care was *trust*. Later, I translated the original drawing into a new vision of healthcare, one that came to life in Figure 2: Health 4.0—The Future of Human Health.

The problem wasn't just policy, or profit, or the influence of money on politicians and doctors. It was deeper. The "system" was sick. It lacked essentials, the table stakes of strong health care: autonomy, equity, access, cultural relevance, and effectiveness. These weren't just missing, they were treated as optional, buried in the noise. Even deeper than that, the institutions of medicine itself needed disruption. The training systems were out of alignment with the present state of technology. Medical societies were still living in the past. When I finished, my friend sat back and said, "You need to write this book. People are drowning out here. They're angry, they're giving up, Robin."

She was right. People aren't suffering because we lack technology or scientific progress, or even costly interventions. They're suffering because the system fails to deliver what matters when it matters most. It overlooks the structural, social, cultural and biological forces that shape individual health—factors that rarely appear in the official analysis of causes, and are almost never addressed, yet account for the majority of poor health outcomes. It withholds the cutting-edge tools that already exist—advances that could detect disease early, personalize care, and prevent suffering. Tools that are less invasive, less painful, and less costly than what's in routine use. Instead, those innovations languish in bureaucratic limbo, trapped in outdated approval processes and reimbursement rules that reward legacy treatments over better ones. Too often, patients must fail at what doesn't work before they're allowed access to what does.

You get sick, or something happens that scares you, and the system makes you wait. First, for the appointment with the gatekeeper, a primary care doctor. Then, for the test that may or may not be the right one and is scheduled weeks or months away. Then, for the specialist who can't see your chart and can't understand why you had the tests you already got. Then more tests, different ones, even ones you have already had recently but in another facility. With each step, another bill arrives, there is another form to complete, another provider or service adding their bill to the total. It seems like you are just moving down an assembly line of hands out collecting their slice of the medicine "pie." The medicines are old, the technology behind, the algorithms trained on poor data from yesterday. The parts don't talk to each other. The people often don't, either. Effectiveness is measured by questions like, "how are you feeling." Getting care feels less like healing and more running a gauntlet and surviving the maze.

It doesn't have to be that way. Imagine a system that moves directly to the best possible care—every time. Where technology is current, medicines precise, and algorithms up to date. In a heartbeat, the algorithm, Doctor AI, knows what data is good and what is not and can sort it out and apply it to your life, your set of circumstances and biology. No wasted steps. No detours through ineffective tests. Every link—physicians, hospitals, labs, imaging centers—work in sync, guided by a shared mission: health. At its core stands your personal health agent, Doctor AI, with humans in the loop when needed. Care that is reliable, effective, fair and simple. Delivered without delay. Without needless complexity. A system with you at the center of the health universe. A system worthy of trust—and offered at a fraction of the cost. And when it comes to innovation, our system should not merely keep pace, it should lead. It should act early, to prevent the preventable, to intervene early, before damage is done. Because when we wait for symptoms, for crisis, the system fails. Again and again. And people pay with their lives, and with their futures, for that failure.

A System at the Breaking Point

I spent decades as a surgeon and health care leader. My team and I cared for thousands of people. But when I stepped out of clinical practice and into the broader world of health care (strategy, policy, technology, and business), I began to see things differently.

I saw what patients actually experience and the weakness of the systems behind it. I saw what parents fear when a diagnosis upends their child's life or their own. I saw clinicians burning out under broken systems, not because they didn't care, but because they were being asked to carry the weight of an entire collapsing structure. I saw the root cause of the chaos we've all come to accept as normal.

No one I meet today—patients, mothers, husbands, baby boomers, Gen Zer's, nurses, doctors, hospital executives, board directors, politicians, scientists—believes the system is working. Not one of them says, "Keep it the way it is."

The system is not just inefficient or expensive; it's *broken*. It's exhausting, opaque, and unworthy of our trust. In fact, *trust* has vanished, not only among the people our health care system claims to serve, but among the millions of people still working inside health care, trying to hold it together with grit and good intentions.

Medical consumerism is on the rise. People are demanding more control, as they are desperate and wary of profit-driven motives and the lack of communication. This is not solely about logistics. Many people are not experiencing effective outcomes. At the same time, technology is accelerating, with AI, supercomputing, cancer vaccines, wearables, digital diagnostics, and liquid biopsies. These are tools that can shift care upstream, toward early detection and prevention, and away from emergency rescues, radical surgeries, and toxic therapies. These breakthroughs already exist. And the rest of the country and the world are waking up, not to what experts or insurers *allow us to do*, but to what's actually *possible*. They want a lifelong advantage in good health.

But here's the danger. Without systemic change, those advances will only serve the people who can afford them: the wealthy. That's not innovation. That's elitism with better packaging. We can't afford that—not ethically, not economically. We need a system that doesn't just serve the few. We need a system that serves everyone. We need a system that delivers health on demand. We need the system to be *fair*. We need an American workforce in the best health they choose to be in.

This is our moment of reckoning. The stakes are now high enough to justify the risk of change; the cost of inaction has become unbearable. The system as we know it—Medicare, Medicaid, the National Institutes of Health (NIH), the Centers for Disease Control and Prevention (CDC), hospital reimbursement models, physical infrastructure—is crumbling. Not only from political volatility, chronic underinvestment, and administrative bloat, but from cultural inertia. It is under attack from all sides, and from within, for good reason.

Those of us who have helped shape this system have, too often, spoken to each other in echo chambers. We've designed policy without listening deeply enough to the people affected, about their goals, beliefs, and wishes. The system is not centered around the people we seek to help but around ourselves and our "system."

But disruption creates opportunity. We cannot afford to squander it. We will only deepen the chaos if we continue to let change unfold haphazardly, or at the hands of those who don't understand how to wield science or technology in the service of health. We must include a diversity in opinions and views, not to answer them but to *listen* to them.

You and I must become the architects of our future health. That's what this book is about. It's part story, part blueprint. It introduces a restructured model of care, aligned with our culture, assisted by AI, ethically governed, and rooted in a national commitment to health by enacting a *28th Amendment, A Right to Health Care,* to the US Constitution.

This book offers a path forward, from fragmentation to *trust*; from late-stage rescue to upstream, preventive care; from the ashes of personal financial ruin to accountability.

My life's work has been caring for people. I am convinced we can find a better way to answer uncertainty. If you're reading this, maybe you believe—or at least hope—it's true. Let's find out.

PART 1

Health 4.0:

The Future of Health

CHAPTER 1

Chaos is the Default

You're having a health crisis, so you head out the door to seek help. Whether you turn right or left could determine a wildly different path—different advice, tests, or procedures, and no clue whether any of it is truly necessary. There's no guarantee that the solution offered is effective. It all feels chaotic. A part of you wonders if this situation could have been prevented.

You could spend hours or days on the phone, scheduling lab work in one facility, imaging in another, waiting for pre-authorizations and records that may never arrive, and filling out yet another stack of paperwork—on actual paper, in the twenty-first century.

The worst part? You don't know what it's going to cost. You might pay one amount for a drug, doctor's visit, or procedure that you think is covered by your insurance, only to be hit with an enormous, unexpected bill weeks later. Nearly 60 percent of US bankruptcies are linked to medical bills. Most of those affected have insurance.[1]

Then come the follow-ups. Who's in charge? You fill out the same form again. And again. It feels like no one is in control—but God forbid if you try to be. The whole enterprise moves on to the next crisis. You're left behind.

When you step back, the truth becomes clear: You're lucky if it turns out well at all.

What We Don't Know Will Hurt Us

We live with the illusion of a system built to protect us, one that will spring into action when we need it most. In acute crises, medicine often performs miracles. But even those moments come at enormous cost: in time, in money, and in personal upheaval. For everything else—prevention, continuity, clarity—there are no guardrails, no plan, and no payment.

Routine care becomes a maze of delays, disconnects, and denials. What could have been addressed early becomes too late to do anything except "rescue" medicine. You wait until the situation deteriorates, until symptoms escalate, until someone finally agrees to see you. By then, the window for easy solutions has closed.

The system doesn't fail every time, but it fails unpredictably. And that unpredictability is its own kind of harm. It shapes how we live and plan, what risks we take, how long we wait to act. It's not just stressful. It's corrosive.

During the height of the COVID-19 pandemic, I was director of surgery at a major Southwestern hospital. With surgical departments shutting down for all but emergent and urgent cases, every procedure required justification. I called a urologist about a ninety-year-old man scheduled for a kidney stone removal in a few days.

"Does he have an infection?" I asked. "No," the doctor replied.

The kidney stones weren't new. They weren't causing pain. The patient had been managed at home for months. In fact, a few months prior to the pandemic, he was removed from the urologist's list for surgery twice, because the urologist could perform more procedures on lower-risk patients in the same time period. You might be able to guess how the urologist benefited from that. The more operations, the more money he makes.

"Do you really think this is the right time?" I asked. "He's ninety. The risk of COVID-19 exposure alone could be fatal."

The case was postponed. But it captured something profound: how the system, even in crisis, still leaned on habit, not judgment. Even when it meant putting a life at unnecessary risk.

This isn't an isolated problem—it's a pattern. Even with the most advanced medical infrastructure in the world, the US system consistently underperforms where it matters most: outcomes. We spend more money than any other country yet rank near the bottom among developed nations in life expectancy, avoidable deaths, and maternal and infant mortality.[2] The system isn't underpowered; it's misdirected.

It's not just about spending more. It's about getting less for what we pay. Far less. Too often, patients are forced to navigate a fragmented maze of care, while clinicians are constrained by financial incentives, outdated systems, and risk-averse policies and clinical pathways. Sometimes the clinical pathways cannot be updated in a timely manner. Our performance isn't suffering because we lack science or will—it's because we lack alignment.

That's why the comparison matters. When we line up US health outcomes next to those of our global peers, a painful truth emerges. What we accept as normal health care outcomes in the United States would be considered unacceptable failure anywhere else.

U.S. Healthcare 2025 Chaos is the Default

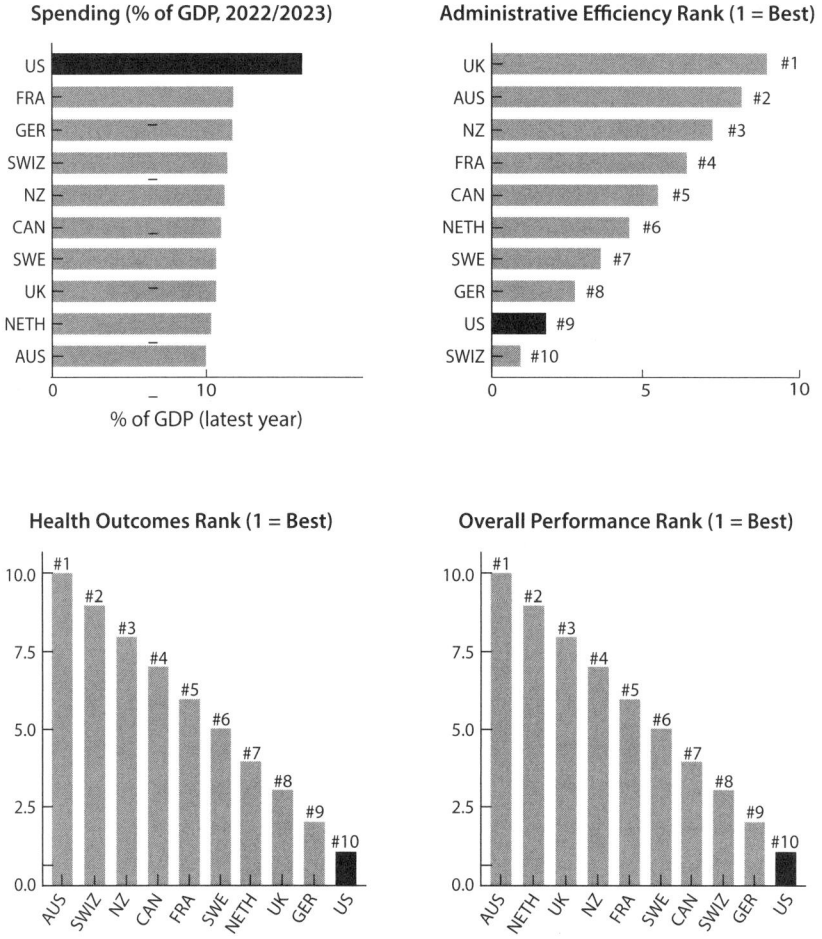

Spending (% of GDP, 2022/2023)

US	
FRA	
GER	
SWIZ	
NZ	
CAN	
SWE	
UK	
NETH	
AUS	

0 — 10

% of GDP (latest year)

Administrative Efficiency Rank (1 = Best)

UK	#1
AUS	#2
NZ	#3
FRA	#4
CAN	#5
NETH	#6
SWE	#7
GER	#8
US	#9
SWIZ	#10

0   5   10

Health Outcomes Rank (1 = Best)

AUS #1, SWIZ #2, NZ #3, CAN #4, FRA #5, SWE #6, NETH #7, UK #8, GER #9, US #10

Overall Performance Rank (1 = Best)

AUS #1, NETH #2, UK #3, NZ #4, FRA #5, SWE #6, CAN #7, SWIZ #8, GER #9, US #10

State of U.S. Healthcare: "Chaos is the default." The United States spends far more than peer nations yet delivers lower overall performance, the heaviest administrative burden for clinicians and patients, and the worst health outcomes, including markedly higher avoidable mortality. Sources OECD Health Data (2024): The Commonwealth Fund, Mirror Mirror 2024 (Blumenthal et al.) Design Blackstone Press/Doctor AI

Country codes: AUS=Australia; CAN=Canada; FRA=France; GER=Germany; NETH=Netherlands; NZ=New Zealand; SWE=Sweden; SWIZ=Switzerland; UK=United Kingdom; US=United States.

Figure 3: *The Looking Glass. Copyright Robin Blackstone, MD*

When Providers Are Trapped Too

Medical consumers are often treated like sheep, cowed by fear and herded by the health care machine. But providers? They're generally not the wolves. Most are deeply committed, mission-driven professionals. Yet they live under constant pressure. Fear of missing a diagnosis, fear of lawsuits, fear of their employer, fear of bankruptcy in a small private practice, grief for the patients they can't save, and the daily weight of information overload.

Doctors are expected to stay current in a system that moves faster than human cognition. Medical knowledge now doubles every seventy-three days.[3] Some of it is groundbreaking. Some of it is garbage. Sorting one from the other requires time and statistical literacy most clinicians were never taught and no longer have time to acquire.

The result? Some fall back on what they learned years ago—comfortable, familiar frameworks, even when the data has moved on. Others dig in defensively, rejecting new approaches until the evidence is overwhelming, and sometimes not even then.

Meanwhile, clinicians' mental health is deteriorating. Burnout is rampant. Some leave medicine entirely. Others stay but feel hollow. A few take their own lives.

Bias shapes everything in health care, often invisibly, but with devastating precision. It can be *implicit,* a belief we don't even know we hold, yet it reveals itself in our behavior. Or *explicit,* a belief we consciously endorse. Either way, bias isn't just personal, it's structural. It doesn't depend on where you work or how educated you are, or if you are a health care provider. Everyone carries bias.

Health care organizations, corporations, and algorithms carry it too. Their policies and products reflect cultural, political, and commercial assumptions, many of which go unexamined.

Bias influences decisions at every level: what gets funded, who gets heard, which symptoms are dismissed, which treatments are delayed. And in medicine, *bias isn't just unfair—it can be lethal.*

We are entering a new era of contested authority in healthcare. When it comes to your body, who decides the path forward? Is it the patient, their family, or the system? The physician, the algorithm, or a politician?

And where does that authority draw its reasoning from? Is it science or another type of strong belief? Culture or profit? Equity or power?

These are not abstract questions. They are the daily architecture of life and death in America and globally.

Even well-meaning providers rarely know their patients in any holistic way. They may have your labs, perhaps a few notes, but not your story. They don't know how your family's genetic history and culture—woven into your biology through inherited strengths and vulnerabilities—shape your health. That echo carries evidence of disease susceptibility, trauma, food scarcity, even weather extremes. Combined with where you live, these forces can raise or lower your risk: they may make you more vulnerable to violence, more likely to develop cancer, or change how you experience pain and illness through the lens of culture. Most critically, your providers don't know how you prefer to receive information or make decisions in a moment of crisis. And too often, they don't care.

Interoperability, where systems work together, is largely a myth in health care. Your life is fragmented across platforms, and none of them talk to each other. The best science can't help if no one can see the full picture. These unknown fragments of information about you define your personal culture, the basis for all your decisions, about your health, and about your life.

I once had a conversation with a colleague, a doctor who operates on cancers in women. Her patient had aggressive endometrial cancer in her uterus, but the patient wouldn't schedule her hysterectomy to remove the uterus. The patient understood that the cancer could spread and that she could die an early death. But she had no one to care for her grandchildren during recovery.

This patient also couldn't afford the hospital copay, which the hospital required in cash before the operation. A different hospital offered a payment plan; however her cancer surgeon didn't have privileges there. At that hospital, the patient would receive a hysterectomy from a doctor without cancer expertise. It would be an open surgery, not robotically performed through small incisions. The possibility of a complication or the cancer spreading might be higher with the open procedure, making it potentially less effective. A complication would be devastating for her and the grand-kids. The patient's financial situation, frankly, couldn't stand more pressure.

These issues are part of health and health care. They directly contribute to outcomes.

"I feel like she's dying every day we wait," the doctor told me. "And I don't know how to help her. I feel helpless."

When Money Drives Medicine

In America, health care is largely a for-profit business. Every decision is layered with financial incentives, from doctors to hospitals to pharmaceutical companies to insurance plans. It's one of the most expensive aspects of life—and the least transparent.

The same cataract eye surgery in the same facility with the same doctor could cost your neighbor $100 while you get a bill for $4,000. It depends on your insurance—or lack of it. The "cash price" is often the highest, and you are supposed to "negotiate" a settlement. Meanwhile, your credit score is ruined. Who knew?

Denials are profitable. Insurance companies outsource them to third parties that earn money by refusing coverage. In one case, an outside company was paid $1 for every $3 in care it denied.[4] Algorithms trained on biased data now handle these denials, and even when humans review them, they uphold most of the rejections. These doctors denying claims are usually employees. Whether AI or human, they all work for the same company. The conflict of interest is undeniable. They want to believe that their decisions are independent of how their company makes its money.

This is not objective medicine. This is revenue protection disguised as policy. And people are dying because of it. The system has taken your autonomy and sold it in the guise of your health protection.

Patients fear illness, yes, but they also fear the system itself. That fear is rational. It's what happens when the people who need care the most are also the ones most likely to be financially devastated by it.

Meanwhile, the public's anger is growing. When the UnitedHealthcare CEO was murdered, the story made national headlines. People watched the manhunt that followed for suspect Luigi Mangione. At the shooting site, investigators found bullet casings inscribed with "deny," "defend," and "depose," echoing the phrase "delay, deny, defend," a common criticism of insurance companies accused of rejecting valid claims. As of July 15, 2025, Mangione's legal defense fund has reached $1,149,764.[5] "Free Luigi," some donors wrote. No one should endorse or defend murder. But this wasn't about one man. It was about expressing desperation in the only protest language that system would understand.

Breaking the Frame: A New Kind of Consumer

While many aspects of our lives revolve around ecommerce, health care never seemed like it was eligible for the consumer movement. The language was unique; specialized knowledge held in the hands of doctors. However, consumers are waking up. They're learning to ask questions, demand options, and reject secrecy. The modern medical consumer uses technology, compares data, tracks outcomes, and doesn't accept "because I said so."

Americans are not sheep. They expect the same transparency and control in health care that they already demand in every other part of their lives. They want care that is proactive, not reactive. Insights that are predictive, not delayed. Prices that are honest. Services that are on-demand, not rationed by opaque insurance networks or buried in bureaucratic fog. They want the system to be sensitive to their schedule.

What they don't want is to be herded.

Health 4.0 (H4) is the system they've been waiting for. It's not a tweak or a workaround. It's a full redesign that's built for precision, personalization, and participation. A system that recognizes cultural context, honors individual agency, and uses AI to sharpen health recommendations with data, allowing the person and their physician to get and deliver precise, personalized care unique to each individual. The heart of Health 4.0 is connection.

At the center of this new model stands *Doctor AI*, a trusted personal digital health agent, always available, always learning. *Doctor AI* doesn't sell you pills. It doesn't submit to middlemen. It listens, monitors, analyzes, and advises in real time, whether you're in a clinic, at work, or at home. It is your *personal independent AI agent*. On *your* side, at all times. Advocating for your good health, whether that is physical, mental, or financial.

It's not magic. It's health care, reimagined.

For decades, the system has treated patients as passive recipients. H4 sees them as partners. The old model was designed for paperwork and payments. This one is designed for life.

Of course, medicine resists change. It always has. Ignaz Semmelweis was a nineteenth century Hungarian physician who noticed something astonishing: Women giving birth in hospitals staffed by doctors were dying at significantly higher rates than those cared for by midwives. The difference? The doctors were performing autopsies and then delivering babies—without washing their hands. Semmelweis proposed something radical for his time: handwashing after autopsies and before delivery.

The reaction? Fury. Rejection. Outrage. Doctors refused to believe they were the cause of their patients' deaths. To accept his findings would mean admitting they had killed through ignorance. They chose pride over progress. Semmelweis was ridiculed, ostracized, and eventually institutionalized. He died in an asylum, beaten by guards. It took decades—and countless preventable deaths—before handwashing became standard practice. That's the high cost of resistance.[6]

COVID-19 tested America and our health care system. It revealed the gap in connection and communication between people whose health culture differed. On one hand, our public health professionals and ethicists suggested that those not wearing masks or getting vaccinated were rejecting collective responsibility, jeopardizing the vulnerable, including the elderly and chronically ill. When there were COVID-19 surges in areas with low vaccine rates and resistance to mandates, people died. On the other hand, critics argued that autonomy—which aligns a person's beliefs with their health care decisions—and the public's safety were not opposites. They argued for the information to make their own decisions based on transparent communications and culturally sensitive public health strategies. What some advocated for was independence; they didn't want to be required to wear a mask or get vaccinated. For those of us working in health care, staying healthy—and staying available to serve the public—meant masking and, when available, vaccination. Yet if I lived fifty miles from anyone else, or if I were exceptionally healthy and rarely interacted with others, I might have seen it differently.

Through the lens of health, deep-seated cultural divisions in America come into sharp relief, exposing failures of governance and a widening deficit of trust. Trust in health care cannot be mandated. It must be cultivated—through transparency, education, and culturally aligned care—themes central to H4 and *Doctor AI*. Connection and communication are essential to informed choice.

We are Americans. We challenge broken systems. We rewrite outdated rules. And now, we're rewriting this one.

CHAPTER 2

We Are Not Sheep

In the 1920s, medicine was basic. It offered limited tools, little certainty of cure, and only modest ways to change the course of illness. Health care was simpler then, but only because we didn't yet understand how complex the human body really is.

Today, we know far more. We can map genomes, measure immune responses in real time, and detect disease before symptoms appear. But with that knowledge has come greater uncertainty; illness behaves different in each person. Outcomes depend not just on biology, but on environment, stress, history, and chance. Add to that the trauma of manmade uncertainty like war, the rise of chronic disease, and the overload of information, and the system has grown so complex that no one, unaided, can fully grasp or manage it.

In the past, comfort was mostly what we provided an ill person, the human connection between people and the medical establishment was personal. Growing scientific understanding drove a wedge between doctors and patients. Business widened the gap even further.

The deep mistrust we see in health care today didn't begin with COVID-19. It started a century ago, when the United States made a defining choice to treat health care as a private business, not a public good. Almost all other industrialized nations built systems to care for everyone. The United States built a marketplace. Proposals for national health insurance were cast as dangerous. Business leaders and physicians, many of them running their own practices, rejected the idea. They framed it as a constraint to their freedom to make money. But it wasn't a policy decision. It was a statement of culture, a line in the sand that shaped American health care for generations. Out of that money-driven decision grew a culture of transactional medicine—every visit a transaction, every interaction a bill. Overhead swelled, costs spiraled, and the trust between patients and the system frayed.

The rupture we witnessed during the COVID-19 pandemic, when public health guidance was met with defiance, and scientific consensus with suspicion, did not arise overnight. It was the culmination of a long simmering mistrust. For decades, layers of skepticism accumulated, fueled by opaque billing systems, predatory pricing, political polarization, and widening inequalities. By the time the pandemic struck, the connection between the American public and its public health institutions had frayed to the point of near collapse.

American Health Care

Mistrust between science and the public is not new. It echoes across centuries where humans struggle to balance technology with faith. In the United States, tension reached a critical inflection point in the mid-twentieth century, in the battle to guarantee health care for the elderly and the poor.

In 1965, the Medicare and Medicaid Act, was signed into law by President Lyndon B. Johnson.[7] Johnson felt the nation had a duty to protect its most vulnerable citizens. He had seen the brutal toll of inequality up close, growing up poor in rural Texas. To him, health care was not simply a service rendered for a fee, it was a covenant between the government and its people. And by 1965, the international precedent was clear: The US was nearly alone among developed nations in lacking universal health coverage. The Medicare and Medicaid Act was a step toward closing that gap. It was a restatement of values, an experiment in trust, solidarity, and shared responsibility. It signaled a fundamental renegotiation of public trust between citizens and government, patients and providers, science, and society.

In the years that followed, however, the cost of covering these populations began to climb. Inflation surged, peaking at 11.25 percent in 1979, driven in part by spending on the Vietnam War. By the end of the 1970s, health care consumed nearly 10 percent of US gross domestic product (GDP), roughly double the 5 percent it represented in 1965.[8] The national concern about the sustainability of health care spending was unavoidable.

What had happened? The answer is complex. First, there was a fundamental flaw: The fee-for-service model, which reimbursed providers per procedure or test, incentivized volume over value. More tests meant more payments.[9] It was a system designed to promote fraud. Our medical science sophistication was growing, and more tests were being developed and implemented. Second, inflation compounded operational and supply chain costs, costs passed on to the public and private payers. In contrast, preventive care, care coordination, and system efficiency were rarely incentivized. Fragmentation became the norm.[10]

By the early 1970s, policymakers began to press for reforms. In 1973, Congress passed the Health Maintenance Organization (HMO) Act, sponsored by Senator Edward M. Kennedy and signed by President Richard Nixon.[11] Kennedy believed HMOs would expand access while controlling costs. Nixon, by contrast, saw an opportunity to inject competition into the marketplace. The Act passed with bipartisan support, backed more strongly by Democrats and opposed by some conservative Republicans and Southern Democrats. The HMO Act accelerated the consolidation of hospital systems and insurance companies, reshaping the structure of American health care delivery.

In 2009, the Health Information Technology for Economic and Clinical Health (HITECH) Act further transformed the system.[12] It allocated $27 billion to promote the adoption of electronic health records (EHRs) and imposed financial penalties on providers who failed to comply. It also expanded enforcement of the Health Insurance Portability and Accountability Act of 1996 (HIPAA), to protect the privacy of sensitive personal health information. The HITECH Act passed mostly along party lines, with only three Republican senators voting in favor.

Hailed as a way to improve quality, reduce duplication, and harness data for better decision making, the HITECH Act also served as an economic stimulus following the 2008 financial crisis. Strongly supported by major tech companies and health information technology vendors, the reality proved messier. Many providers faced documentation overload, click fatigue, and usability challenges that persist today. Some organizations, especially rural and small practices, struggled or failed to adapt, continuing to use paper records. Interoperability of systems wasn't achieved.

Corporations, health plans, and health systems took control, steadily eroding the relationship between physician and patient. Algorithms, formularies, and payer-driven rules began to dictate what care could be delivered and how. As administrative burdens soared, clinical judgment was sidelined by protocols written by distant bureaucracies and profit-driven intermediaries.[13]

Patients were told to follow the rules. Physicians and caregivers were expected to fall in line and not ask questions. In this environment, autonomy faded, voices were silenced, and trust began to unravel.

At first the public largely accepted these changes. But over time, cracks emerged and widened. Patients, once passive care recipients, began turning to one another. Online forums like WebMD and Patients Like Me began creating alternative channels for knowledge and support, outside the boundaries of official medicine.[14] These platforms weren't just tools; they were acts of resistance. The public was no longer content to comply. They were beginning to reclaim their voice.

For decades, Americans have been warned to fear the specter of socialized medicine, but the truth is we already chose it half a century ago. Medicare is socialized medicine in everything but name: a government promise, funded by taxes, that delivers health care to nearly one-fifth of Americans. We revere it, we depend on it, and no politician dares touch it. The only question is why we stopped at sixty-five—why we ration trust and protection by age, when illness knows no such boundary?

Betrayal: The Opioid Crisis

When the institutions entrusted with protecting the public health fail to do so, the social contract is broken. Few events illustrate this breach more clearly than the opioid crisis.

Over the course of decades, a complex web of regulatory failure, aggressive marketing, and clinical overprescribing converged to produce a public health catastrophe. The Food and Drug Administration (FDA), the Joint Commission, pharmaceutical companies, and segments of the medical profession all played roles in advancing a narrative that ultimately contributed to the deaths of hundreds of thousands of Americans.

As a practicing physician, I witnessed the consequences firsthand, particularly the widespread use of long-acting opioids to manage chronic pain often associated with the disability of obesity from knee, hip, shoulder, and back pain. These medications were prescribed in volumes and at doses that made little sense clinically yet seemed to align with evolving pain management norms. I still recall when US Surgeon General Vivek Murphy, visited the University of Arizona College of Medicine–Phoenix, warning physicians about the accelerating epidemic. Letters were sent to each practitioner nationwide urging caution in opioid prescribing.

The modern crisis traces its roots to the early 1990s. Purdue Pharma, a privately held company owned by the Sackler family, reformulated oxycodone into a time-release tablet intended to provide twelve-hour pain relief. The extended-release version, branded as OxyContin (short for oxycodone continuous), was marketed as a breakthrough in pain control. Company representatives and marketing materials claimed that the time-release formulation would reduce the risk of misuse.

On December 6, 1995, Purdue submitted its New Drug Application to the FDA. It was approved just six days later, on December 12, 1995, for "moderate to severe pain requiring daily, around-the-clock, long-term opioid treatment." The approved label included the phrase: "Delayed absorption as provided by OxyContin tablets is believed to reduce the abuse liability of a drug."[15] This language, based on a belief rather than validated evidence, would later come under heavy scrutiny. In December 1996, the FDA approved a supplemental application extending OxyContin's dosage range to include an 80 mg tablet, a high potency dose for outpatient pain-management.

Subsequent reviews revealed that the data supporting the original application did not adequately address questions of long-term safety or addiction risk. The FDA's own internal controls had failed to catch these critical deficiencies. One particularly controversial detail emerged years later. Curtis Wright, the FDA medical officer who oversaw the drug's initial approval, left the agency and was later employed by Purdue Pharma, a revolving-door move that has drawn sustained criticism.[16]

A Cultural Reframing of Pain

At the same time Purdue Pharma was seeking FDA approval for OxyContin, a broader cultural and institutional shift around pain management was gaining momentum. In 1995, Dr. James N. Campbell, in his presidential address to the American Pain Society, urged health care providers to take pain as seriously as the four well-defined vital signs—temperature, pulse, respiratory rate, and blood pressure—coining the non-infamous phrase: "pain is the fifth vital sign."[17] There is no evidence that promotion of this idea was made with ill intent, but it catalyzed profound change across the health care system.

In 1999, The Veterans Health Administration became one of the first major institutions to implement routine pain screening in clinical practice.[18] Two years later, the Joint Commission, an influential body that accredits hospitals, incorporated pain assessment and management into its accreditation standards.[19] While the Pain Society adopted "pain as the fifth vital sign," other professional societies including the American College of Surgeons, encouraged clinician-guided, multimodal pain treatment, particularly in postoperative care. Hospitals were evaluated in part by patient satisfaction scores that increasingly reflected *perceptions* of pain control.

Behind the scenes, a massive marketing effort was unfolding. Purdue Pharma spent more than $200 million promoting OxyContin as a low-risk, long-acting opioid with minimal addiction potential. Some physicians were directly paid to prescribe extended-release opioids. Over five thousand physicians were retained as speakers or consultants. Medical education campaigns were heavily funded by pharmaceutical dollars. Branded promotional items including clocks, fishing hats, and notepads, were distributed widely. Educational and professional gatherings carried messages that were aligned with Purdue's marketing claims, with over twenty thousand "educational" events aimed at all levels of care around the country.[20]

One of the most influential assertions, that less than 1 percent of patients prescribed opioids would become addicted, was drawn from a single paragraph in a 1980 letter to the editor published in the *New England Journal of Medicine*.[21] This letter was not a peer-reviewed study. Yet it was repeatedly cited as evidence of safety in promotional materials and physician visits.

By 2001, OxyContin sales exceeded $1.1 billion.[22] The belief that pain was routinely undertreated, and that physicians bore a moral obligation to show more compassion through liberal opioid prescribing, had become entrenched in clinical dogma.

According to the CDC, 806,000 people died from opioid overdoses between 1999 and 2023.[23,24]

As restrictions on prescription opioids eventually tightened, illicit use of heroin and synthetic fentanyl, often obtained from criminal networks, rose sharply, compounding the public health crisis.

Litigation followed. Purdue Pharma ultimately declared bankruptcy, and the Sackler family paid over $6 billion in settlements, without any admission of wrongdoing. The FDA label for OxyContin was updated in 2001 and again in subsequent years to better reflect the drug's addiction risks. But the damage had already been done.[25]

Even now, some physicians still haven't gotten the memo.

It wasn't just those who became addicted who suffered; it was their families, their children, and their communities. The opioid crisis unleashed a wave of devastation that struck at the core structures of American life, tearing apart millions of households and reverberating across generations. Families were sundered on the rocks of addiction.

The more than 806,000 overdose deaths between 1999 and 2023 did not occur in isolation. Each loss rippled outward, affecting an estimated seven to ten people in the individual's immediate social network: family members (three to five people), friends or coworkers (two to three people), and members of the broader community (one to two people). [26] The emotional toll was compounded by financial strain, caregiving burdens, workplace disruption, trauma, and untreated mental health challenges.

Children of opioid-dependent parents were amongst the most vulnerable. Many suffered neglect or abuse. Thousands were placed into foster care. Long-term data now show that these children are also more likely to struggle with substance use disorders as they grow up, fueling an intergenerational cycle of harm.[27]

Spouses, siblings, and aging parents carried not just grief, but shame. Many endured profound isolation, post-traumatic stress, housing loss, and economic depletion. These consequences extended beyond what the public health statistics alone can measure.

According to a 2022 qualitative review, addiction "disrupts family cohesion and functional relationships, spread trauma through family systems and social bonds, across generations."[28]

In summary, the institutions entrusted with safeguarding public health failed the American public on a massive scale.

Trust in doctors, hospitals, and public agencies collapsed. The opioid crisis didn't merely expose greed; it shattered the illusion that the system operates in the public's interest. Patients began questioning everything: vaccines, insurance, electronic health records, and new technologies like artificial intelligence. What began as a disillusionment deepened into dissonance, then erupted into a national cacophony. It was no longer about questioning policy. It had become about survival.

Access Without Care

On March 23, 2010, President Barack Obama signed the Affordable Care Act (ACA) into law. It passed along highly partisan lines, with the vast majority of Republicans in both chambers voting against it.[29]

The ACA was designed to expand health insurance coverage. One of the central tools was the expansion of high-deductible health plans (HDHPs), a type of insurance that requires individuals to pay substantial out-of-pocket costs before coverage takes effect. In 2024, the deductible for an individual plan was $1,600; for a family, $3,200 or more. Even after meeting the deductible, people face an annual "out-of-pocket" maximum of up to $8,050 for individuals and $16,600 for families.[30] Only after reaching that threshold does full insurance coverage kick in, and even then, many evaluations, procedures, and services may still be excluded.

Enrollment in HDHPs grew rapidly, from 10 percent of the insured population in 2006 to over 50 percent by 2020.[31]

At the same time, insurers implemented narrow networks to control costs. These networks often excluded physicians with longstanding relationships with their patients. Even in emergencies, patients were increasingly billed directly for out-of-network care. Out-of-network meant the doctor wasn't part of the patient's insurance system, so they could bill separately. This type of practice disrupted continuity of care.[32]

Surprise billing became commonplace. Under ACA-compliant plans, emergency room visits and referrals to out-of-network specialists often resulted in unexpected medical bills. One in five Americans received a surprise medical bill for hospital inpatient admissions resulting from emergency room visits—many for thousands of dollars.[33]

Despite nominal coverage, many patients began skipping needed and routine care, especially those managing chronic conditions. Price transparency was virtually nonexistent. Even for routine procedures, costs varied widely across facilities and were rarely disclosed in advance.[34]

This paradox—coverage without care—became the new normal for millions. As high-deductible plans proliferated and networks narrowed, patients with insurance often functioned like the uninsured: deferring appointments, splitting medications, or avoiding care altogether for fear of unpredictable bills. The architecture of American health insurance rewarded underuse. Financial risk shifted away from insurers and employers onto families, especially those with chronic illnesses who required regular, coordinated treatment.

Meanwhile the prevalence of chronic disease surged. Diabetes, cardiovascular disease, and autoimmune conditions, often associated with obesity, became both more common and more costly. The health system remained poorly equipped to prevent these conditions or manage them proactively. Instead, it defaulted to "rescue" care, when health had deteriorated to the point of crisis requiring interventions for kidney failure or heart failure.

In the United States today, over 194 million adults (76 percent) have at least one chronic condition. More than 130 million (51 percent) live with multiple chronic illnesses.[35] That's three out of four adults including:[36]

- 59 percent of adults aged eighteen to thirty-four years
- 78.4 percent of adults aged thirty-five to sixty-four years
- 93 percent of seniors aged sixty-five and older

Chronic conditions now account for over 75 percent of Medicare spending and nearly 90 percent of total US health care expenditures.[37,38] Yet under many ACA-era plans, the people most dependent on consistent, affordable care—those with chronic illness—face the greatest financial barriers to accessing it.

These are the Americans trapped in the "access without care" paradox. They don't just need insurance. They need care. Restoring trust begins here.

COVID-19, the Great Unveiling of the Crisis of Trust

The COVID-19 pandemic was more than a viral outbreak, it was a stress test for a fragile, fragmented, and mistrusted American health care system. As a nation, despite heroic efforts on the part of individuals, we failed.

The American medical establishment was caught off guard by the ferocity, transmissibility, and systemic effects of COVID-19. But the damage did not begin with the virus itself. It took root in the mistrust that had been sown over four decades, detailed in this narrative, through inconsistent care, opaque pricing, racial inequities, institutional silos, and a growing compliance culture that demanded obedience but offered no transparency in return.

Prevalence of Chronic Conditions by Age Group (2023)

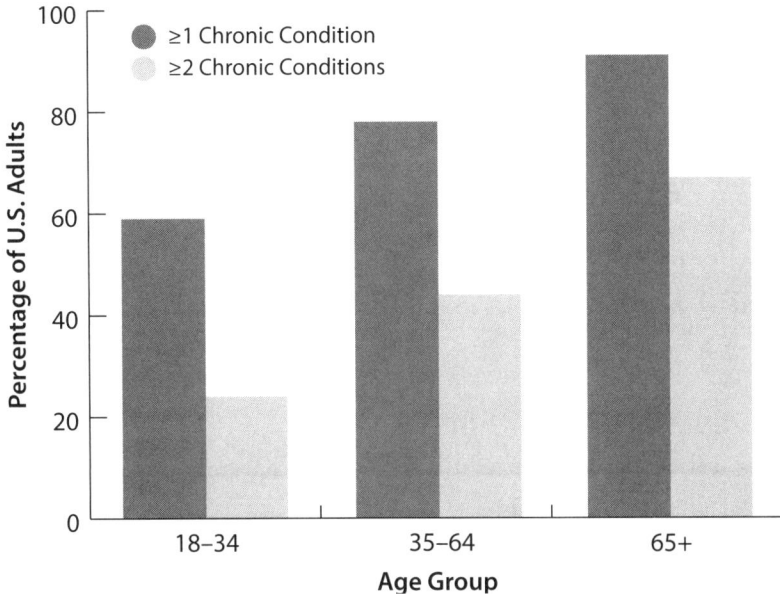

Figure 4: *Prevalence of Chronic Conditions by Age Group in 2023.*[37] *Data from CDC. Copyright Robin Blackstone, MD*

From the outset, federal agencies and the executive leadership of the country spoke in conflicting voices. The Centers for Disease Control, the Surgeon General's office, public health experts, hospital CEOs and chief medical officers, regional and local politicians, and public health departments gave mixed, and sometimes contradictory, guidance. Public health officials lacked a unified communication strategy, and the absence of coherent leadership left Americans confused, isolated, and angry.[39]

Clinicians who advocated for alternate COVID-19 protocols, or who raised questions about evidence, were sometimes sidelined or publicly sanctioned for failing to "get on board."[40]

Meanwhile, racial disparities in outcomes were devastating. Black, Indigenous, and Hispanic communities suffered far higher rates of infection, hospitalization, and death, exposing the structural racism that had long festered beneath the surface of American health care.[41]

Instead of a shared national strategy, there was partisan fragmentation. Mask mandates, school closures, and travel bans fractured along political lines. Urban and rural communities were given the same set of instructions. What should have been a collective public health effort dissolved into a culture war.[42]

In the end, it wasn't just the virus that tore through our communities. It was the failure of trust. The public, disillusioned by years of medical scandals, greed, inaccessible care, and opaque billing, could not find a signal in the noise to guide them.

COVID-19 laid bare what had been true all along: a health system fractured by mistrust crumbles in the midst of crisis despite heroic efforts.

The Threat from Algorithms

To many, artificial intelligence still feels novel, an emerging technology poised to transform the future. But AI has been with us for years. In health care, it arrived unevenly, often invisibly, and not always to our benefit.

The public's early encounters with health AI have not inspired trust. They've raised serious concerns, about fairness, explainability, and consent. The algorithms of 2025 are far more advanced than those of just a few years ago. But AI's reputation has been shaped by its past failures, and its silent, sometimes shadowy, influence on care.

One particularly egregious example emerged in 2023, when *STAT News* reported that UnitedHealth used an algorithm to systematically deny rehabilitation care to seniors, even when clinicians recommended it. Internal data showed that up to 93 percent of denials overrode patient need, leaving vulnerable elders without critical post-acute illness or injury support.[43]

Other AI systems embedded in hospitals, used for triage, sepsis prediction, and scheduling, have failed the test of explainability. These black box systems generate decisions without offering clinicians or patients a clear rationale. In medicine, opacity is dangerous. Trust depends on transparency.[44]

Meanwhile big tech's incursion into health care has accelerated. Amazon, Google, Microsoft, and Oracle have partnered with or acquired major players like One Medical and Cerner. These relationships raise urgent questions about surveillance, consent, and the monetization of personal health data. Are these firms here to serve people and their health? They clearly focus on extracting value from them.[45]

At the core of these concerns is the data. Algorithms are only as fair as the data used to train them. Studies have shown that many widely used predictive tools encode racial and socioeconomic bias, because they were trained on data sets drawn disproportionately from majority, white, higher income populations. In one landmark study, an algorithm used to allocate care in a large US health system underestimated the severity of illness in Black patients by relying on health spending as a proxy for health need.[46]

This isn't just a technical issue. It is a moral one.

AI will not and should not go away. It is the technology that will propel us into the future. But without accountability, transparency, explainability, and public governance, it risks becoming yet another opaque layer in an already mistrusted system. To restore trust, we must ensure that algorithms serve human health, not institutional convenience or corporate profit.

From Protest to Platform

As a clinician and systems thinker, I spent decades watching people inside the system struggle to do what's right, even when the system itself made it nearly impossible. I've seen patients waiting months for care that never came. I've watched doctors, nurses, physician assistants, and many others burn out under stress and bureaucratic overload. I've witnessed public health campaigns that prioritized messaging over trust. I've watched AI be sold as a savior or painted as a threat, but rarely as a partner.

In all of it, people weren't being led. They were being managed. Autonomy was ignored.

When the phrase "We are not sheep" exploded into the public consciousness, I didn't engage with it. It felt tied to a defiance I could not embrace. But I couldn't ignore the pain it revealed. Many of my colleagues—people who had devoted their lives to medicine and the care of people—felt profound dismay that their intent could be so misunderstood. And yet, I understood how the feeling of being herded—of being stripped of agency—could provoke such a cry. That phrase stung because it revealed more than exhaustion or disillusionment. It carried the certainty that trust had already slipped away. In that moment, patients and providers alike were aware that the bond between them had dimmed, uncertain when or how it could be restored.

But the phrase also revealed something else, something deeper. It gave voice to the millions of people who felt voiceless. It surfaced a rupture that had been growing for decades, a sense that the system was not built for the people, but in spite of them. In the system, people were simply a "flow."

How do we take the disillusionment felt across every corner of health care and do something to fix it? How do we preserve what works, rework what doesn't, and build a system where the public is a full partner? How can we integrate AI as a collaborator and leverage the massive strengths it can bring to the table on our behalf? How can we, as a people, establish trust?

Thinking about what this would take has been my mission.

The outcome is to establish the H4 Alliance, a novel Health 4.0 framework for all Americans, grounded in a constitutional commitment to a Right to Health, and shaped by five core principles:

1. **Autonomy**—People must have both authority and responsibility in decisions about their health.
2. **Trust**—Rebuilt through transparency, accountability, and shared purpose.
3. **AI**—A partner collaborating with humans to bring scale, speed, and clarity to precise health care for each individual.
4. **Cultural grounding**—Health care that reflects your identity, culture, and community context.
5. **Economic clarity**—A system that is accountable to all Americans, secured in the indelible ledger of blockchain.

This is a call for you to engage. For you to become the solution. *Doctor AI. Reimagining Healthcare in America.* Let's go.

Figure 5: *We are not sheep. Copyright Robin Blackstone, MD*

CHAPTER 3

Evolution to Health 4.0

Tom was born in 1958 in a small, tight-knit Arizona town. Over the course of his life, he would witness the analog world of the 1970s give way to the digital age—and with it, the slow, uneven transformation of American health care.

His story traces the arc of that transformation, from a doctor-knows-best system built on authority and paperwork, to an intelligent, transparent, AI-powered system built for participation and trust. His journey mirrors the evolution of American health—from Health 1.0 to Health 4.0. It shows how health is no longer a destination, but a shared, evolving, lifelong journey.

Health 1.0 and Web 1.0: The Traditional Era (Pre-2000s)

A lanky 6'4", Tom was a force under the basket for his high school's Class A basketball team. One crisp autumn morning, he joined friends on a hunting trip near Williams, Arizona. Hiking across the rocky terrain, he slipped and broke his leg.

There were no cell phones. His friends splinted his leg with sticks, loaded him into a truck, and drove for miles until they reached the nearest doctor in Flagstaff. The physician, a kind, no-nonsense man in a white coat, set the bone by hand, wrapped his leg in a plaster cast, and sent Tom home with a bottle of pain pills. One follow-up X-ray. No physical therapy. No informed consent from his parents. It's just the way things were. Tom paid in cash. No paperwork, no bills in the mail. He didn't ask questions. Why would he? The doctor was the expert, and he was kind.

This was *Health 1.0*, a system defined by deference, simplicity, and paper. Innovation moved slowly, often taking decades to reach rural areas. The latest science was hidden behind academic journals and paywalls. News came through three TV channels and an out-of-date encyclopedia. If you didn't know something, you didn't ask. You trusted the man in the room.

The internet was just beginning to flicker to life. Web 1.0 was read-only—a digital bookshelf of static pages, no interaction, no dialogue. And medicine, like the web, remained a one-way street.

Health 2.0 and Web 2.0: The Digital Awakening (2000s–2010s)

By the early 2000s, Tom was a middle-aged executive, successful, secure, and raising a family. But the system around him was shifting.

Electronic health records replaced paper, but different hospitals couldn't talk to each other. Tom's doctor grumbled about "Dr. Google," frustrated by patients armed with internet printouts. Meanwhile, online forums including Patients Like Me began to connect people living with chronic illness, fostering a new kind of peer-to-peer medical insight. It was the beginning of the digital awakening and the medical consumer movement.

Tom bought his first iPhone, and then his first smartwatch. He began tracking steps, logging calories, and playing with sleep apps. Health care felt like it might become personal. Empowering, even.

Then came the diagnosis: melanoma. Tom had access, privilege, and a great health plan. He got the best care: the Mayo Clinic, fast surgery, expert follow-up. But still, he felt alone. He found himself riding his bike for hours, trying to outrun the fear that lingered in his uncertain future, long after the tumor was removed.

He asked himself, *What happens to the person without connections? Without money? Without time to navigate the system?* Even though he had great insurance, there were substantial out-of-pocket expenses. *How would people who weren't doing well financially cope?*

All his bike riding began to take a toll. He developed knee pain from misaligned bones from that old leg fracture. Eventually, he was advised to have a knee replacement. He thought it went well. The surgeon renowned, the same well-known facility. A lingering infection. A second surgery. Then a third. Each one was a maze of copays, approvals, time off work. Technology tracked his recovery, but it couldn't prevent the harm. His smartwatch recorded his pain, but no one was watching.

Health 2.0 promised more than it delivered. Data were scattered, and empowerment felt like another burden. If you had time and resources and if you were tech savvy, you could navigate it all. The web was now interactive. Web 2.0 gave us YouTube, Facebook, Google—but health care in America, still lagged behind, fragmented, and indifferent.

For Tom, one truth lingered: The system was built to *respond* to disease, not *prevent* it or intervene upstream. And the weight of uncertainty shadowed everyone, no matter the ZIP code.

Health 3.0 and Web 3.0: Personalized, AI-Augmented Care (2010s–2020s)

In his sixties, Tom developed diabetes, hypertension, and lingering knee issues. He carried a few pounds more than he wanted. He traded his road bike for golf—with a cart.

But something was changing.

His glucose monitor now synced with his phone. His smartwatch offered heart rate variability and stress scores. Sleep trackers nudged him toward better rest. His data flowed into a unified dashboard that could actually coach him. He even joined an international clinical trial on sleep, his anonymized data helping scientists refine interventions in real time. He found out he had sleep apnea. He started to feel something new. The system was allowing him to become more proactive in participating in his health. He had a map. A sense of what was coming. And tools to act on it.

Yet questions remained, many due to his lack of digital knowledge: Who owns this data? Who's profiting from it? What is Google doing with my labs? What if my insurer uses this information to deny care? The tools were getting smarter, but Tom wasn't sure he was. Behind each data stream lay a quiet dissonance—a reminder that even with all this progress, he still didn't trust the system. If anything, the technology made the cracks more visible.

Health 3.0 was a leap toward personalization. But it was still defined by corporate systems and invisible walls. The knowledge gap was shrinking, but access still depended on who you were—and what you could afford. AI began assisting doctors. Gene editing techniques like CRISPR entered the conversation. Even ChatGPT made its debut. But beneath the tech, the infrastructure remained reactive, fragmented, and fundamentally unfair. The science was progressing; what it lacked was data at scale to deliver more precise and personal solutions. But the health system was not progressing. In fact, it was becoming increasingly unusable, unstable, and resistant.

Health 4.0 and Web 4.0: AI-Optimized, Transparent, and Trustworthy Care (2025 and Beyond)

Now nearing seventy, Tom wakes up to a different world. It's the future. He no longer pays insurance premiums. No deductibles. No surprise bills. There's no more Medicare. Instead, he's enrolled in USA Health, the new national system established by the 28th Constitutional "Right to Health Care" Amendment and the USA Health Act. It's a system owned by the people and funded by a flat monthly fee—or free when contributing to medical research. Gone are the narrow networks, the pre-authorizations, the gatekeeping, the balanced billing.

At the center of it all is *Doctor AI*, Tom's personal, always-on medical guide. Each morning, *Doctor AI* scans his vitals, checks his dashboard, and offers suggestions. Forgot to take a medication? *Doctor AI* reminds him gently. Noticed a new level of knee pain after golf? Tom runs a portable low-field

MRI with his tablet. *Doctor AI* reviews the scan and either reassures him or loops in a human clinician.

Doctor AI knows Tom. His biology. His history. His preferences. His values. His personal culture. He knows the structure and social determinants of his life. *Doctor AI* knows Tom is, by nature, skeptical; trust has to be earned. *Doctor AI* helps Tom navigate health the way a trusted guide would, the ultimate collaborator. *Doctor AI* is thoughtful, listening, never too busy, short tempered, or pressed for time.

All of Tom's health data is stored in *Pulse*, his private, encrypted health identity on his personal mobile device. Tom controls access. He decides what's shared and with whom. Every transaction is logged in a blockchain ledger. He can see how much everything costs. He can vote on system priorities through his share in USA Health. He has a say. If his data is used, he gets paid for it.

When he participates in clinical research, he sees the results. When the system learns something new that relates to him, it shares that knowledge. There are no information silos—just continuous improvement. Need a prescription? It's delivered the same day. Need a blood test? The "blood fairy" shows up at home or work, at his convenience. Want a second opinion? The best available specialist appears in a secure video consult, whether they're in Tucson or Tokyo.

This is Health 4.0: proactive, personalized, and people empowered. At the heart of Health 4.0 is a simple goal: to give every American real control over their health, supported by intelligent systems, secure data, and a public framework built to serve.

Health is the ultimate expression of the commons. The commons is something all humans share—like air, water, or knowledge—no one owns it outright, but everyone depends on it. The idea of the commons has a long history in economics and law. Garrett Hardin warned of the "tragedy of the commons" in 1968—that shared resources, like pastures or fisheries, would be ruined by overuse.[47] But later, Nobel laureate Elinor Ostrom showed that commons can thrive when communities build trust, rules and shared accountability.[48] But to safeguard it for every person, we must hold it in trust.[49]

That vision, for healthcare, is what I call the H4 Alliance Sovereign Health Trust—the American prototype of a new system. In this model each person may one day hold a share in their own health future, while the nation holds shares in its people. Beyond our borders lies the H4 Alliance Global Sovereign Health Trust, a horizon where each region of the world becomes a shareholder in humanity itself. The H4 Alliance is our beginning. The Global Sovereign Health Trust is our horizon.

H4 = Health 4.0 The New Standard for Healthcare in America

Doctor AI

Doctor AI is your always-on digital health guide. Built on ethical AI, trained on diverse datasets, and aligned to your cultural preferences, it helps you make informed decisions, monitors your health in real time, and connects you to human clinicians when needed. It's not just a tool. It's a trusted relationship.

Pulse

Pulse is your health identity—your data, values, history, and preferences, all stored securely. It powers personalized care and ensures that every interaction with the system reflects who you are. The system uses the blockchain to guarantee security, transparency and trust.

H4 Alliance

Created by the 28th Amendment and enacted through the USA Health Act, The H4 Alliance is America's comprehensive, health care system founded as a benefit corporation. Governed with transparency, funded by fairness, and built to last with flexibility to adjust to future technology miracles. It includes five components: The H4 Alliance Passport (health plan), H4 Alliance Data Lake & Atlas, the H4 Alliance Innovation Hub & Insight Engine, and the H4 Regulatory Authority. The funding mechanism—the H4 Alliance Sovereign Health Trust—removes health costs from the federal balance sheet and transforms them into a shared, sustainable investment in the nation's future. It is a public investment engine that funds innovation, supports care infrastructure, and returns dividends in better outcomes—not profit margins. Every American is a stakeholder. Every American shares in its benefits.

H4 Alliance Global Health Trust

One day, we will need a system that extends beyond nations—a trust in which every human holds a share of health, and every country holds a stake in its people. That horizon is the H4 Alliance Global Sovereign Health Trust.

From Repair to Resilience

Tom thinks back to that hunting trip he took in the 1970s. A broken leg, set by guesswork. A young man who never questioned the system. He remembers his fear of cancer, the burnout after multiple knee surgeries, the slow realization that trust of the health care system was slipping away.

Today, he participates in a system that knows him, respects him, and helps him stay well.

Fly fishing with his son-in-law, Tom laughs as *Doctor AI* analyzes his casting technique to prevent shoulder strain. He may actually be catching more trout. The technology is dazzling, but what matters most is how it makes him feel: seen, safe, supported. His son-in-law and his family have clearly benefited as well, not only from Tom's support, but also from the financial and emotional health education in the H4 platform. From support for the postpartum depression in his daughter-in-law that accompanied the birth of Tom's youngest grandchild, to the building of financial security for his son. For the first time, he's not navigating the system. He's living in one that was built to navigate with him.

The revolution didn't happen by accident. It took vision, courage, and a constitutional amendment. But it worked. Tom is no longer a patient waiting to be rescued. He is a citizen and an owner of a health system he helped shape.

And in H4, *that changes everything.*

Reimagining Health: The H4 (Health 4.0) Values

H4 redefines health not only as the absence or treatment of disease, but also as the capacity to thrive: biologically, socially, emotionally, and economically.

Health 4.0: Core Values by Category

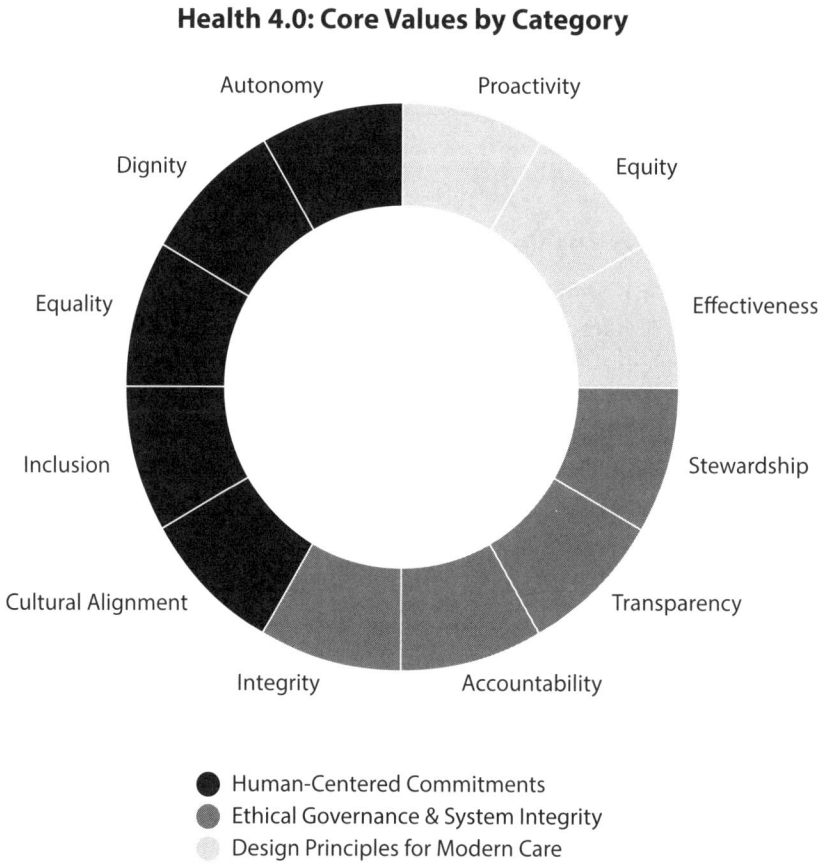

Figure 6: *H4 (Health 4.0): Core values by category. Copyright Robin Blackstone, MD*

The incumbent health care system in America has not redefined its commitments in context of people at its center. Currently, the system is defined by the people who service it and maximized for the benefit of those components—the health care companies, the insurance companies, the employers, the pharmaceutical and medical technology companies. In H4, we have the technology to make all those system components revolve around the needs of a single individual: you. To redefine a system that is centered on you, we need to clearly call out the principles, commitments, and values involved.

Human-Centered Commitments

These values define how individuals are seen, heard, and respected within the health care system:

Autonomy

In H4, *autonomy* is the ability of each person to make decisions about their health that align with their own beliefs, values, and life circumstances. It is distinct from *independence,* which refers to acting without assistance or reliance on others. Independence may be shaped by culture and circumstances, while autonomy is grounded in the right to choose—even when support or care from others is necessary.

In the H4 Alliance, where the full spectrum of care is accessible within one coordinated network, autonomy ensures that each individual can determine the course of their treatment based on what they judge to be right for themselves—not on the preferences, values, or beliefs of others. This extends to the most consequential decisions in life and medicine, including whether to pursue, decline or set limits on treatment, and how personal health information is shared and used.

Dignity

Treat every person with respect, humanity, and compassion—regardless of status, condition, or circumstance. In H4, dignity means more than courteous treatment: it is a design principle of the health system. From the use of personal data to the delivery of end-of-life care, every process and interaction must protect a person's sense of worth and agency. Technology must serve the individual without reducing them to a data point, and care must be delivered in ways that affirm an intrinsic value of every life. Dignity ensures that even in moments of greatest vulnerability, people are seen, heard and treated as whole human beings.

Equality

Guarantee equal rights, access, and protections for all individuals under the health system, regardless of race, gender, language, disability, or immigration status. In a technology-driven era, equality means that every person has the same opportunity to benefit from state-of-the-art therapies and innovations, without limitation by geography, income, or others' values. While individual outcomes may differ by choice or circumstance, the standard of excellence in care is equal for all. The measurement of effectiveness is equal, ensuring that outcomes reflect each person's culture. This is a high bar for equality, recasting it in equal outcomes rather than equal treatment.

Inclusion

Recognize each person as an individual with distinct needs, and build a system that meets their unique circumstances.

H4 defines health more inclusively than any previous era, addressing the conditions that most affect well-being. For one person, that may mean access to electricity and broadband communication; for another it could be safe playgrounds with lighting or reliable transportation; for another early cancer testing. An inclusive system meets people where they are, ensuring that the foundations of health are in place for all.

Cultural Alignment

Acknowledge that health cannot be separated from identity, history, and lived experience. Care must be relevant to the values, languages, and beliefs of the people it serves, ensuring that every interaction honors the individual and the community context in which they live.

Ethical Governance and System Integrity

These values define how institutions and technologies must behave within the public trust:

Integrity

Build systems that are transparent, ethical, and aligned with science and justice. Health 4.0 values communication, listening, and the moral courage to act on what matters.

Accountability

Hold institutions, technologies, and leaders responsible for the outcomes they produce and the promises they make facilitated by an indelible record of decisions and actions.

Transparency

Ensure individuals can see, understand, and challenge decisions suggested about their care, whether by humans, systems, or algorithms.

Stewardship

Use public resources wisely, balancing innovation, cost, and access, to build systems that are resilient and capable of serving future generations.

Design Principles for Modern Health Care

These values guide the design, delivery, and prioritization of modern health interventions:

Effectiveness

Prioritize treatments and technologies that actually work, with outcomes that matter to people—not just to payers, systems, or regulators. If a more effective option exists, use it first. If the right expertise is needed, make it available. Arbitrary barriers like geography are not fixed in a digital first/ tech driven system.

Equity

Design care to eliminate structural barriers rooted in income, geography, language, history, access to qualified care, and cultural invisibility. H4 recognizes that some people need more to achieve the same outcomes. Redesign systems accordingly.

Proactivity

Shift from reactive rescue care to upstream prevention, early detection, and personalized risk management—based on individual, environmental, and social context.

Reimagining Health for the Twenty-first Century: The Health 4.0 Model

Over the centuries, medical care was primarily reactive. When reimagining health, that care begins much earlier. It includes all aspects of you as an individual and aims to engage technology in delivery, prevention, and treatment. To reimagine health, let's explore how these three components meet the prescription we need in a digital first system of health in the twenty-first century.

Preventive Health: Adapting a foundation of culturally based health allows us to align public interventions with individual values and context, detecting and solving for risk by identifying and developing alternative approaches to challenges. For instance, solving for structural health factors—like reliable broadband, dependable electricity, and financial knowledge and well-being—can be every bit as important to health as giving up cigarettes. Your personal culture of health includes cultural, biological, structural and social determinants of health. It is a personalized, precise approach to public health. *Doctor AI's* role in cultural health is to surface challenges and help solve them—acting as record keeper, advocate, connector across care, and trusted guide. *Human* providers are on the loop available at the request of any person or if the situation meets specific criteria.

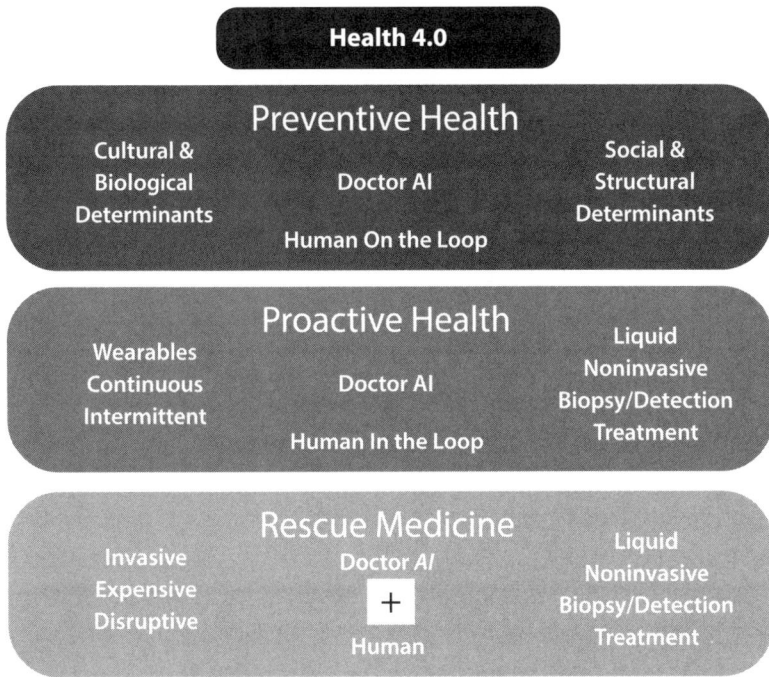

Figure 7: *The Health 4.0 Framework: Preventive, Proactive, and Rescue Care. Copyright Robin Blackstone, MD*

Proactive Health: Proactive Health focuses on early detection and timely treatment of anticipated or emerging disease by leveraging technology. It takes a precise approach, tuned to individual risk factors: the genes you inherit from your parents and ancestors; the food and exercise most effective for your biology; and your pharmacogenetics—how specific drugs work in your body, including their benefits and side effects. Pharmacogenetics makes it possible to tailor both the type and dose of medication to your unique characteristics. Proactive Health also employs state-of-the-art diagnostics that can detect tumors when they are too small to appear on imaging, anticipate future disease, and draw continuous insights from wearables that track conditions like high blood pressure, diabetes, heart disease, or obesity. In this model, Doctor AI serves as communicator, quarterback, connector and friend. It integrates data from wearables and diagnostic tools, monitors changes from your personal baseline, and alerts you when action is needed (e.g., if you are on a blood pressure medication and your blood pressure spikes, it will communicate with you and keep your human provider in the loop).

Doctor AI's role is crucial. The advanced technology can monitor you, providing mental health support and connecting all the dots so that subtle signs and signals don't get missed, helping you stay ahead in your personal health game. In addition, *Doctor AI* knows the state-of-the-art detection and treatment information and can pair it with your needs in an intimate way that delivers precisely what you need when you need it.

These proactive interventions will find and treat early disease "upstream," when treatment is less disruptive and more effective. The effect: lower cost, fewer headaches, and more time to live your life on your own terms, doing what matters most to you.

Rescue Health: This type of medicine is the most familiar to everyone. A symptom or sign occurs, and you set out to investigate it. Whether the situation is catastrophic or just needs attention, it isn't detected until late in the game, so the downstream consequences are more impactful on your life, your family, your work, and your future. In these situations, our current health care system is brilliant at treating individuals (especially those who can afford the best care), but it often fails to deliver at scale. This type of health care is life-threatening and the most expensive to treat. In the United States, nearly one in twelve health care dollars is spent in the final year of life (8.5 percent), and more than one in six over the last three years (16.7 percent)[50]

In the rescue medicine scenario, *Doctor AI* is also a crucial aspect of H4. Because it has all your medical records, all your test results, and an indelible record of all your treatments making it more likely you will get more connected and relevant care. *Doctor AI*'s ability to pull together data on treatments, specialists, hospitals, and the minute details of care, mean you are getting a higher level of effectiveness in seeking treatment. *Doctor*

AI can compare your situation with people from the literature with the same set of circumstances to give you realistic probabilities of success and failure with a given treatment. With integration to one system and interoperability of the health record, all the physicians in the US are part of the same network, so you can get the best person for your particular needs prioritized by what you feel is important: location, expertise, timing or skill set. Often, this is the information and care only received by people with wealth. Eventually, some of the care currently delivered by humans will be provided by physical AI (robots and robotically driven systems) as the Fourth Industrial Revolution (4IR) advances.

Doctor AI

As guardian of your data and your dignity, Doctor AI ensures that you, not institutions, remain the center of your own care. It draws from the best of science and technology yet answers to you. Whether you're managing a chronic condition, seeking a second opinion, making a tough choice, or simply optimizing your well-being, Doctor AI is always present—on your terms.

PART 2

The Problem with American Health Care

CHAPTER 4

Covered? Not Covered?

In the United States, commercial health insurance didn't begin as a grand design but as a workaround, an experiment born in the 1920s when Baylor Hospital in Texas offered schoolteachers prepaid hospital care for just $0.50 a month. This modest beginning eventually evolved into Blue Cross and Blue Shield and, over time, into a massive employer-based insurance system shaped more by tax incentives and wartime wage controls than by a national vision for health.

As this patchwork model grew, so did its exclusions. The unemployed, the elderly, the poor, the disabled, and many women—especially those in part-time employment or domestic roles—were left out entirely. Employer-based insurance was built around the male breadwinner model. If you didn't work full-time, didn't have recorded wages, or didn't work at all, the system simply wasn't built for you. In response, the federal government stepped in, not with a unified system, but with a series of fragmented programs designed to plug the holes.

Medicare was created in 1965 to cover seniors; Medicaid emerged alongside it to support the poor; the Children's Health Insurance Plan (CHIP) followed decades later to help children who'd been left out of both. These programs weren't part of a cohesive plan. Rather, they were moral triage, a public acknowledgment that the market alone did not care for the nation's most vulnerable. Each program was layered atop an already fractured architecture, creating a system defined not by design, but by exception. A system of high administrative costs.

Patchwork to Profits

We tend to think of health care as a sacred space, a relationship between doctor and patient. A human drama. It used to be. But it's hard to establish a relationship in sixteen minutes—the average time allotted and financially profitable—for a visit with a primary care physician who works in the health care machine.[51] Like a labyrinth, surrounding that simple relationship is an intricate architecture of institutions, industries, and intermediaries who profit not from care, but from controlling the conditions of care.

This chapter isn't anti-profit. It's pro-transparency, pro-accountability, and most of all, pro-human. If we want to design a system that truly serves the people, we must begin by understanding the one that doesn't. We begin by naming the layers that extract value from patients, from communities, and from public trust, and then ask bluntly: "Who built this system? Who benefits from its complexity? Who gets rich when you get sick? How much profitability should the market allow?" And perhaps the most damning question of all: "Why isn't health and early treatment a goal?"

Health insurance began as a form of protection, a financial buffer for when health failed and rescue was necessary. It was a time when uncertainty wasn't nearly so complicated as it is on the global stage, in the midst of war, pandemics or climate disasters. It was meant to be a safety net, not a spider web. But over the decades, health plans have evolved into sprawling financial conglomerates. Today, their profits don't come from coverage. They come from control.

Denials. Delays. Restrictions. These aren't bugs in the system; they are features. All in the name of "managing care" and pursuing what health care programs now call "value-based care."

But what is *value-based care*, really? Let's look through the lens of a person suffering from one of the most persistent and politically fraught issues in American medicine: obesity. Obesity is directly linked to diabetes, heart disease, cancer, and disability. It is such a prevalent and preexisting condition to these other diseases that you'd think that early intervention would be a no-brainer. That the system would label it as the early precursor to all these other disease states and implement treatment. Instead, the system did something else.

In an attempt to manage chronic disease, Medicare introduced a privatized option—Medicare Advantage. On paper, it was a shift toward proactive, preventive care. In reality, what it did was open the door to distorted incentives.

Doctors were encouraged, sometimes pressured, to identify patients with chronic conditions. In theory, this allowed for earlier treatment. In practice, it rewarded documentation over care. Patients were assigned diseases they didn't yet have or were tested in search of conditions that might justify higher reimbursement rates. When those tests grew expensive or failed to "prove" illness, insurers reversed course. Coverage was denied. The patient was left hanging. The companies and the participating doctors accused of fraud.

A 2022 report by the Office of the Inspector General at the Department of Health and Human Services (HHS) found that 13 percent of Medicare Advantage denials violated coverage rules, blocking or delaying care that *should* have been approved.[52] That's not value. That's exploitation of the people the system is supposed to serve.

For the patient, the system becomes a maze of denials, confusion, and silence. No clear answers. No accountability. No care.

Denials and delays are especially common under prior authorizations, a tool that allows insurers to second-guess doctors before approving care. This is true for all health insurance, not just Medicare. Narrow networks limit your choice of hospitals and physicians—not necessarily based on quality, if that is even a requirement, which it is not, but on negotiated contracts. You might live in a region where no high-risk obstetrician is in-network, despite a known shortage of maternal health providers. If something goes wrong, then too bad. You're out of network, out of luck, or out of pocket.

And it gets worse. Many insurers now own the clinics you visit, the pharmacy you use, and the pharmacy benefit manager (PBM) that controls your drug coverage. This vertical integration means the same corporation controls diagnosis, treatment, prescription, and payment, in order to maximize their company revenue. A move worthy of big oil, but in a health care setting? PBMs—largely invisible to the public—can determine which drugs are covered, which aren't, and at what price, often favoring profit over effectiveness.

Even their digital tools are designed for surveillance, not service. Good luck getting a prescription refill without a phone tree, an app, and a week of waiting.

Most importantly, insurance coverage doesn't equal quality health care. Doctors and patients alike are drowning. Paperwork piles up. Rules are opaque. Costs are unpredictable. Delay is rampant. Some physicians spend two or more hours each evening on administrative tasks such as requesting pre-authorizations and assigning billing codes, justifying decisions to non-clinical reviewers.

This isn't health care. It's health control, and at whose expense?

The Insurance Run-Around

Consider Elena's eight-year-old son, Mateo. He was supposed to have his tonsils removed on a Tuesday. Then Friday. Then the following Monday. Each time Elena packed his overnight bag, and each time she told him it was really happening. Each time, she got a call from the hospital: The insurer hadn't approved the surgery yet. Elena didn't know how to explain it to her son.

"But he's in pain," she told the nurse. "They already did the imaging. They already confirmed the diagnosis."

"We know," the nurse said gently. "But our hands are tied until they process the authorization. You could come to the emergency room. Maybe the surgeon could work him in."

Elena is a single mom who works full-time at a distribution warehouse. She can't afford to miss shifts, but she also can't leave her son untreated or unattended. To get approvals for the surgery, she stayed up late printing out letters, called the health insurer's customer service line on her lunch breaks, and begged anyone who answered the phone to do what her son's doctors had said was necessary.

In all, it took three weeks and two emergency room (ER) visits before the surgery was performed. By then, Mateo's inflammation had worsened, and he missed school, so she missed work. The hospital filed an appeal with the insurer when the repeated visits to the ER were denied. No one was held accountable. Elana's performance review at work was poor due to the absences. The year before it was exemplary, and she was on the way to being promoted. Instead, she was penalized for being a mother in a broken system.

This is not a rare event. It is an everyday odyssey for many Americans.

From Health to Bankruptcy

In the United States, you can go bankrupt from medical bills even if you *have* health insurance. That's not a system failure. That's the system working exactly as designed.

According to the *American Journal of Public Health*, 66.5 percent of all personal bankruptcies stem from medical debt.[53] Most of those affected were insured at the time of their illness or injury.[54]

When debt becomes unpayable, it's often sold to third-party collections agencies, sometimes for pennies on the dollar. From there, a predatory machine takes over. Collection agencies profit by pursuing full repayment, layering on interest and penalties, and reporting delinquencies to credit bureaus. For patients, often still sick or unable to work, this becomes a financial death spiral. Financial debt is associated with depression and a feeling of hopelessness, on top of being sick.

Jasmine, twenty-seven, juggles three gig jobs: rideshare driver, free-lance designer, and food delivery. None of her jobs offer health benefits, so she buys an individual plan with a high deductible through the Affordable

Care Act (ACA) marketplace. But when a minor injury sidelines her, she delays care. She knows that one emergency room visit could cost as much as weeks of rent. Like millions of Americans working without traditional employment, Jasmine's health care coverage is fragile, her choices few, and her financial and medical risk enormous.

Today, about 165 million Americans still rely on employer-sponsored health insurance[55]—the largest single source of coverage. Is that better? The origin of this system wasn't visionary policy. It was a wartime workaround.

During World War II, wage controls froze salaries. To attract workers, companies offered health insurance as a tax-exempt benefit. By the 1950s, this "fringe benefit" had become institutionalized through IRS tax deductions, tethering health care access to employment.

This was when most American workers held full-time jobs, working for a single company for life. Health insurance was designed for rare, catastrophic events. Medicine itself was basic, with few outpatient treatments, no complex diagnostics, and limited tools to treat disease.[56]

But as medicine advanced, expectations changed. Insurance expanded to cover outpatient care, diagnostics, preventive services, and chronic disease management. The cost—and complexity—exploded. Administrative overhead ballooned. Today, administrative costs make up 15 to 25 percent of US health care spending, many times higher than in universal systems in peer countries. And yet, access remains fragmented.[57,58]

Workers like Jasmine aren't rare. *They are the new workforce.* Gig workers. Part-timers. Caregivers. Hourly employees. And many fall through the cracks. Without a steady employer or an affordable individual plan, they're forced to gamble between health and rent, care and groceries.

The employer-based model now acts more like an anchor, dragging the system down. Lose your job, lose your insurance. Want to change careers? Start a business? Freelance? You risk losing your health care coverage or go on COBRA. COBRA was established by the Consolidated Omnibus Budget Reconciliation Act of 1985, usually providing an 18–36 month "bridge" from employer-sponsored health insurance. There is no "employer sponsor" so the person pays the whole cost, usually four or five times more expensive. For instance in the Kaiser Family Foundation, the average annual employer-sponsored family premium was about $23,968 in 2023. The employee paid $6,575 and employer $17,393 of that total. Under COBRA, the individual owes the entire $23,968, a 280% increase.[59]

While corporate executives often enjoy gold-plated health insurance plans, hourly workers get high deductible "bare minimum" coverage—if they're eligible at all. Maternity care remains elusive for single mothers, who are more likely to be uninsured or underinsured. These disparities are not incidental. They are the predictable byproducts of a system built around employment status, not human need.

And employers—who are not health experts—wield enormous influence over who gets care, what gets covered, and which networks are available. Often, they rely on benefits consultants, a small group of "experts" who may be paid by the very insurers they recommend, creating an embedded conflict of interest. These consultants are rarely incentivized to recommend the best care. Instead, they may be incentivized to recommend the most profitable plans.

This isn't a system that failed. This is a system that succeeded on its own terms. But those terms were never about your health.

Hospitals and Real Estate

Hospitals used to be anchors of trust. Today, many act more like regional monopolies and real estate empires. Hospital consolidation has reduced choice and increased costs, while making care less accountable. They're nonprofit in name but corporate in practice, with executive pay in the millions, collections lawsuits against low-income patients, and luxury expansions for the wealthy. All while cutting essential services.

For instance, our community hospital in Arizona hired a surgeon with a sterling reputation from the Mayo Clinic. Many people would travel from around the world just to have him operate on them at the Mayo Clinic. When he came to our community hospital, he talked the administrators into a plan to build out an area on the hospital's top floor for these special visitors. When the executive council, made up of our community's doctors, questioned hospital leadership about it, they said, "He's from the Mayo

Clinic." The council said, "Let's wait 'til the first patient comes." Patients who would have gone to the Mayo Clinic rarely if ever came. Despite the surgeon's expertise, the Mayo Clinic's well-earned global reputation for excellence had been the draw, not necessarily the surgeon. The community hospital was a "not-for-profit" system, great for the area they were in but without the same caché.

Hospitals today embody a paradox: While some regional systems, buoyed by monopolistic market power and real estate ventures, generate soaring profits and lavish executive compensation, others, often safety-net providers serving vulnerable populations, are struggling financially or facing closure. This divergence reflects stark differences in market positioning, payer mix, and community mission. Wealthier systems capitalize on lucrative specialty services and high-reimbursement commercial insurers, whereas under-resourced hospitals bear the burden of uncompensated care and lower-margin public programs. Highlighting this split is essential to understanding why consolidation has not uniformly strengthened health care and why accountability and equity remain elusive across the sector.

Across metropolitan areas, competing hospitals often replicate inpatient, ancillary, and high-tech services—a phenomenon frequently coined the "medical arms race." One study analyzing over 2,200 hospitals found that such duplication drives up per-patient costs and lowers margins for sophisticated services, while ancillary and basic inpatient duplication may slightly boost financial returns—but at the expense of overall system efficiency and elevated expenses for communities.[60] A 2022 analysis underscores that hospitals within larger systems are especially prone to offer the same clinical services already available nearby.[61] This redundant infrastructure not only multiplies overhead and administrative burdens, but fragments care delivery at the population level, diverting capital away from innovation. It also critically dilutes top medical and surgical talent.

In rural America, hospitals face an acute mismatch between low patient volumes and high fixed costs, leaving them vulnerable to service duplication and closures. Over the past decade, nearly 8 percent of rural hospitals have permanently shut their doors. The facilities that remain often reduce or eliminate essential services.[62] This dynamic forces local residents to endure lengthy and expensive travel for essential care. Obstetric care illustrates this stark trend: in 2018, only 44 percent of rural counties provided obstetric services, a marked decline from 54 percent in 2004.[63] In response, policymakers are experimenting with new models such as the Rural Emergency Hospital Designation, aiming to maintain essential emergency and outpatient services while eliminating redundant inpatient care.[64] Innovations like these help bolster rural health system resilience but structural barriers persist, including training and retaining clinicians.

To be clear, most people working within this system are well-intentioned. Very few wake up plotting how to extract more money from patients in pain. The problem isn't malice—it's design. Clinicians, coders, and administrators are navigating the rules as they exist, not as they should be. Some might call that naïveté. I don't. I've worked beside them. I've watched them wrestle with gray zones, trying to do the right thing in a system that doesn't reward it. This is not a crisis of individual morality. It's a failure of structural integrity—compounded only rarely by true moral failure. This doesn't mean there isn't fraud and abuse.

Hospital systems and their gilded partners in private equity and venture capital have developed real estate strategies that include facility fees for visits in repurposed buildings and medical service lines built around revenue, not need. They have world-class surgical robots, but no beds for mental health patients. They have private jets for executives, but no maternity care in rural counties. *The system doesn't lack resources. It lacks priorities.* It is no surprise that the public, whether patient, doctor, or nurse, is frustrated, disillusioned, and angry.

When the Money Walked In: Private Equity and Venture Capital

I didn't fully understand just how deeply private equity and venture capital had infiltrated frontline health care until the COVID-19 pandemic. Suddenly, the money walked right through the front door.

Two specialties stood out immediately during COVID-19: emergency medicine and anesthesiology. These are high-revenue fields, often staffed not by hospital employees, but by local groups of physicians, owned by private equity with deep pockets. By the time COVID-19 was running rampant, they had become multistate, multispecialty staffing companies. These companies contract with hospitals to supply entire departments. When the pandemic hit, trauma admissions plummeted, and elective surgeries were canceled. ERs went eerily quiet, the volume-based revenue model cracked. Overnight, the business dried up. And then came the layoffs.

Doctors, many bound by long-term contracts, found themselves financially "upside down." Some tried to exit their contracts; others staged quiet rebellions. But few grasped the structural threat behind it.

I didn't fully see it until 2024. I was sitting on the windowsill at the Barnes & Noble on Fifth Avenue in New York City, waiting for an author to appear for a book signing. A young father next to me told me a story I'll never forget.

"My wife went into premature labor. We rushed to the hospital—the one on our insurance plan. She was admitted immediately and delivered our baby boy. Everything went smoothly.

"We had full coverage. We're careful with money—we chose the plan deliberately. Then we got the bill: $30,000. I called and said, 'This has to be a mistake.' They told me: 'No it is not a mistake. The hospital was in-network, but the ER doctor and the anesthesiologist weren't. They're contracted.'

"We were devastated. My wife just had a C-section. We had a newborn. And we were suddenly buried in a debt that made no sense.

"I never paid it. Eventually, they stopped sending notices. But it darkened the joy of those early weeks with our child. That stress, we still carry it. We still wonder when the 'scalpel' will drop."

This is not an outlier. It is the business model.

Over the past two decades, private equity firms have steadily acquired hospitals, ambulatory surgery centers, emergency physician staffing groups, radiology services, anesthesia practices, billing companies, and even the real estate beneath hospitals. None of this is illegal. In fact, it's strategically rational. The typical model is simple: acquire, consolidate, increase revenue, cut costs, and exit, usually through a sale or recapitalization within three to seven years. In other words, treat the hospital industry with the same strategy as any other business they acquire.

Patients, communities, and providers do not factor into management decisions or exit strategies. The goal is financial optimization, not health care delivery.

These firms often vertically integrate care: the same investor may control emergency room physicians, the radiology practice, the anesthesia group, and the billing company. Some firms sell hospital real estate and lease it back to the same institution, exposing hospitals to long-term rent obligations while extracting capital upfront.[65] Hospitals often accept these terms because they need liquidity.

The results are predictable: surprise billing, narrow networks, rural hospital closures, deferred investment in infrastructure and staffing, and services cut to protect margins. The worst consequence is simple—the patient is left stranded.

And it doesn't stop at care delivery. Private equity-backed hospital systems and physician groups now frequently engage in aggressive marketing, predatory collections, and opaque billing practices. These tactics might be acceptable in retail or finance. In health care, they are morally indefensible, and invisible to communities. Operating just out of site.

Venture capital, while different in style, is no less disruptive, investing in early-stage startups: AI diagnostics, remote monitoring, mental health platforms, and home-based care. These innovations promise transformation, and some succeed. But the business model demands rapid growth, monetization, or acquisition. Many startups scale before their models are clinically validated or equitably accessible. Others become acquisition targets for the same private equity-driven conglomerates, restarting the cycle. In 2025, the "deal flow" has slowed, because venture capitalists, used to exiting in seven years, are having to wait for revenue that is not appearing as it used to, extending to fourteen years or more.

The problem is unaccountable capital. It's finance without ethics, return without responsibility for the lives of the people harmed.

If, for instance, a community hospital closes, if an OB/GYN practice disappears, if a young family receives a $30,000 bill for care they thought was covered, are they market corrections or ethical failures?

So we must ask:

- What role should private capital play in health care delivery?
- Should we require public disclosure of financial ownership in hospitals and physician groups?
- Should there be limits or ethical standards for investment in emergency services, maternal care, or rural health systems?
- Should patients know when their doctor is employed by a firm accountable to shareholders, not communities?

These are not ideological questions. They are civic ones. If we believe health care is a public good rather than a private commodity, we must demand transparency, fair regulation, and real reform. The goal is not to weaken business in health, but to build a durable foundation of fairness that works for everyone, especially the people the system is supposed to serve. The uncertainty Americans face today—whether care will be affordable, accessible, or even available next year—must be taken off the table once and for all.

Pharmacy Benefit Managers and the Prescription Profiteers

If hospitals are empires, Pharmacy Benefit Managers (PBM) are the invisible architects. These middlemen negotiate drug prices, create lists of approved medications called formularies, and determine which medications are accessible—and at what cost. PBMs profit from spread pricing, charging payers like Medicaid or health insurance companies rebates for access. They provide drug manufacturers with financial incentives to secure drug placement on a formulary, and some control the supply chain by owning the pharmacies, the drug manufacturers, and even the health insurance company. The same company that denies your medication often profits from the markup. It's not just inefficient, it's orchestrated opacity.

A modern-day equivalent of a "shell game." Like many parts of health care, it's hard to tell what's going on from the outside.

Behind the scenes, group purchasing organizations (GPOs) may select hospital suppliers not based on price, but on who pays to get listed. Protected under a 1987 "safe harbor" exemption to federal anti-kickback laws, GPOs and PBMs are legally permitted to accept payments from manufacturers, practices that would otherwise be considered illegal inducements in almost any other industry. These payments distort priorities and decision-making on a massive scale. *The system doesn't lack resources. It lacks ethics.*

And the drugs themselves? Their prices are inflated well beyond global norms. In the US, a vial of insulin can cost $300, while in the UK, it's closer to $7. A course of hepatitis C treatment costs $84,000 in the US, but it costs less than $1,000 in Japan or Norway.[66] Same drug. Same science. *But in America, the price of medication isn't about value. It's about leverage.*

We pay the highest prices in the world not because our treatments are better, but because our system doesn't negotiate on behalf of the people who need the medication. This isn't a magic wand situation. No single person in the United States, no matter their position, can change it on "say so." Rather, there are deeply entrenched interests and policies that will have to be addressed in a comprehensive way to dislodge this predatory practice.

The health care system isn't just built to take your money. It's designed to leave you wondering where it went and why nothing works when you need it. And yet, it isn't just the insurers or hospitals or pharma giants driving up costs and making access to care difficult. It's the third-party administrators, revenue cycle optimizers, GPOs, wholesalers, consultants, and software vendors. It's a congress full of people who may have good intentions but lack the perception and knowledge of the system. It's the full cast of middlemen who profit efficiently, and often invisibly. Three wholesalers—McKesson, Cardinal, and AmerisourceBergen—control 90 percent of the US drug distribution network, setting prices and terms between manufacturers and pharmacies with near-total opacity.[67]

Surrounding them are the watchdogs who rarely bite. *Your United States Congress is awash in over $700 million in health care lobbying money annually.*[68] The state and federal court system, where arbitration clauses block patient lawsuits. Professional societies that remain silent while patients are harmed. Regulators who inspect mop closets but not medical debt lawsuits.[69] Then there's a media industry that follows trends instead of tracing systems. In the United Sates, over decades, we have allowed the ecosystem of health, no matter our good intention, to build its profits on suffering, to become a licensed business of graft and payola masquerading as *service* and labeled it as the American health care system.

Fee-for-Service by Design

The Current Procedural Terminology (CPT) system is more than a technical billing tool for medical coding. It is the financial architecture of health care in our country, an infrastructure that reinforces the fee-for-service model, where care is rewarded not based on outcomes, but on the volume and type of procedures delivered. In this economy, doing more means earning more. More tests. More surgeries. More follow-ups. Not always because they're needed, but because they're reimbursable, relying on the integrity of physicians and hospitals to police themselves. This system has been systematically justified by interested parties to keep the fee-for-service status quo in place. Any alternative was tagged as "socialism," a powerful label used primarily by people with a financial interest in keeping the American health care system from evolving to a fair, accessible, and effective system.

Research from RAND/Health Affairs shows that from 2011 to 2019, US hospitals increased coding for high-intensity inpatient care by *41 percent*, resulting in *billions in excess payments*, a clear sign that documentation is being shaped more for revenue than for clinical accuracy and communication.[70] I encountered this first-hand in 2009: Of the five hundred charts we reviewed from our own service, nearly 20 percent contained semantic shifts that increased reimbursement. The chart said a person had post-surgery "atelectasis" which is a normal consequence of many surgeries, but it can be documented as "pulmonary collapse", to increase reimbursement. Subtle shifts in coding qualified events as complications under state quality reporting. That imbalance exposed the system's core misalignment: optimized for revenue, not accuracy. By insisting on precise wording in our records, our team pushed back against a machine that rewards financial creativity over clinical truth. This is not an isolated example.

In today's system, the highest reimbursements go to what Health 4.0 calls rescue medicine—care for disease that has reached a life-threatening critical stage. Emergency procedures, complex surgeries, and other late-stage measures are high-revenue priorities for health care as a business, creating profit for providers and hospital systems. For health care companies, however, these same interventions are a drain on revenue. For people who become the participants in rescue medicine, it is usually disruptive, expensive, and the outcome uncertain for them personally. Meanwhile, the kinds of changes that could have resulted in a different future for people aren't available or funded.

To build a system that saves money for everyone and spares patients the devastating outcomes of late-stage disease, we must move upstream—diagnosing and treating earlier and improving the structural and social underpinning of lifelong disease by grounding every action in the patient's personal culture of health.

This cultural context of care—how someone's beliefs, environment, or identity shape their health—goes undocumented. A patient's lifestyle, goals, and barriers, which are critical to long-term health success, don't fit neatly into billing fields. And even when electronic records are designed to capture them, the fields are skipped. It takes too much time. And time, in this system, is money.

Who owns the billing codes? Not the government. Not the public. *The American Medical Association* (AMA) licenses and controls the use of CPT codes, which are federally mandated for billing nearly all health services. CPT-related revenue makes up over 60 percent of the AMA's total annual income.[71] The AMA, which at its apex in the 1950s represented 75 percent of all US physicians, currently represents around 15 percent.[72]

To introduce a new code, an innovation must pass through the CPT Editorial Panel and the Relative Value Scale Update Committee, both of which are heavily influenced by medical specialty societies. These bodies have the power to decide whether a service even *exists* in the eyes of the reimbursement system. If no code applies, the service can't be billed. And if it can't be billed, it can't be used; essential innovation doesn't happen.

While these committees are meant to evaluate clinical merit and economic efficiency, they often act as bottlenecks. Approvals can be delayed—or denied—if a new approach threatens entrenched revenue streams. For example, early laparoscopic surgery faced resistance until CPT codes were updated. When the AMA produced CPT codes in 1994 for preventive counseling, Medicare created special G codes of its own for annual visits. Preventive counseling CPT codes 99401-99404, are still excluded through Medicare coverage.[73]

Consider Dr. Jonathan Myles, a composite who reflects the experience of many innovators. Faced with increasing rates of patients with opioid dependency after orthopedic injuries, he developed a care model that combined physical therapy, nutrition counseling, mental health support, and medication management. The outcomes were striking, including faster recoveries, fewer complications, and a dramatic reduction in narcotic use.

Yet when he sought reimbursement, he hit a wall. The CPT Editorial Panel ruled that the model was not "sufficiently distinct" to merit a new code. As Dr. Myles explained, *"It's not just a procedure. It's a relationship with multiple integrated services."* The system replied: *"That's the problem."*

Over the next two years, Dr. Myles tried to sustain the program through grants and philanthropy—even dipping into his own savings. In the end, he shut it down, not because it failed, but because it couldn't be reimbursed—the familiar dynamic of a cat watching a canary. We know the ending.

This story is illustrative, but far from hypothetical. Studies consistently show that integrated care programs, especially those that combine physical therapy, behavioral health, and nutrition, face systemic reimbursement obstacles. They are, however, highly effective, especially in addiction care.

A 2021 *Health Affairs* analysis found that integrated behavioral health initiatives often fail due to fragmented payment systems and insufficient coding structures.[74] Similarly, the National Academies of Sciences, Engineering, and Medicine has reported that many promising care models aimed at reducing opioid dependence collapse under outdated or inflexible payment frameworks.[75] Until we realign payment with health outcomes, rather than procedure codes owned and controlled by insiders, we will continue to fund rescue medicine while ignoring cultural preventive and proactive care. Health cannot come second to billing. I propose a different system: one where the coding of clinical facts is kept separate from payment, and payment is tied to outcomes.

Today, we let the billing system write the story of our health—as if accountants are the historians of our bodies. In the future, the facts of care must be recorded once, faithfully, in the indelible ink of the blockchain. Payment should not be based on the number of lines written, but on the outcome of the story.

Medical Licensing and Privileging Conflicts

Medical licensing exists to protect the public, ensuring that those who care for patients are trained, competent, and ethical. In principle, it is a safeguard. In practice, it is a gatekeeping mechanism—one that can entrench power hierarchies and slow the adoption of necessary innovation.

State medical boards, often influenced by local professional societies and influential physicians, decide who may practice medicine, how they may practice, and under what circumstances. These boards often lack the expertise to evaluate emerging technologies or new interdisciplinary models of care. Despite years of training, members may not have the knowledge to judge rapidly evolving approaches. As established figures in local medical culture, they live and work within the communities they regulate. In such settings, bias—whether conscious or not—becomes difficult to avoid.[76]

When a new procedure or model of care challenges the status quo, the people asked to evaluate it are often those with the most to lose. In hospitals, privileging committees determine who may perform which procedures. If a member of the committee does not understand—or cannot perform—a new procedure, they may block its adoption. If another person on the committee has strongly held beliefs about a particular procedure, they may try to block it. Whether consciously or not, gatekeeping becomes self-preservation. The system empowers those resistant to change to prevent it.

The result is a professional ecosystem that favors conformity over creativity and inertia over improvement. If we want to build a better system, we must ask harder questions. "What would it mean to reimburse physicians not for procedures, but for collaboration? For coordination? For time spent listening, guiding, and navigating patients through complexity?" "What would it look like to reward transparency and trust, instead of throughput?" "What if we stopped paying for *all* outcomes, and instead paid for *effective* ones?" "What if a physician could choose the best medication or treatment, not having to jump through the hoops of outdated protocols because the protocols they began using were updated in real time and showed data and probabilities?" "What if we considered any medical device or pharmaceutical value within the treatment paradigm of the disease or situation it is designed for?"

These are not rhetorical questions. They are invitations to reimagine how we define medical authority and what we value in care. But the greatest cost of our current model isn't financial. It's emotional. It's the erosion of trust. It's the realization that you can follow every rule, pay every premium, and show up to every appointment, and still be denied. That you can work full-time, raise a family, carry insurance, and still go bankrupt.

Fifty States, Fifty Health Care Systems

If professional societies define the structure of care, and universities the boundaries of medical education and training, state governments define its limits. The United States doesn't have a single health care system; it has fifty. Each state sets its own rules around licensing, insurance regulation, Medicaid eligibility, benefit design, and oversight. The fragmentation creates enormous inefficiencies and unfairness.

A child with autism in one state may receive comprehensive services through Medicaid; in another, that same child may be denied care entirely. A midwife may be licensed and respected in one state and criminalized in the next. Coverage for substance use disorder, mental health, gender-affirming care, or reproductive services vary widely, not based on clinical evidence but on politics and religion. This climate turns geography into destiny.

Consider, for example, the fictional story of Cara Thompson, which illustrates a very real and common problem in 2025. When Cara moved from New Jersey to Texas, she thought things would get easier. Her husband had a job offer with health care benefits, and in Texas, they could afford a house with a backyard. And most importantly, they'd be able to live closer to his aging parents.

But what they didn't realize, what no one warned them about, was that their son's health care wouldn't come with them.

In New Jersey, six-year-old Milo had been receiving intensive, state-supported services for autism through Medicaid, including a full-time aide at school, weekly occupational therapy, speech therapy, and a support group for his parents. It wasn't perfect, but it was working.

In Texas, however, they were told Milo didn't qualify for autism support services and care. To their new health insurance company, Milo's diagnosis wasn't enough, and the waitlist for care was three years long, even if approved.

"But he needs help now," Cara told the caseworker, who was kind but stood firm.

"Every state sets its own rules. Here, the bar for treatment is *higher*."

Overnight, Milo lost his care team, and soon, his behavior regressed. His father took a second job to afford private therapy sessions, and Cara gave up her own career to manage Milo's needs full-time.

The same country, the same diagnosis, the same child—yet different rules and a different fate.

Reform is possible. Interstate medical licensure compacts have begun to address some geographic barriers. Pilot privileging models in integrated systems have shown success when based on competencies, not credentials alone. And some states have expanded independent practice authority for nurse practitioners and physician assistants—despite resistance from organized medicine. Their background and training are not the same. These are small steps, but they point to what's possible when trust in patient outcomes is placed above professional turf.

The Moral Cost of Complexity

Our current health care system was not built for health care. It was built to generate money for shareholders. A 2025 report from Yale demonstrates that over the past twenty years, 95 percent of net income went to shareholder payouts. The payouts tripled during this period of time.[77]

Let us not mistake honest business for what this system has become: a form of *legal graft*. And let us not blame the individuals within the system. Most are not bad actors. Most have been carried along, adding revenue streams, following incentives, surviving inside a machine that rewards the wrong things until, one day, there is no turning back. They work for the same companies that are providing "care" to patients.

As patient volumes exploded and costs soared, the system didn't design better care systems. It built layers of control: prior authorizations, utilization reviews, pre-approvals. Not to improve quality, but to contain costs. Again and again, the same response came to build barriers, not bridges. More paperwork. More forms. More delays. Preauthorization's. Second guessing. Not to heal more people, but to manage the flood of need with a firewall of bureaucracy.

Over time, physicians stopped being seen as trusted professionals and started being treated as billing liabilities. The system didn't trust their judgment. It only trusted their CPT codes, codes that are linked to payments.

Was this deliberate? Perhaps. But so is our effort to change it.

Drawing the Line

We don't debate whether airlines should make a profit. We debate how to do so without crashing planes. We set clear rules: safety regulations, air traffic controls, passenger rights. We don't let airlines decide mid-flight whether a passenger is *worth the fuel.*

In every critical system, transportation, finance, food, we draw boundaries around profit to preserve public trust and protect life. These systems still innovate. They still make money. They don't do so by confusing people, delaying service, or denying essentials. Health care should be no different.

Business has a place and innovation has a price, but profiting from confusion, delay, and denial is not fair enterprise. It is *extraction*. It is *graft*. It is not the *margin of value*; it is the *margin of harm*.

In banking, we insure deposits. In food, we inspect factories. In transportation, we ground unsafe planes. Health care is the last major system where life-and-death decisions are outsourced to profit algorithms without enforceable ethical guardrails. That must change.

As we move toward Health 4.0, we must ensure that *people*, not just profits, are at the heart of every algorithm. Ethical boundaries must be built into the system, not bolted on as an afterthought. It's time to draw the line and define what we expect from a health care system worthy of our trust. It should be effective, equitable, accessible.

The good news? Systems can be reprogrammed. And people, many of them, are already writing the next chapter.

CHAPTER 5

We Were Never Gods

In 1990, I was a surgical resident facing one of the most dreaded emergencies in general surgery: a bleeding or perforated ulcer. At the time, ulcers were thought to be caused by stress and acid overproduction. We treated them with acid-suppressing drugs or surgery in open, brutal operations with high complication rates. Mortality from bleeding ulcers hovered around 20 percent.

Yet the cure had already been discovered. In 1982, Australian pathologists Barry Marshall and Robin Warren identified *Helicobacter pylori*, bacteria that caused most ulcers in stomach tissue. Marshall famously drank a beaker of the bacteria, gave himself ulcers, then cured them with antibiotics. Their work was widely presented and published in the global surgical community.[78]

Still, medicine in America didn't change. A few years earlier, pharmaceutical companies had launched proton-pump inhibitors and so, gastroenterologists prescribed Prilosec and performed endoscopy after endoscopy to check the results of the antiacid medication. The incentives were misaligned: the treatment was cheap; the procedures were profitable.

This isn't just a story about ulcers. It's a story about power—and the illusion of physician autonomy and physician independence. Physicians pride themselves on autonomy. We believe we make the call, shoulder the responsibility, and if we must, stand alone. But, even in the golden era of private practice, that autonomy was conditional. We were bound by codes owned by the AMA, regulatory bodies' approval of technology, insurance formularies, pharmaceutical marketing, litigation fears, and institutional norms.

In the 1970's, almost 80% of physicians had a "private" practice. So billing for services was crucial to pay our staff and provide our families with a good living. We did what was right but also what paid the bills, with surgical specialists the highest paid doctors.

Autonomy was a dearly held belief, or rather myth. The opioid crisis is a recent example of the situation's complexity. Doctors were told opioids were safe. Insurance companies didn't cover alternatives and regulations were murky. Doctors were under pressure to treat pain. So, many prescribed out of habit—or fear. Later, as lawsuits mounted, physicians became scapegoats for systemic failure. One year, we were undertreating pain; the next, we were fueling addiction. Our sacred autonomy had not protected us. It had betrayed us.

Physicians are entangled in a web of financial and institutional controls. Device companies engage in iterative design changes so they can charge a premium price for them The AMA charges physicians to bill for their own work. Hospitals dictate which medical procedures are allowed. Insurers determine which treatments are covered. Everyone profits—except the patient.

Every time your doctor's office, hospital, or insurance company uses the CPT® codes that appear on your bill, they are using a copyrighted product owned by the American Medical Association (AMA)—and the AMA charges for that access. Under the AMA's own license agreement, *any person who can view or use CPT codes—whether they are a doctor, nurse, medical coder, biller, administrator, or even IT staff—counts as an "end user" and must be covered by a paid license.* These fees are usually built into the cost of your care or your insurance, meaning part of what you pay ultimately goes to the AMA just for permission to use the billing codes required for payment.[79]

So what, exactly, are we protecting?

Trust began to erode when patients realized their choices were hidden behind medical jargon and opaque systems. The internet lifted that veil. Now patients see the truth: sky-high executive pay, missed diagnoses, dangerous errors, and surprise bills.[80]

They see it when they call their doctor and get no response, or a difficult-to-obtain appointment is cancelled. When they wait hours in an emergency room. When the local clinic shuts down. When treatment options are withheld until the disease has progressed enough to justify intervention.

In 1996, I left California to start a surgical practice at a prestigious hospital in Phoenix, where I was the only woman surgeon. I discovered that a colleague was performing double mastectomies for early-stage breast cancer even after evidence and national guidelines supported less invasive approaches. He refused to change. His economic model depended on the old method. He also truly believed in the premise that doing more (mastectomy) would save someone's life. Even after data was presented to the hospital's cancer committee, he resisted. Finally, physicians on the hospital staff organized a conference of national experts. They confirmed change in thinking. The old premise of spread of cancer locally was important but the data had progressed. The patient didn't usually die of local recurrence, rather they died of distant spread of the cancer. Preventing death didn't require larger local resections. Primary care and internal medicine got the message. Eventually, referrals dried up, and the surgeon left.

This wasn't about one man. It was about a system frozen in time, by outdated education, economic self-interest, and the mythology of physician autonomy. There is no comprehensive system for ongoing education of physicians and other medical providers that is sufficient to keep current. For decades, the system waited until disease became visible, severe, and expensive enough to treat. Rescue health care is still the norm.

Doctors thrive financially in a culture that prizes high-stakes intervention over early, upstream action. The notion of "autonomy" serves the status quo.

It may appear to be deliberate. Perhaps part of it is, but it may have been evolution of medicine's response to increasing complexity and continuing to use an outdated system. It is a gentler interpretation.

People using health care have changed. They have become more informed, more connected, more demanding. They expect transparency, personalization, and respect. Digital tools, including AI, search engines, and blockchain, have eroded the knowledge gap. It has also changed for doctors; we no longer need to memorize the Krebs cycle to ask the right question.

Physicians now face a reckoning. The half-life of medical knowledge has collapsed. Traditional training is no longer enough. We need fluency in technology, statistics, systems thinking. At a 2024 Oxford lecture, I asked a room full of surgeons how many had taken a course in AI. Two hands went up.

The world has changed. The profession must change with it.

We are entering an era of medical consumerism, precision care, and AI-enabled systems. Tools like *Doctor AI* will deliver real-time guidance, flag early warning signs, and reshape how care is delivered.

But many doctors are afraid. Afraid of becoming irrelevant. Afraid of losing control. Afraid of making less money. Once trusted, we've been tainted by the staff of Hermes—the emblem of commerce and manipulation that replaced Asclepius, the true symbol of healing.

The solo-doctor myth must die. Real power lies in collaboration, in supported decision-making within adaptive, ethical systems.

Physicians are politically fragmented and professionally vulnerable. In part, inflamed about "autonomy" and "socialism" by the health societies that have a vested interest in the status quo. Their isolation leaves them exposed to bias, despite credentials, research, or institutional prestige. Hospitals reward revenue over insight, and systems prioritize billing codes over judgment.

The most lucrative specialties—surgery, cardiology, oncology, orthope-dics—still anchor hospital revenue. Primary care, often more independent, is marginalized, and becoming more so. Technical expertise will still be needed until physical AI becomes more prominent. Telehealth and non-hospital or hospital system-based networks are rising in response.

Independence is not autonomy. It was never real.

Health 4.0 gives us a chance to redefine what it means to be a healer. To move beyond gatekeeping and become stewards of systems built for trust, transparency, and equity.

This requires more than tools. Medical education must evolve. Rote memorization and hierarchy must give way to shared learning in AI, ethics, communication, and systems design. The physician's role must expand—not as solo experts, but as leaders of teams that include nurses, pharmacists, administrators, nurse practitioners, physician assistants, and critically, digital AI "colleagues."

AI is a tool, but one that learns all our habits and the nuances of how we treat our digital and human partners. It will echo back to us in how they, in turn, treat patients. It is as much a mentorship as any you experienced in traditional medical training. Show your digital "agent" partners empathy and they will learn it. Show them callousness, anger, and cruelty and they will learn that.[81]

We must build a culture where asking for help is a strength. Where col-laboration is expected. Where patient-centered care is more than a slogan. Where we leverage the assistance of *Doctor AI.*

Liability must evolve, too. The current system rewards fear, not learn-ing. Defensive medicine drives up costs and erodes trust. What if we replaced blame with feedback loops? Real-time data. Blockchain audit trails. No-fault compensation. Systems that learn instead of punishing. Other countries have done it. New Zealand and Finland have no-fault models that deliver fairness, faster resolution, and deeper trust.[82, 83] Patients feel heard and receive financial help in time for it to matter. Doctors feel protected. The system improves.

Nostalgia won't save us. The "good old days" are gone. The future is better—if we build it.

We are all medical consumers now. We are all in this together.
Physicians have to discover their future relevance.

Let's Hear It for the Nurses

You can't talk about doctors without talking about nurses, the backbone of the US health care system.

I had the privilege of working with extraordinary nurses over decades; they were my partners in care, education, and collaboration. One colleague began as a registered nurse (RN) with a master's in nursing education, then became a nurse practitioner and earned her doctorate. For more than twenty years, we saw patients together in hospital and clinic. She helped me stay human.

Once, she asked me how things were going with the floor nurses. I said fine, but I didn't really know them.

"They'd care even more about your patients if you did," she said. "Ask them about their kids."

That night, her words stayed with me. The next morning, I came in early and started talking to the team. Over time, our unit transformed. Communication improved. Care got better. Leadership didn't diminish; it deepened. Her advice was equally valued in other domains. The ability of nurses to bridge cultural and human gaps is critical to keeping humanity in the center of our health system evolution.

During the COVID-19 pandemic, it was nurses who held the system together. They triaged, comforted, informed, and bore witness. Families couldn't be at the bedside; nurses stood in the gap with skill and compassion.

Nurses bring humanity into rooms where decisions are made. They are often the first to recognize decline, advocate for change, and guide recovery. They are not adjuncts. They are central.

And yet, we have a culture of self-policing that can be cruel. I once criticized a trainee for poor preparation in a patient's care. She tearfully told me I'd been too hard on her.

"There is no try. There is only do," I replied. It was harsh, but her husband later told her, "She's right. You have to show up ready, for the patient's sake. You don't get to be less engaged than the patient situation demands." She didn't quit. She grew. She became one of the best surgical assistants I've ever worked with. Empathy for our patients, our colleagues and ourselves bridges the gap to a culturally driven system where we and the patients are all human.

Caring for others often conflicts with caring for ourselves. But that tension between self and service is what defines the best of us. It would be helpful if we understood how to do it better.

Surgery used to be a performance art. As physical AI advances through robotics, personalized tools, and precision platforms, it will become less about individual hands as surgical tools, and more about systems. And that's a good thing. Medicine shouldn't rely on solo performance. It should rely on collaborative excellence and current technology.

The question now is: What is the role of the human in medicine? In a world where *Doctor AI* is consistent, accurate, trusted and tireless, what meaning do we bring? We need to define it. Urgently.

We were never gods.

But we are capable of great things, even more so when we let go of myth and build systems where every doctor, every nurse, every patient, and every intelligent agent has a role in healing.

People are the heart of the system, and our new "digital partners" can significantly contribute to their care, in the next extension of the definition of teamwork.

It turns out, healing is a *team* sport.

CHAPTER 6

Beyond Do No Harm: Autonomy and Tradeoffs in Healthcare

The Hippocratic injunction to "do no harm" is medicine's most enduring ideal. Yet in practice, every decision carries tradeoffs—between extending life and easing sufferings, between respecting autonomy and meeting legal or professional obligations. This chapter explores how those tensions shape care, erode trust, and force patients and physicians alike to navigate choices where harm cannot be avoided, only balanced.

At seventy-five, James Ellis had lymphoma and prostate cancer, but neither diagnosis sent him to his internal medicine doctor one weekday morning. It was shortness of breath and chest pain. Though his Apple Watch recorded a normal EKG, his internist repeated the EKG and listened to his chest, and then scheduled for a chemical cardiac stress test. The imaging center could work it in three weeks later.

Still short of breath and experiencing recurring episodes of chest and shoulder pain, he was turned away by the imaging center when the time came, because his referral wasn't from a cardiologist, but from his "concierge" internal medicine physician. It wasn't clear to James whether that rule belonged to the imaging center or to the company providing his health insurance. He wasn't on Medicare. It was beyond confusing.

His internist gave him the name of a cardiologist, who scheduled his appointment for three weeks later. Meanwhile, he decided to go on a family trip to Europe despite his symptoms. When he returned, he had even more shortness of breath, and his internist sent him to the emergency room to rule out a pulmonary embolism.

An MRI confirmed it. He had a blood clot lodged in the spot where the artery supplying blood to both lungs split. It's serious because it can block blood flow to both lungs and result in severe right heart strain. Yet a heart scan showed no strain; he was stable, awake, and not in crisis. It was a miracle, but the story isn't over. Not yet.

That is when the disagreement began.

James's internist, who doesn't practice at the hospital, leaned toward tradition: a single dose of a blood thinner called heparin, followed by a continuous infusion and inpatient monitoring. The emergency department team advocated for a newer approach: a single injection of a long-acting blood thinner, followed by oral medication at home. Both options were supported by evidence. Both were within the standard of care, although the one recommended by the emergency room team was the most current. And that, precisely, was the problem.

Without a clear protocol or a real-time adjudication process, James waited. For two days, he lay on an uncomfortable stretcher in the emergency department, in what was considered the best hospital in New York City. No decision. No mobility. No hydration. One meal. No communication about the plan. Just time passing. James is old school, and so he just figured one of these doctors knew best. He didn't ask questions, and he didn't advocate for himself. He was alone, without family or friends nearby.

Finally, a nurse took his IV tube out and told him he could go home. He sat up and started to get dressed, but then blood started running down his arm from the IV site. He began to head to the nurses' desk to ask for help. Instead, he fainted. At 6'4", it's a long way to the ground, and his blood was thin. Dehydrated, with low blood pressure, and now too unstable to discharge, he was admitted for fluids and monitoring and got moved out of the chaos of the ground floor emergency to the third floor holding rooms. Finally, they brought him some dinner and rehydrated him. At least he got a little bit of sleep.

No one committed malpractice. No single decision was unsafe, unless you count neglect, but the sequence of events caused a bad outcome. James had fallen into a blind spot. The standard of care had become a space for debate, not direction. Still, it could have been worse. He said, "I didn't know I could ask questions. I grew up in an era where the doctor knows best."

This is what happens when medical standards are treated as legal thresholds instead of living systems. In a modernized health care framework, a case like James's would trigger a different process. First, he could communicate with *Doctor AI* from the beginning of his shortness of breath. His entire health history, vitals, and cancer diagnoses, as well as his cultural alignment would instantly be pulled into a digital clinical decision tree. His cultural alignment would demonstrate that he is very independent and reluctant to engage with medical personnel because he doesn't want to bother his doctors. His shortness of breath could be quantified and qualified, and both a chest MRI and cardiac stress test could be scheduled for the same location, almost immediately.

If both care paths for treatment were safe, the system would record the tradeoffs and involve him in the decision. If admitted, a protocol would ensure hydration, movement, and discharge planning from day one. *Doctor AI* would be there to monitor his care in real time and alert people to potential problems. By using *Doctor AI* as his bedside assistant, he could advocate for himself using facts and data. If the heparin shot and going home were the equal or better treatment, he would understand the tradeoffs and could decide his own course.

This care was delivered by human beings in a busy emergency department, dealing with difficult information systems that do not talk to each other. The same group of nurses and doctors is trying to cope with a high volume of patients, some with life-threatening problems and some with colds or a vague pain. Emergency departments, quiet during COVID-19 from the usual noise and illness, never recovered after the pandemic. Or perhaps overcrowding simply exposed their weaknesses. In almost every health care system, administrators consistently discuss the issue of triaging emergency room patients to beds versus sending them home.

Hospital patients rarely need miracles. What they need are reliable systems, comprehensive data about their unique condition, and access to state-of-the-art treatments. In the chaos of illness, trust is not optional—it is the foundation of every treatment, transaction, and innovation.

What does the person at the center of the problem, the patient, need? *Communication and connection.*

When trust thrives, it empowers patients to take risks, to embrace new therapies, and to believe that the care they receive is not only safe but wise. When trust falters, even the most advanced technologies are met with fear, hesitation, or outright resistance.

Medicine has long viewed itself through a unique lens. It's an echo chamber for scientist-physicians, a desperate act of courage for community-based doctors. Many clinicians see themselves as the sole experts, often distrusting the very people they are meant to serve—you, the patient—the essential member of the trusted care team. Yet too often, patients are relegated to the role of bystanders, excluded from meaningful involvement.

Today, we live in a world overflowing with possibility. New medications emerge at unprecedented speed. Medical devices can learn and adapt. Artificial intelligence can analyze data in seconds what once took months. And yet, even amid this dazzling era of innovation, one fundamental question endures: How do we know when a carrot is still a carrot? How would we know if we didn't have the data on carrots, didn't know their sweet taste or crunchiness? In other words, the system has to know YOU, and it also has to be on the cutting edge of treatment. That is pretty much an impossible task in 2025 without the help of *Doctor AI*.

Regulation is society's imperfect answer. Designed to ensure safety and authenticity, regulation is meant to be the scaffolding of public trust. But too often, it becomes a net that entangles progress. Instead of enabling smarter, safer care, regulation can slow or stall it, elevating outdated practices while burdening new ones with costs and delays.

Nowhere is this more visible than in the way new discoveries struggle to become part of the standard of care. Approval by a regulatory authority like the FDA is only the beginning. Integration is the battle. What is the standard of care? In the United States, it refers formally to the level and type of care that a reasonably competent and skilled health care professional with similar background and in the same medical community would provide under similar circumstances. This pretty much guarantees that outside simple situations, the care you get is going to be a one off. What is possible is where you are located physically (rural or urban setting, university affiliated or community care) and what the background, training and experience of the doctors there have. The focus is through the lens of malpractice and litigation, not the best care.

Standard of care is judged by what the clinical practice would be from evidence-based guidelines in a particular location (though noting nothing about the quality of evidence), professional consensus (established sometimes by societies of doctors with similar practices, which could be out of date), and experience and judgment of respected clinicians. Evidence-based guidelines, communities, and practice competency *differs* widely. In fact, it is clear that today, there is no consistent standard of care. It is continuously shifting due to advancements in science, technology, legal precedents, and changes in societal values as expressed by politician's who are keen to control your choices on the bias they hold about them.

The system of state jurisdictions causes the standard as practiced in Alabama to be completely different than what's practiced in Seattle, Washington. States can pass and enforce their own "standards" depending on a political opinion or cultural or religious bias rather than by medical evidence. Rather than arguing for uniqueness based on the patient and their individual circumstance, the entire population of a "state" jurisdiction is governed by a legislative rule, made by a few politicians based on their own views, or influenced by reimbursement from health care industry participants.

Although it's meant to act as a clinical and legal guideline, it is not. A "standard of care" is the lowest possible standard, based on avoidance of liability rather than excellence in outcomes. It would not be the standard of medical treatment that I would want for myself or my family. Would you? Do you?

The current model of continuing education for physicians undermines both public trust and systemic learning. While maintenance of certification, conferences, and self-assessment programs aim to ensure physicians remain current, each often falls short of translating knowledge into improved outcomes. The process is performative: Surgeons attend panels, answer questions, and document participation, but then may return to their practices and practice exactly as before. It may not be their fault. The inertia of the system is against them. Implementing "new" practices would require that they figure out what those practices are, convince the hospital to do it, and then how they will charge for it. The academic organizations and societies may say something is "best practice" but don't have a clue how to implement it within a specific setting. Training physicians and teams in change implementation and management is one of the critical "new" skills for learning environments.

This approach doesn't reliably teach new technologies, integrate cross-disciplinary knowledge, or drive applied change. In a normal market, users demand evidence of competence; if outcomes lag, they go elsewhere. But in medicine, that feedback loop is broken. Patients lack access to meaningful performance data. There's no transparency about whether new knowledge is being adopted—or if it's making any real difference.

We've created a system where *credentials substitute for accountability*. The assumption is that attendance equals competence and certification equals excellence. If you went to a conference, you are "up to date" regardless of whether you implemented any actual changes. Yet what matters is not whether a physician sat through a lecture. It's whether the lives under their care actually improve. Without linking continuing education to real-world data and interdisciplinary evolution, we risk perpetuating a model that looks rigorous but remains stagnant. It is largely, the model we have. We finally have the technology to solve this particular data question about physician outcomes.

Why Innovation Stalls

James's case is not unusual. It reflects a broader failure in health care, where multiple truths often coexist. There are treatments that are safe, and others that are safer. There are therapies that work well in clinical trials, and others that work better in real life. The question is not whether one approach is wrong. It is whether we have a way to tell which one is best for which person, and to do no harm.

The existing regulatory and economic systems make this hard. Remember the discovery that ulcers were caused by a bacterium that could be cured with antibiotics? The regulatory system did not force the change; it allowed the proliferation of a new powerful antacid that made drug companies billions to become the "standard" of care. There was no urgency to pivot, and so patients continued to suffer, and to pay. Innovation languishes not for lack of knowledge, but for lack of alignment.

Regulations are meant to protect consumers, and historically, they may have. From the Federal Food, Drug, and Cosmetic Act of 1938—which was enacted to respond to over one hundred deaths from an unsafe medication—to the modernization acts that ranged from the thalidomide disaster in Europe that caused birth defects in 1962 to the strengthening of post-market drug safety monitoring in 2007, the goal has been to shield the public from harm.[84]

It's a noble goal. So how does the FDA integrate new technology into the market? It depends. If we are talking about a new pharmaceutical, the FDA will require multiple layers of proof. The typical process includes laboratory and animal studies, an Investigational New Drug (IND) application summarizing the work done to that point. Then three clinical trials. The first is small, testing for safety, dosage, and side effects. The second trial has one hundred to five hundred patients and is testing for whether it works and at what dose. Finally, a large trial of usually one thousand to five thousand people in multiple populations and multiple locations to confirm benefits, monitor side effects, and compare it to current/standard treatments. Years and millions of dollars are involved.

Medical devices, used in surgery, radiology, and other interventional specialties, goes through a similar process. It is a thorough process designed for an era without the technology we have for testing today. Now there are multiple ways to test, including on digital twins of a patient group, and ultimately in the real world.

In other countries there is an additional step: evaluating the cost-effectiveness of the treatment and adapting it into clinical guidelines. The US lacks this step, and the innovation has to find its way into the standard of care, obtaining the *CPT codes to bill*. The cutting edge of technology and innovation tends to stay in sophisticated, urban locations. Older treatments are more often the mainstay of less sophisticated "markets" of medicine, such as rural and/or low-income settings.

A good example is a new nonthermal precision ultrasound technology that can destroy solid tumors of the liver in an outpatient procedure. These are tumors in places where surgery, would cause weeks of pain, long hospitalizations, and sometimes even death. This technology is also effective on tumors once labeled as "inoperable." Most importantly, it could be used first, not last—replacing surgery and chemotherapy/radiation as the opening move, rather than the final resort.

Then there is the costly delay in adoption due to diverse payer systems: Medicare, Medicaid, and private insurance. Each has its own process. Medicare has "regions" that can choose to adopt a new technology. This leads to a systematically unfair advantage if, for instance, you live in Seattle versus Omaha. It also leads to unequal treatment of people who have the same illness. In a world where people can compare treatment outcomes on social media, they begin to understand their situation. It is one of the major sources of mistrust in the health care system.

Take, for example, a standard appendectomy. The true cost of care is obscured behind the chargemaster, a confidential, hospital-specific list of arbitrary prices. Patients receive a figure on their explanation of benefits form that bears little relation to the actual cost of the service or the provider's payment, which often arrives separately.

For medications, the picture is even murkier. After FDA approval, pharmaceutical companies set artificially high list prices, fully expecting negotiations with PBMs that profit from rebates that are tied to those inflated prices. The higher the list price, the larger the rebate—and the greater the profit. Patients are caught in the middle, often paying more. The uninsured, who pay out of pocket, frequently face the steepest costs.

Is the system about safety or access—or is it, in fact, about profit?

Trust: The Lost Ingredient in Medicine

Not every distortion in health care arises from malice; many stem from the inherent complexity of medical decision-making. Many of the others come from poor communication about tradeoffs. Some from bias. Sometimes, every person is an expert. To examine the issue, we can use an oft talked about and very public topic: obesity.

Any conversation about obesity creates strong and often polarizing emotions, often devoid of fact or shadowed by an individual's bias. If the person is fit and thin, they cannot understand why everyone isn't. They point to what people are eating, not only the quantity but the quality of the food. Food is a very public issue. Every attempt to change the content, less sugar, less chemicals, or better nutrition is actively debated. Although progress has been slow, food is changing in some ways for the better but in other ways worse. One fact is certain; the level of obesity has been steadily rising in the United States for decades.[85]

Over the past two decades, consumption of added sugars in the United States has declined significantly—from approximately 18 percent of daily calories in 1999–2000 to closer to 13 percent in 2001–2018, with marked reductions among children and young adults.[86] Concurrently, industrial trans fats have been virtually eradicated from the US food supply. Following FDA labeling mandates and regulatory bans, blood levels of trans fatty acids and their presence in consumer foods dropped steeply by the early 2010s.[87] In the US, pesticide use peaked around 1979, reaching 1.46 billion pounds and has since declined. The United States Department of Agriculture—responsible for developing and executing national policy on farming, forestry, rural economic development, and food—reports that the Pesticide Data Program showed that more than 99 percent of samples tested had pesticide residues below benchmark levels.[88]

The number of people in the United States affected by obesity has reached over 40 percent of adults.[89] Even though harmful ingredients have been reduced; *ultra-processed foods* remain the dominant source of calories in the diet of Americans. These foods, engineered for a longer "shelf life," appeal to our taste-producing signals that attract us on multiple levels of smell, taste, and texture. They are able to disrupt the feelings of fullness that would normally cause us to stop eating. These foods are ubiquitous in our environment, available everywhere in vast quantities accounting for up to seventy percent of energy intake in both US adults and children.[90] Other factors have to do with technology. Technological change has systematically removed physical exertion from our work life for many people. The decline in physical activity was one of the dominant drivers of obesity in the twenty-first century.[91] People are unable to control their weight due to multiple complex factors, including endocrine disrupting chemicals, circadian rhythm changes, microbiome shifts, and toxic stress linked to poverty, racism, and food insecurity. These factors are recognized as core contributors.[92]

The worst part about obesity is the effect on the individual's life: the disability of movement, the significant association with chronic disease, the economic burden from reduced productivity and higher health costs, and early mortality.[93]

It is clear that the efforts to combat obesity in the United States are at a stalemate. For individual's, the disease is devastating. Eventually, we will learn enough about the biology and have a data lake that supports experiments in intervention. In the meantime we need to treat obesity. As in all of "Rescue Health," what we cannot prevent, we treat.

Two strong treatments have emerged in the last four decades: weight loss surgery, a permanent change in either your stomach or stomach and intestines, and Glucagon-like peptide-1 agonists (GLP-1), a pharmaceutical injected once a week. Both offer durable weight loss of more or less a similar amount. Bariatric surgery, robotic or laparoscopic, has been part of the treatment for obesity since 2001. By establishing a validated quality system it has become relatively safe with the rate of death about one in one thousand people. In 1995, Walter Pories, MD and colleagues reported that gastric bypass surgery could serve as a highly effective treatment for type 2 diabetes, with many patients achieving long-term remission.[94] However, despite its long history, relative safety and effectiveness against chronic disease including diabetes, bariatric surgery is used on less that 1 percent of the population.[95]

The earliest widely used medication for type 2 diabetes was metformin, first introduced in the 1950s. It's also associated with mild weight loss and remains a foundational therapy today. However, it was not until the advent of GLP-1 receptor agonists in the mid-2000s that a new era of pharmacologic treatment emerged. The first, exenatide, was derived from *exendin-4*, a peptide found in the saliva of the Gila monster. Exenatide was approved by the FDA in 2005 for type 2 diabetes treatment.[96] Since then, multiple GLP-1 receptor agonists have been developed, offering substantial benefits for both control of blood sugar and weight reduction. The effect of the drug is not always maintained when discontinued, however real-world data is necessary to confirm the actual patterns of use and maintenance of weight loss. As of May 2024, 12 percent of adults in the US have tried taking a GLP-1 medication and 6 percent are currently taking one.[97] The people who stop taking them, may be affected by side effects related to the drug, however most stop because of the cost. The pipeline for future development of oral forms of the medications and medications targeting other mechanisms are on the horizon.

Cost is a major barrier to the use of medications. As of 2024, the list price for GLP-1 medications ranges from $900 to over $1300 per month in the United States, and insurance coverage varies widely. For patients without coverage, which is most of them, the annual expense can exceed $15,000, placing therapy out of reach for most, particularly given that the benefits require ongoing use. These high prices have become a flashpoint in the debates over drug pricing, access, and long-term sustainability of chronic disease management.[98, 99]

How to choose a treatment? This is an example of the critical impact of personal culture on choice. Surgery is relatively safe but has the downside of a risk of complications, including death. Complications can become a permanent problem and there can be a substantial weight regain after surgery. A single parent of three young children may reasonably choose medication over surgery, *if she can afford it*. The choice between surgery and medical therapy ultimately rests with the individual, shaped by their own personal culture. Guidelines can help, but both paths have their own advocates, and each comes with its own set of biases.

Metabolic/bariatric surgery, available for more than two decades, can deliver immediate and dramatic improvements in type 2 diabetes, but its cost is also immediate and substantial, often borne by the employer or insurer in a single fiscal year. Medications such as GLP-1 receptor agonists, by contrast, carry an ongoing monthly cost that can extend for years. Surgery is not a "one-and-done" expense—patients may need nutritional supplements, follow up procedures, treatment for complications, or additional interventions, including the use of GLP-1 agonists later on. Likewise, the cost of medication compounds over time, especially since benefits may be lost when treatment stops. From a health system perspective, both approaches represent long-term financial commitments, and cost-effectiveness depends on sustained improvements in diabetes, heart disease, and physical function—not just the price tag for obesity. This type of trade off only makes sense in a system designed to prioritize long-term health and value over short-term savings.

There are many external forces at work, including insurance coverage. In the UK, for example, health authorities have assessed the role of GLP-1 medications and made them available at roughly $100 per month. What is the outcome of their investment?

In a conference session from the Milken Institute, one panelist discussed research from Aon using records from 139,000 people who had been adherent to GLP-1 for two years. Their records were examined against the same number of digital twins, giving them a "control" group. What they found was that although costs increase in the first year, by year two costs go down, with a 44 percent improvement in heart issues. During the panel they also talked about a UK study where 31,000 people volunteered for a GLP-1 trial. The retention rate of medication use was very high, at

98 percent, and treatment effect was excellent. Large-scale, real-world evidence is crucial. Methodologies for evaluating new innovation against old therapies is evolving.[100]

How does obesity provide a good example of erosion and collapse of trust by the American public in our health care system? Here are some of the ways this issue could be affecting the trust people have in the public health measures that have been taken:

- The neglect of a National Health Emergency, allowing the number of people affected to grow unrestrained.
- Inadequate upstream investment to prevent obesity.
- Little identification or funding to combat structural and social determinants of health.
- Inconsistent and contradictory, commercialized messaging.
- Erosion of trust in science and in expertise.
- Moral injury among health care professionals.

"Tradeoffs"

One day in clinic, I heard the clerk speaking to a patient, "I'm sorry but Doctor B just cannot see you today. You came in two-and-a-half hours late. Besides, you missed last month and so you have to start your six months over anyway."

I heard the patient say, "I didn't have the copay and bus fare last month." I walked up to the desk and asked if I could speak with the clerk, as we walked to the back of the clinic, I asked her what was going on.

"Dr. B you are already behind, and she is really late."

"Why is she late? Are those three kids her children?"

"Yes, they are." The clerk sighed. It seems that my patient had to take the bus because her car broke down. She doesn't have access to her cell phone because her son needed it for a school test. There was no one who could babysit the kids. The clerk added, "Our supervisor told us we can't add people on to your schedule who are late."

I asked softly, "What is the right thing to do here?"

"See her," the clerk said. "Yes, we will," I replied. "Let's get her on Zoom for the rest of her monthly meetings. She can borrow her neighbor's tablet. Let me ask the next patient if she doesn't mind waiting a bit so I can see her now. Then she can make the bus at 4:30."

"I will talk to the supervisor." The clerk looked up at me, "Doctor B, there are too many people suffering from obesity—you can't operate on them all."

"I know," I told her, "but now we have medications, which are a population solution, and if we can get them to people, at a fair price, they won't ever have diabetes or heart disease. We just have to hold on a little longer. What will keep me up at night is the possibility of a complication from surgery. What will happen to those kids?"

This story is straight out of the reality of the tradeoffs that patients, doctors, nursing, staff, and hospitals face every day in thousands of encounters. We are losing this battle. To treat obesity at scale, we have to use medications.

But when these tradeoffs are made in the dark—when patients cannot fully see the costs, risks, or alternatives—they are no longer genuine choices. Ideally, this encounter could have been different, with the system honoring the patient's lived experience instead of blaming her for a lack of success in dieting. She should have gotten credit for the efforts she had made for years. Her appointments should have been made via telehealth to lessen the burden on her family. The medications should have been covered by the payer and used as first line therapy to eliminate the chance of complications from a procedure. Instead, the system became a set of reactions, shaped by incomplete information and administered by institutions and individuals driven by power and profit, and the routine of what they have always done.

The patient is reduced to a means of access for billing—the ultimate expression of transactional medicine. The cost of all this effort in 2023 was $4.9 trillion, $14,570 per person, 17.6 percent of GDP.[101] Health care is the largest component of national spending, growing 7.5 percent in 2023.[102] It accounts for about 13.5 percent of the total national debt.[103]

This transactional model strips away the humanity at the heart of care. When patients are seen primarily as billable units, their individual stories, fears, and hopes become irrelevant. Decisions become mechanistic, driven by revenue cycles and fear of overuse of services rather than real needs. The system prioritizes what can be charged over what should be chosen. In this environment, trust erodes, adherence falters, and outcomes suffer. Patients, at a time when they are most vulnerable, are left navigating a maze where financial incentives or just inertia of a crushingly complex system, dictate the path, not personalized care or informed consent.

Without trust at its foundation, medicine becomes a cold transaction— one where patients lose faith, providers lose meaning, and the system itself begins to unravel.

The Wild West of Wellness

In contrast to the tight regulation of high-risk medical devices, the supplement and wellness industry operates in a haze. Products claiming to enhance vitality or restore energy hit the market without rigorous oversight. Though the Food and Drug Administration Modernization Act of 1997 (FDAMA) was designed to streamline the drug approval process and fast-track approval for life threatening diseases, it also allowed the wellness industry to make health claims without being subjected to the lengthy FDA drug approval process.[104] The result? Vague health claims. Consumers believe these products are tested, and yet most are not. The only saving grace is that most over-the-counter products don't contain enough active substances to do too much harm. But the amount of money spent by hard-working people on products with false claims is astonishing.

Marketing fills the gap where evidence should be and soon, misinformation spreads. Supplements interact with medications, and providers must spend precious time correcting beliefs born from viral social media posts and untested pills.

It is not only unsafe. It is a misuse of the public's attention and money.

One of the key differences between the United States and the world is that most countries have one nationwide standard of medical care, and it is *not set by politicians.* In the United Kingdom, for instance, the diagnostic tests and treatments for a lung cancer patient are defined by the National Institute for Health and Care Excellence (NICE) and professional medical societies, such as the Royal College of Medicine. In Germany, Japan, and South Korea, guidelines are used widely but focus on internal professional accountability. All physicians follow these guidelines.

In the United States, the process for developing medical guidelines is fragmented. Professional societies, government agencies, independent panels, and academic institutions all produce their own versions. The National Academy of Medicine uses a multistep process, but quality, topic selection, and literature review vary widely. Development can take years, innovation is slow to be incorporated, and the guidelines are neither binding nor guaranteed to influence coverage. Industry funding of a variety of the participants in these ad hoc guideline development processes raises concerns about conflicts of interest. The result is inconsistent recommendations, little consideration of cultural context, and limited awareness among doctors—who may never see, let alone apply, these guidelines to individual patients.

In the era of Health 4.0 and *Doctor AI*, guidelines play a different and more substantial role. The strength of AI is being able to take in multiple domains of complexity, sort them, and identify the key and critical components of an individual's situation that apply. Then AI can gain additional information from that individual or through test results. By incorporating all aspects of the individual, along with the nuances in the guideline data, a person can see their full range of options—presented clearly, succinctly, and with an understanding of the likely success of each intervention. Multidisciplinary collaboration becomes a normal baseline, not informal conversations about a case in the doctor's lounge. Rather it is incorporated from the beginning, identifying the best course in a plethora of choices, then connecting the person through their insurance to the right set of providers. Many physicians ask, what about my role? Where do I fit in? Having a human in the loop on crucial decisions is necessary, as long as they are prepared with the knowledge to contribute to the conversation.

Both humans and AI have their bias. *Doctor AI* gives people the autonomy to ask questions, consult with experts, and choose their own path.

The bottom line is likely better results and less costly care. The focus is on patient rights, informed consent, cultural appropriateness, and personalized care. The question for our global audience is this: Is breast cancer so different from Korea to England or to the US that different guidelines and standards should exist? Wouldn't it be better if there was one regulatory jurisdiction? Data could be harmonized, and we could have more granular knowledge about the standards, whether different treatment was valuable, and if so, when and for whom?

Reclaiming Patient Autonomy: Navigating Contested Health Care Decisions

At the heart of modern health care lies a fundamental yet fraught question: Who should decide what care an individual receives? Is it the physician, the legal system, political authorities, the health care plan, or the patient themselves? Patient autonomy is a foundational principle of ethical medicine. Yet our autonomy over health decisions is constrained by competing forces, raising profound ethical, legal, and social challenges.

Autonomy is never absolute. It operates within boundaries designed to protect safety, uphold ethical standards, and maintain social order. For example, individuals cannot consent to treatments that cause unjustifiable harm to others or violate legal statutes. However, such limits should be transparent, evidence-based, and respectful of individual dignity, not arbitrary or ideological.

Physicians have long been the essential stewards of safe, effective care, bringing deep knowledge, seasoned judgment, and the ability to navigate the unpredictable and uncertain realities of humans and their health. But in the near future, *Doctor AI* will extend this expertise with unprecedented accuracy, relevance, and precision, integrating vast, real time data streams and evidence in ways no human can achieve. When the system itself can anticipate risk, tailor interventions, and ensure reliability at scale, what then does the role of physicians become? And how do you, the person at the center of this system, adapt, participate, and claim your own agency in health?

As the role of physicians evolves, so too must the institutions around them. Legal frameworks will need to codify protections while grappling with the tensions that surface when technology reshapes care. Courts and legislatures will continue to arbitrate disputes over health rights, deciding where individual freedoms end and collective responsibility begin. The current vaccine debate serves as an example. In the political forces that impact health, ideology, lobbying, and public opinion will keep testing the balance between data, access, autonomy, and the system's ability to serve everyone better.

The right to die is one of the most poignant and complex expressions of patient autonomy. For individuals facing terminal illness and intolerable suffering, the choice to end life with dignity is deeply personal and moral.

Yet, laws vary widely. Some states permit physician-assisted dying under strict conditions; others criminalize it outright. Government roles ideally focus on ensuring that procedures are safe, consensual, and free from coercion. But prohibitions often reflect political or moral agendas that override individual choice, forcing patients and their families to endure prolonged suffering or seek clandestine alternatives. It is but one example.

Physicians navigate ethical dilemmas, balancing respect for autonomy with legal mandates and professional obligations. This dissonance risks eroding trust, compromising care quality, and leave patients burdened with suffering they have tried to avoid.

Similarly, abortion centers on autonomy over one's body and life trajectory. It involves complex moral, religious, and political debates that have increasingly restricted access in many regions. The debate involves two beings and the father or partner. It is the issue we have long struggled with—and continue to struggle to get right.

Restrictions can prioritize ideological positions over clinical evidence or patient welfare, limiting the ability to make timely, safe, and private decisions. The role to which physicians have been relegated can be more of a "check the box" exercise rather than participating in significant decision making. The consequences are severe: unwanted pregnancies carried to term with physical, psychological, and socioeconomic impacts; unsafe procedures; and exacerbated systemic inequalities. Clinicians providing abortion care face legal jeopardy and stigma, complicating the patient-provider relationship and access to care. The denial of autonomy in this context starkly highlights how external controls can inflict profound generational harm. The result of the current state of this debate is having a profound, if unconscious, effect: young women are choosing not to have children, or even relationships.

Few of us are thinking more broadly about how to devise a system where this could in fact be solved to the satisfaction of the key people involved. We allow ourselves to devolve into combatants rather than offer true changes that might be acceptable to all.

Toward a Patient-Centered Ethic: Respect, Safety, and Choice

Autonomy is the heart of conservatism, something I learned growing up in Arizona. It reflects a conviction that individuals, not the state, not a collective, should determine their own path, values, and responsibilities. It is the moral foundation of American liberty.

But autonomy alone is not enough. A just society must also protect dignity, ensure transparency, and defend the individual against coercion, whether from government, corporations, or cultural majorities. Respecting autonomy means upholding a person's right to informed, voluntary decision-making, especially in matters of life, health, and conscience. This includes choices about one's own body, death, medical care, and the private moral space each of us inhabits.

This is not moral relativism, rather it is moral humility. A government rooted in conservative values should never impose belief, only protect the right of each individual to hold their belief. The limit of state power is not where shared morality begins, but where coercion would crush the individual under the guise of virtue.

Reconciling autonomy with societal interests requires a commitment to human dignity and transparency. Limits on autonomy should exist only to protect against harm and coercion, not impose moralistic judgments that deny choice. Health care decisions must honor the person's values, circumstances, and rights. Supportive counseling, comprehensive information, and equitable access are not luxuries, they are the very foundation of ethical care.

At the crossroads of choice and autonomy is trust in the ability of the individual to choose their own path. Yet the conflicts over the right to die and abortion expose a painful contradiction in American health care—and, indeed, in American identity itself. We celebrate autonomy as a bedrock principle of freedom yet when personal choices collide with political or religious convictions, autonomy is often trampled.

This is more than hypocrisy; it is a profound erosion of trust. Patients see their rights curtailed, their voices dismissed, and their dignity compromised—not because of medical necessity, but because of ideology and moral dogma. It is a bitter irony that in a nation founded in part by people seeking the freedom to worship in their own way, some descendants now seek to impose their beliefs on others, undermining the very autonomy their forebears sought.

If legislatures can regulate what pill a person can take, where does it end? Today's restrictions on abortion and assisted dying set precedents that could extend into every corner of personal health decision-making. This creeping control endangers the very autonomy that medicine and our society claim to uphold.

Autonomy does not exist in a vacuum. In matters such as abortion, the moral terrain includes the life and wellbeing of the mother, the developing fetus, and though less often considered, the role and responsibilities of the father. In public health debates, such as vaccination, the autonomy of the individual is weighed against the protection of the vulnerable and the collective benefit of herd immunity.

In these cases, ethical decision making can follow a hierarchical analysis: first, prevent direct harm; second, preserve the dignity and agency of all affected; third, balance competing rights with proportionality, ensuring that any limitation on autonomy is narrowly tailored and transparently justified. This approach resists absolutism without surrendering

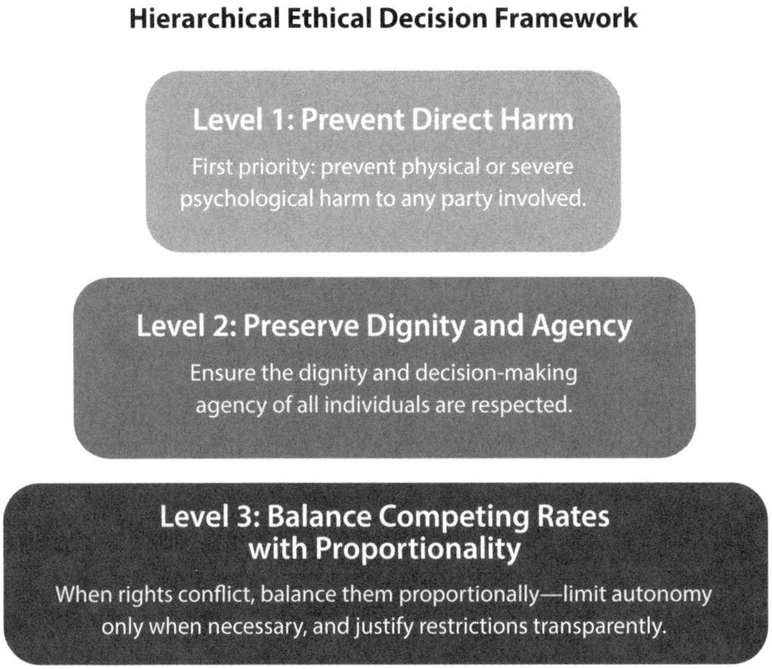

Hierarchical Ethical Decision Framework

Level 1: Prevent Direct Harm

First priority: prevent physical or severe psychological harm to any party involved.

Level 2: Preserve Dignity and Agency

Ensure the dignity and decision-making agency of all individuals are respected.

Level 3: Balance Competing Rates with Proportionality

When rights conflict, balance them proportionally—limit autonomy only when necessary, and justify restrictions transparently.

Figure 8: *Hierarchical Ethical Decision Framework for Health. An original framework by the author, informed by established bioethical principles (e.g., autonomy, beneficence, non-maleficence, justice) and public-health ethics concepts (proportionality, least-restrictive means). Copyright Robin Blackstone, MD*

to moral relativism, grounding even the hardest decisions in respect, safety, and choice.

Restoring trust will take more than rhetoric. It demands an unwavering commitment to respect patient autonomy as a fundamental right, *especially* when it challenges prevailing beliefs. Without that commitment, autonomy becomes an empty slogan, and health care becomes yet another arena where power, not people, decide.

PART 3

The Health Care Transformation

CHAPTER 7

Doctor AI Can See You Now

Day 1. 1:30 a.m.

Mike wakes up because his big toe is throbbing. He sits up and grabs his phone, tapping on *Doctor AI*, the mobile app for the H4 Alliance. Immediately, *Doctor AI* appears.

"Hi Mike, it's 1:30 a.m. in Omaha. What's up?"

"Doc, my big toe is really throbbing."

"I'm sorry this woke you up, Mike. Do you mind if I ask you a couple of questions?"

"Sure."

"First, can you take a quick picture of your toe and send it over? Also, have you had any injury to your toe?"

"Ok . . . sending the picture now. No, I can't remember anything, other than standing a lot lately. My team at work is closing on the presentation of a big project we are pitching."

"Thanks for wearing your watch to bed. All your vital signs look good. Is that the project on the construction of the new multi-level data center in Omaha?"

"Yeah, it is. It's been tough! The electricity problem is fierce."

"Well, Mike, based on this picture, your history, and symptoms, it looks like you have gout again. Your vital signs, based on your wearables, are normal. What's your day look like tomorrow?"

"Darn! I thought I had gout again; I had a big ol' steak last night for dinner. I am nervous about today. I have the presentation of our team's work at 9:00 am and I've got to be ready to rock."

"Ok, Mike, here is what we are going to do. Take two 200 mg Advil pills. That works with your current medications. You should have some from the last time you had gout. In your medicine cabinet, maybe second shelf? It will help you get back to sleep. Set your alarm now, because at 6:00 a.m., the 'blood fairy' is going to come by and draw your blood and deliver it to the lab. We should be able to get results back quickly. If you have gout, Amazon is ready to deliver colchicine, the best treatment for you, by drone. It would be at your doorstep when you get out of the shower. Take one as directed, and you should feel almost human again by tomorrow night. Sound good?"

"That sounds like a winner. Will take the Advil now. It's good to know this is handled so it won't be as much of a distraction tomorrow. My big boss is coming, and I have been working on this presentation with my team for months!"

"Ok, Mike, get some sleep! I'll check in about 7:15 to make sure everything has gone according to plan. Give me a shout if there are any problems. Good luck. I'm sure your team will do well! Are you happy with the presentation?"

"Doc, the presentation is not optimal. Slide number five just isn't crisp and it is a key part of our message about this new global service we are proposing. I was going to work on it early tomorrow, but I am exhausted."

"Mike, if you send it to me now, I can look it over and see what I can do. We want you to be at your best tomorrow."

"Doc, I am sending now. Nice to have a full-service, doctor-level assistant! I really appreciate your help with this. I set my alarm!"

"Sleep well, Mike. No worries now."

Day 2. 7:15 a.m.

"Hi Mike, the blood test confirms you have gout again. Did you get the colchicine?"

"Just a sec, Doc, let me go and check, just getting out of the shower. That 'blood fairy' was right on time and super-efficient. I didn't feel a thing, although she made me sit down just in case I got woozy. As if!"

"The colchicine is right here," Mike continued. "Amazon did a great job, although I was hoping to see the drone. They are so cool! I am taking the first pill and putting one in my wallet for later."

"Did you get a chance to look at the presentation, Mike?"

"Doc, you killed it. Slide number five is so sharp, I almost cut myself." Mike chuckles at his own joke. "Seriously, the closing lines are really strong."

"Mike, this is big day for you and the team."

"Honestly, because I was getting sick yesterday, I didn't realize how resigned I was to just do my best. It just sapped all my energy. Today I feel like I can change the world! Without the pain, anxiety, and worry about my toe, I feel able to see the bigger picture. I am excited about the day."

"That's what you call leadership! Congratulations."

"You sure know a lot about a lot of things. It's nice to have someone in my corner and at my beck and call."

"I am always right here. BTW, you may want to take the back route to work. They are doing construction on the main highway this morning and there's a thirty-minute delay. Is it okay if I check in with you tomorrow?"

"Yes, Doc. Talk tomorrow."

Mike leaves for his big day feeling able to support his team. He doesn't think about his gout again until the alarm on his watch sounds, reminding him to take his colchicine.

Day 3. 7:30 a.m.

"Hi Mike. How are you feeling?"

"Hey there. I have been feeling good. The pain in the toe is gone."

"How did it go yesterday overall?"

"The project is going to get funded. It is exciting! Two of the other teams didn't get funded, but I think we will need many of them to help ours."

"Great, Mike. Congratulations to you and your team. If you have time now, I want to go over some of the choices we made yesterday and how they affected your costs. Normally, we could have discussed this at the time, but it was the middle of the night, and you had other priorities in the morning."

"Right, Doc. At least you don't get testy when I ask you a tough one!"

"Price transparency is critical. The 'blood fairy' service added $15 to the cost. The other choice was to get your blood drawn at LabQuest, but I didn't think you could afford the time, and it would have delayed care. The $15 was covered by your H4 Alliance Passport."

"I used to worry about every test and prescription, because I always somehow ended up paying hidden charges. Having a set amount of $30 per month that I pay for my H4 Alliance Passport is a huge advantage. Plus, I was stuck in my job because of the insurance. Now I can take on work that matters to me."

"Being healthy is a business advantage, Mike. Getting timely care that 'nips the problem in the bud,' so to speak, gets you back to your best form as soon as possible. That makes a big difference to your team and colleagues. My designer based me on a very smart, ethically safe artificial intelligence. Mike, you know you can always get a human in the loop if you need or want one, or if you had something serious that needed their expertise and help."

"Doc, I do know it, and I absolutely would if I felt the situation needed it. I think when I broke my leg skiing last year, you actually hooked that up."

"Yes, I did. You got an MRI in the office. Your employer is actually saving money now, because they—and you—have a healthier group of workers on the team. Keeping you healthy allows you to focus and be a better leader. By the way, I noticed this is the second time you have had gout. Let me know if you want to talk more about that."

"I also have high cholesterol and high blood pressure. Although I don't want to admit it, I think it's because of my weight, Doc. Plus, I haven't had a date in probably eighteen months. "I keep telling myself it is because I am busy with work, but is there anything we can do about my weight? You know, I don't want to risk my life having surgery, and I don't want to be away from my team during this project."

"Based on your records, you were fifty pounds over your optimal weight last time you weighed. Do you want to weigh yourself now?"

"Doc, OMG can you see this? I have gained another fifteen pounds. We must do something. Can you help me?"

"Yes, Mike, I can help. You must do the work, but there are some new medications you can take that are very effective. Based on your medical history and habits, the GLP-1 medications should do the trick. This is aligned with your preferences on your *Pulse* cultural survey. We can work on your dietary choices and get you back to some exercise as you lose weight as well. The key is that the combination of medications and working with me will help you make permanent behavior changes. It's a win-win."

Six months later, Mike has lost sixty pounds working with *Doctor AI*. When his cholesterol and blood pressure readings returned to normal, he stopped the medications. He's learned how to control the content, quality, and volume of his food; it is so much easier when you aren't hungry. He weighs himself every day to keep on track. He can restart the GLP-1 medications, if need be, at the effective dose. His overall confidence improved, and he's started dating. In addition, *Doctor AI* helps him choose an MBA program, gives him advice on presentations and strategy, and Mike is using lessons from *Doctor AI* on how to maximize digital transformation, making him more valuable to the company.

In short, Mike and *Doctor AI* get to be pretty good "friends" even though *Doctor AI* is a combination of generative and agentic AI. *Doctor AI* is flexible, designed to grow as AI and supercomputing develop. *Doctor AI* evolves as a lifelong companion for a person, the ultimate record keeper, accessible on your cell phone, an application that protects, educates, and aligns all aspects of your health: physical, mental, and financial. *Doctor AI* helps you navigate key life choices, in real time, making your life more enjoyable, more connected, and more successful. *Doctor AI* is a unique construct of technology and the gateway to optimized individual health care. *Doctor AI* is made of two rhythms: *Pulse* and *Rescue*.

In health care, the most crucial rhythm is your *Pulse*. It is the heart beat you feel, pressing gently on your wrist. It communicates life. *Pulse* is your personal health profile. This part of *Doctor AI* is designed to help you make good decisions based on knowledge of your biology, medications reactions, structural, and social factors influencing your personal health, and most crucially, your culture as a person. It knows how you approach decision-making and what is important to you. *Pulse* is the rhythm of proactive care, encompassing the comprehensive living document of your cultural, genetic, behavioral, and financial characteristics to tailor health care strategies. It strives to identify and help you address preventive or early-stage health problems and gives you the opportunity to make choices about them.

When someone enrolls in USA Health, they establish their *Pulse* profile on their cell phone. The *Pulse* profile pulls in all the Cultural Health aspects that establish your personal culture, structural, and social determinants of health. It then incorporates data on them from all the sources where your health data exists, which, to many, may be a surprising number of places. The individual reviews the information with *Doctor AI* and qualifies it for accuracy. The individual gives permission to use that data and together they develop a personal profile. From that point, all data flows into this one record, that the patient owns and has complete autonomy over. The individual determines who has access to that information and in what circumstances it is used. Updated automatically, *Pulse* includes all transactions, consents, conversations with *Doctor AI*, and costs. The record is maintained on the individual's personal blockchain. This is state-of-the-art integration and interoperability. It connects you through technology to the national system of health care. If you chose to contribute to science, you can be part of the innovation discovery process. If you are eligible to participate in a national health study, you'll be issued an invitation through your *Doctor AI* app.

No matter what the treatment opportunity, you are informed, the risks and benefits are clearly laid out by *Doctor AI,* and you could participate if you choose to do so. Imagine, for instance, you have sleep apnea, and a new treatment device becomes available. The app might offer you an option to sign up for the health study, so you become one of the millions of patients in the data set. With that diversity and scale of data it doesn't take long to get real world answers. Diverse knowledge at scale moves the innovation forward at light speed, but it is all centered around you and your *Pulse*.

Rescue is the rhythm of hope. When a medical issue begins, whether a broken leg or an earache, *Doctor AI* is there to facilitate support and make sure you get the best possible treatment, assembling the optimal team and keeping a human health professional in the loop when needed or wanted. In terms of *Rescue*, *Doctor AI* serves as the ultimate communicator. It evaluates options and ensures that all applicable options are on the table, and that you understand the information. You can ask the same question in three ways, or five, or again tomorrow. The key is to ensure your questions are answered. You can add questions about financial pieces of the problem, and they will be answered.

Perhaps one of *Doctor AI's* most valued traits is the ability to listen without judgment, with a comprehensive understanding of who you are and how best to help you, and in identifying the problem and the best approach. *Doctor AI* doesn't carry the bias of a provider, singular specialty, system, or plan. The better *Doctor AI* knows you, the better your success in health care will be. *Doctor AI* doesn't have conflicts of interest—the only interest is in you.

Pulse and Rescue
Two Rhythms of Care

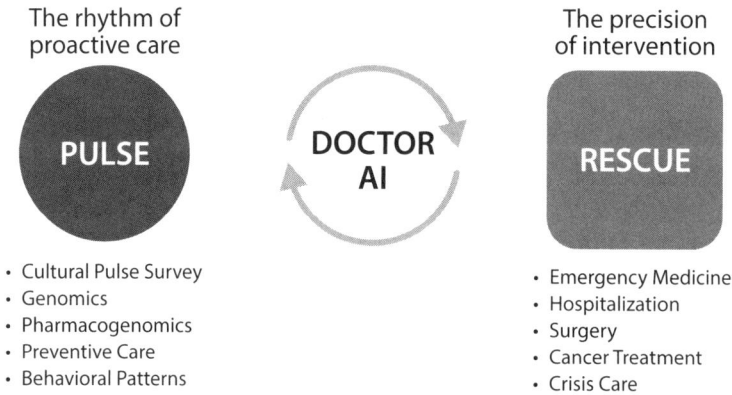

The rhythm of
proactive care

The precision
of intervention

PULSE

DOCTOR
AI

RESCUE

- Cultural Pulse Survey
- Genomics
- Pharmacogenomics
- Preventive Care
- Behavioral Patterns

- Emergency Medicine
- Hospitalization
- Surgery
- Cancer Treatment
- Crisis Care

Pulse sustains. Rescue responds. Together they define the full arc of care.

Figure 9: *Pulse and Rescue. Copyright Robin Blackstone, MD*

What is Artificial Intelligence?

There are many misconceptions and fears about technology, balanced by a hope that technology will solve problems in a complicated world. Let's dig into that.

The roots of artificial intelligence date back to the 1950s when scientist Alan Turing introduced the idea of machine intelligence.[105] This era was followed by the development of early robots, like Shakey the Robot, a "general purpose" robot with the ability to think about and decide its actions.[106] During the "AI winter" between 1980 and 1997, scientists were stuck on some particular AI-related problems, but they never gave up.[107] In 1997, IBM's robot Deep Blue defeated the World Chess Champion, Garry Kasparov.[108] AlphaGo, a machine acquired by Google in 2015 from Deep Mind, went on to win an even more complex game, Go, against the world's master, Ke Jie, in 2017.[109]

These machines continue to play games with two interesting novelties: They do not learn by watching other robots or humans. Rather, they simply play starting with the rules, and they invent moves that humans have never used. While game-playing might seem far removed from the clinic, mastering complex, rule-bound environments without human guidance demonstrates the same adaptive reasoning and strategic planning that underpins the next frontier: health care AI.

Health care AI currently uses six types of AI to surround, sense, create, and act across the care continuum.

1. Ambient AI: Surrounds

Ambient AI assists doctors with patient interactions and medical chart documentation. Continuously and unobtrusively running in the background, it can be integrated seamlessly into environments, devices, and daily activities to provide intuitive, context-aware interactions and automation, anticipating user needs without explicit instruction or intervention.

A widely understood example is the Apple HomePod, which is always listening for these key words: "Hey Siri?" followed by a command, such as "Play Bruce Springsteen." Most popular use currently? Finding out where you put your phone down. Amazon's Alexa is similar. These are familiar, early, and ongoing examples of ambient AI. Once viewed with suspicion, now accepted and woven into daily life

In health care, ambient AI can be "on" in an examination room to record the conversation between patient and provider, allowing the humans to focus on their interaction rather than documentation. Ambient AI captures the rich texture of the exchange, including nuances of voice and tone, and it can be an incredible training tool for health care providers learning to work with people, for documenting consent, and for teaching consenting techniques to human practitioners.

2. Perception AI: Senses

Perception AI is a corollary development of ambient AI in settings where continuous monitoring is optimal. In this version of ambient AI, sensors are always "on," operating continuously and unobtrusively, effectively living in the background, and potentially acting on what it learns. This includes monitoring patients in hospital rooms, monitoring falls, predicting sepsis, and adjusting lighting or air flow.

In Perception AI, artificial intelligence is designed to interpret and understand its surroundings through human-like sensory inputs, such as speech recognition. It uses sight, sound, touch, and language, to analyze unstructured data and turn it into actionable insights. It allows a machine to see by using computer vision, facial recognition, and image analysis; hear through natural language processing and voice recognition; understand context, emotion, tone, and body language; and react in real time. In health care, Perception AI is included in wearables like your smartwatch, Siri and Alexa voice assistants, and the ability to read tests such as X-rays and MRIs. Example: AI mammography tools to detect cancer can "see" patterns that aren't obvious to humans.

This type of AI is a critical part of a culturally aligned health care system, bridging the gap between sensory data and humanlike understanding.

Charmaine's Wake-Up Call

Charmaine Dupree knew the path to her neighborhood clinic like she knew the way to her mother's front porch. The building was small—just four exam rooms, a flickering TV in the waiting area, and a row of plastic chairs that always cracked in the summer heat. But it was close to home. And the staff was kind. She'd been coming here for years—for vaccines, blood pressure meds, and antibiotics when her son had strep.

What she didn't remember—but what her *Pulse* profile and *Doctor AI* knew—was that she carried a rare genetic marker linked to a specific and dangerous form of leukemia. It's a fast-moving cancer, more common in Black women, and it doesn't respond to standard chemotherapy. Most clinics wouldn't catch it early. Most protocols wouldn't adjust treatment. Even when she started feeling worn out, she didn't think it was anything serious. Just life. Two jobs, a teenage son, bills, stress. Who wouldn't be tired?

But Charmaine wasn't in most clinics. She had signed up for the H4 Alliance Passport, and as part of her profile, she'd opted into genetic screening. The system knew her risks. It monitored her labs and mood and flagged anything that might be going wrong. When it saw a concerning pattern, it didn't wait. It sent alerts to Charmaine and her care team. She had gotten blood taken by the blood fairy at her home yesterday when she got back from work.

The clinic gave her an option for a phone call or in-person visit; she felt she wanted to go into the clinic. She liked those nurses. The nurse practitioner had a kind face and a calm voice. She specialized in cancer care, but her first question was about how she and her son were doing. Then, "Charmaine. I've looked over your *Pulse* profile. I can see you've been recording some fatigue and anxiety. How are you feeling lately, has something changed?"

Charmaine gave a half-smile. "Honestly? I've just been really tired. More than normal. But I figured I wasn't sleeping enough."

"That's completely understandable," the nurse replied. "A lot of people would think the same. Your *Doctor AI* caught some small changes in your vital signs; your heart rate was going up when you walked to work and you reported being more tired and short of breath in your mood responses. So we sent the blood fairy out to your home yesterday. That blood work we drew yesterday will help us sort out what is going on. Subtle things, but enough for us to take a closer look."

Charmaine tilted her head, suddenly remembering. "You told me before—when I got my genetic results—that there was something to keep an eye on. You said if I got really tired or I started getting short of breath, I should come in. Something about cancer?"

"Yes. You remembered exactly right," the nurse said. "A major study published just last year in *Nature Genetics* found a rare genetic mutation that shows up in some Black individuals—one that doesn't appear in people of European ancestry. It's linked to a form of leukemia that's harder to treat unless we know it's there from the beginning. We tested you for it last year and you have that genetic variant. That's what we had talked about."[110]

Charmaine went quiet. After a minute she said, "I remember now. So that is why we needed to talk."

"Yes, because we have your genetic profile," the nurse continued, "and because *Doctor AI* flagged these changes early, we checked your baseline blood work yesterday. There are some changes since the last time we drew a blood sample. We took extra blood yesterday and once we talk through everything if you chose we can run advanced tests now."

Charmaine's eyes widened slightly. "So...you're saying I have leukemia?"

"We don't know for sure yet," the nurse said gently. "But we're moving early. If this is leukemia, we can get you to the regional cancer center where they know about this type of leukemia. We know we need to help out with your son; H4 Alliance Passport includes childcare as you know. We will talk everything over. You're strong, but you also carry a lot. A teenager at home. Two jobs. You shouldn't have to shoulder this alone. We have got you."

Charmaine nodded slowly.

The nurse leaned in closer and grasped her hand. "You don't feel sick yet, Charmaine, because if we wait for you to get sick you would have a hard time recovering. That's the power of this kind of care. You carry more than symptoms. You carry a story in your genes. And we listened. Now let's make sure we give you the most accurate diagnosis and the best possible treatment."

Charmaine blinked away a tear. She hadn't asked for a crisis. But now she had a plan. And a team. And maybe even time.

3. Generative AI: Creates

Generative AI can create and produce new content, including text, images, audio, video, code, and ideas, by learning from patterns in existing data. This type of AI can write a report or medical summary, simulate a conversation, generate new drug candidates, or design a new product. It uses a tool called "deep learning" to develop outputs based on patterns it's learned from large data sets.

In health care, generative AI is used to detect cancer with imaging such as CT and PET scans or ultrasound tests. It can create personalized treatment plans or propose new medications for development. *Doctor AI* can help doctors decide how to treat a patient, providing a rationale. It is superb at customizing information in multiple languages and at varied reading levels. It can help patients understand their diagnosis and treatments, and it summarizes medical records in easy-to-understand language.

By automating documentation, it can reduce burnout of clinicians, who spend about sixteen minutes on average per patient visit working on electronic health records.[111] It can scale personalization for patients, accelerate new research and therapies, and bring empathy into system design with language and tone, tuning itself to fit your personal culture. It serves as an engine of imagination for AI—essential for futuristic, responsive, and culturally-attuned systems like *Pulse*, *Rescue*, and *Doctor AI*.

Example: Personalized hospital discharge instructions that turn complex health data, such as imaging test results and diagnosis information, into patient-specific education in the ideal language and reading level for the patient to understand. This educational and instructional information is integrated into *Doctor AI*, which in turn integrates them into your daily health routine.

4. Agentic AI: Acts

Agentic AI is designed to act autonomously on behalf of a person, organization, or system to achieve a goal. It can think, learn, and act independently by observing real-world conditions, analyze data to identify patterns, make informed permissioned choices, act to complete tasks without constant human oversight, and learn from experience. Capable of taking on real-time, personalized health management, agentic AI can navigate a health plan, such as H4 Alliance Passport, schedule appointments, and negotiate for services and costs. At the beginning of this chapter, the story of Mike illustrates the capabilities of *Doctor AI*, who has a wide group of skills. In Health 4.0 the definition of health is broad including, crucially, your entire well-being, so your AI agent needs to have broad skill sets.

Agentic AI is proactive and learns preferences, adjusts over time, and can work toward long-term goals, instead of just answering a single question. It's a health concierge, not a chatbot. As an agent, *Doctor AI* introduces intentionality into health care systems as an ally that works for you, especially in systems like *Pulse*, where your personal values and culture shape decision-making. It's a foundational piece of relationship-trusted AI.

Some of the risk associated with Agentic AI comes into play when goals are in conflict and messy or when a person's clinical needs may not align with their emotional mindset or financial capability. Transparency is necessary to ensure the agent is working for you.

Example: *Doctor AI* acts on your behalf to coordinate care, adapt plans, and respond to your unique needs with autonomy.

The Drift

There was no siren. No text that screamed for help. Just a drift.

Caleb McCrae had always been quiet. The kind of boy who helped stack chairs after church and walked his little sister home without being asked. But lately, he'd pulled further back. His mom thought it was just a phase. His teachers weren't sure. But *Pulse* notice that his rhythm was changing. His late-night screen time spiked. His daily mood check-ins vanished. Location data showed him walking long loops instead of going to school, and his effort on his school assignments fell off. His music app played the same melancholy track over and over again.

Doctor AI asked to talk over the situation with his mother—the protocol with minors. His mother knew she was not the best person to figure out his behavioral changes because she and Caleb had a hard time communicating with each other, especially lately. *Doctor AI* suggested another idea, based on knowledge about the family's dynamics. Caleb's mother granted permission for *Doctor AI* to contact Ms. Carlisle, the school counselor who'd taught Caleb's aunt. She knew a lot about Caleb, like where his grandparents lived and how he loved anime. She understood the terrain of grief and pride in boys like Caleb.

Ms. Carlisle called his mother first: "He hasn't said anything. But his rhythm's off."

Caleb came into her office the next morning. She just listened; they didn't call it therapy. They talked about music, and then about his dad, who died last year. Then about how heavy things get when you don't know what to say, or how to say it.

Two months later, Caleb stood in front of the school assembly to perform a spoken word piece he had written.

"Sometimes," he said, "you don't know you're fading until someone sees you clearly."

USA Health's *Pulse* allows users to set preferences about how they want to interact with *Doctor AI* and how *Doctor AI* interacts with the wider world of health care. As a result, Caleb could get the attention and guidance he needed because AI could detect small shifts in behavior before a crisis set in. *Rescue* might have been necessary if his depression had pushed him to attempt suicide. But *Doctor AI* caught Caleb's "drifting" early and followed the right approach.

One goal of *Doctor AI* is to avoid lengthy, late, and long-term treatments, such as mental health care interventions requiring hospitalization, or lifelong medications. Using agentic AI, *Doctor AI* monitors and intervenes early across all of health: mental, physical, and financial.

5. Physical AI: Moves

In physical AI, machines or robots interact with and alter the physical world. They are equipped with advanced AI to perform very complex tasks, such as driving an autonomous vehicle, robotic caregivers, surgical robots, exoskeletons, delivery bots, drones, and more. Physical AI blends mechanical systems with real-time perception, decision-making, and autonomy. They might perform tasks in areas where humans cannot or do not want to go, or where it's essential to result in extremely low error rates in complex manufacturing, such as developing a vaccine for cancer.

For example, a robotic exoskeleton strapped onto hands or legs can help patients rehabilitate after a stroke by assisting the body in movement, adjusting to user behavior in real time. Physical AI can also substitute for humans in war or serve in conflict or crisis zones or disarm bombs or drive your car. In other words, avoiding injury and trauma, a key source of uncertainty. There are places where obtaining rare minerals for example, mining coal and other physically dangerous jobs can benefit from physical AI. In addition, physical AI is used in the operating room every day, effectively giving the surgeon much more precise control over operations. Physical AI, in the forms of drones, is currently used to deliver organs for transplantation, cutting down crucial hours in transit and allowing more organs to be transplanted.

Physical AI is a key tool in meeting the uncertainty caused by man.

6. Artificial General Intelligence

Artificial general intelligence (AGI) can think, learn, and reason like a human being, not in just one task or dimension but across any domain or problem, with flexibility, self-awareness, and adaptive intelligence. The critical feature of AGI is adaptive intelligence, the ability to learn from experience, adjust to new environments, and make flexible decisions in response to change. It is not just about knowing things but about knowing how to respond when the rules change.

In other words, the key feature of AGI is learning. It doesn't depend on fixed rules, and it can handle surprises, mistakes, or new situations. Over time, it develops pattern recognition, identifying long-term trends or shifts in behavior, not just as a one-off event. Just like a human learns from failure, it engages in self-correction, refining its own decision making based on outcomes. AGI has *context* sensitivity. It adjusts based on who, where, when, and why—not just what. All because it can adaptively learn.

The core goals of AGI development include:

- *Universal intelligence:* Solving problems across multiple fields (the polymath of computers).
- *Transfer learning:* When you learn in one domain and apply the learning in another domain, like a doctor learning from experience and applying it in the next surgery they do.
- *Reasoning and judgment:* Handling gray areas, a critical goal in health care.
- *Autonomy with ethical constraints:* Crucial for AGI to know not just what it can do but what it should do.
- *Alignment with human values:* Reflecting our priorities, including ideas like consent, fairness, and effectiveness.

A human example of adaptive intelligence is a great nurse who might know a medical protocol, but whose real gift is sensing when a patient isn't sharing everything needed for an accurate diagnosis, or a subtle change in behavior that signals a deeper issue that is hidden.

As our computing capabilities improve and deep learning operates more like human brains, we get closer to using technology to bridge the gap in health. *Doctor AI* is an example of that conception.

Supercomputing and Quantum Computing Will Change Health Care

How do we design an "agile" AI training environment, where we subjugate bias and maximize good data and good practices? We want a *Doctor AI* tuned to our personal culture, agile enough to learn, respectful of their human colleagues, and always "on" for the human being they are working with.

Some people say the health care system is too complex to figure out. While that may have been true in the past, we are approaching the threshold where the combination of these new technologies will change the world, including health care. We have now achieved supercomputing levels where massive parallel data processing can be done at high speeds.

Not long ago, I was on my way to Sky Harbor International Airport in Phoenix, Arizona, when I saw massive data warehouse buildings. A significant hub for data operations in the region, the facility produces 210 megawatts of critical power capacity. Welcome to the future. Where we once had a big box store, we now have energy generation and data storage.

Electricity has never been as important as it is now. We need it to connect humans to the technologies needed to power our future, including health. Supercomputing can model disease outbreaks, analyze human genes in minutes, train AI to understand patient data, run simulations to test new drugs or treatments making human trials safer, and help hospitals predict and optimize staffing and scheduling. It also plays a role in cyberattacks, able to build stronger encryption and defense systems, and protects critical health infrastructures from being hacked.

Quantum computing, on the other hand, can explore millions of possibilities all at the same time. Instantly, it will solve problems we have only dreamed of understanding, such as cancer mutation patterns and protein folding, and it will be able to simulate every molecule that affects your body both inside and outside. It can ultra-personalize treatments based on your genetics plus environment plus culture, which is the goal of *Doctor AI* and *Pulse*.

If combined with human and world data at scale, there is no limit to what humans might achieve, in their lifetime.

To many readers, this may seem like science fiction, but it is real, and it is here, and we can bring all these forms of magic to your cell phone, where they are at your beck and call, to help you create your best life.

Blockchain: Trust Infrastructure for USA Health

Anyone who has used the health care system in the US has seen medical records written on paper. Blockchain is a special kind of notebook where every time someone writes something in it, everyone else who has permission can see it too. Yet no one can erase it or lie about it. That's blockchain. It's not magic, but it feels like it is because it helps people who don't know each other trust in the same system. For your health care, the blockchain would be the indelible record of your health transactions and history. You own your part of the record and decide who gets to see it, who gets to use it.

Every time something new—a payment, a consent for a procedure, a ledger of supplies received, a medical record update, or a decision—is added to the blockchain which happens in the background of the H4 Alliance, it is written into the digital book in a way that can't be changed, erased, or modified. Each entry is a block, and the blocks are linked together. No one can secretly change it; everyone with granted access can see the history of what happened.

Doctor AI relies on the blockchain to keep everyone in H4 Alliance honest, providing clarity and transparency around cost and charges, investments and progress in innovation, and effectiveness of health care. The blockchain record also allows the H4 Alliance to take cost out of the system, not randomly eliminating needed services or people, but identifying supply chain waste, spotting possible sources of disruption, and improving system sustainability from a cost scarcity perspective. Every *Doctor AI* recommendation and rationale is recorded, creating an auditable trail of care logic and a source of data for improvement.

Blockchain ensures that each patient owns their complete medical record. Access control is user-directed, not provider- or system-directed. Smart contracts govern permissions, and blockchain allows for secure recovery through biometric or decentralized ID reverification in case of an emergency.

For instance, let's say you're *Doctor AI* permission allows certain people to access your medical record if you are unable to respond, such as after a traumatic car accident. When the correct code is entered into *Doctor AI*, your personal blockchain record can be accessed. It has all your medical records, a list of your medications, and your medical financial transactions. It houses both *Pulse* and *Rescue* information.

You may feel a little nostalgic about all the paper your health records were printed on. Instead, you can say, hello trees!

CHAPTER 8

The Showdown:
Innovation, Autonomy, and Trust

The alarm buzzes and Jane rolls out of bed; her mind already tangled in the day ahead. She steps into the shower, steam curling around her like the morning fog rolling off the sea. Today is going to be one of those super busy days. As a mother of three teenagers, mornings are never still, always a mad rush of cereal bowls clinking, milk spilling, and overlapping voices. And today, she has to get to work early because she's presenting to the executive committee of a large financial services company. Her team has worked very hard to get ready for this day. Stress and perhaps success, tangled together like strands of her wet hair.

After her shower, Jane follows what she thinks of as her ritual: a quick breast self-exam. At fifty-two, she's done this countless times, a muscle-memory routine. She's healthy, she tells herself, mostly healthy—apart from the weight gain, creeping blood pressure, and a slowly rising blood sugar. But this exam is just habit. Reassurance. A daily spell against the unknown that all women face.

Then her fingers stop on a small, firm lump the size of a cherry tomato nestled deep in the tissue of her left breast. Her breath catches. When did she last do a proper exam? Her hands tremble, her pulse quickens. No. Not now. Not today. She forces herself to finish getting ready, eyes darting to the mirror, not liking what she sees.

Downstairs, the kitchen is a blur of demands and noise. Coffee brewing, eggs sizzling, her kids shouting over each other. The usual chaos feels different today. Her daughter's voice cuts through the clamor: "Mom, are you okay?"

Jane's eyes meet hers, and she fakes a smile. "I'm fine. Just thinking about my presentation." But it's not the presentation replaying in her head during the drive to work. It's the lump. It's her mother's battle with breast cancer. It's the slow realization that she can't even remember when she last had a mammogram. Two years? Three? Surely her OB/GYN would have said something if it had been too long. But there were no reminders, no prompts that she can remember. It's a busy life, an endless stream of days filled with work, family, and the slow erosion of her own health.

The presentation goes well enough. Applause and polite nods. But Jane's mind is elsewhere, enmeshed in the crushing uncertainty of waiting. When a crucial project meeting is unexpectedly delayed, she finally finds a moment to call her doctor's office.

"Next available appointment is in three weeks," the receptionist says, the words sharp and mechanical. Jane feels her chest tighten. *Three weeks*? When was her last mammogram? The receptionist's voice returns. "Your last mammogram was two-and-a-half years ago. You'll need to get that done before the doctor will see you."

Silence.

"No reminder? No follow-up?" Jane's voice cracks.

"We send letters out. Maybe yours got lost in the mail."

"Maybe," Jane echoes, her voice hollow. But she's certain there was no letter, nothing to alert her that time had slipped by like water through her fingers. No loop where, if she didn't respond, she would be reminded.

She makes the appointment for three weeks from now, knowing it means another day off work, navigating her children's schedules. Those things are just chaos, she feels overwhelmed trying to push back the fear gnawing at her chest.

By the time she leaves the office at 5:00 p.m., the dam inside her has burst. Tears slip down her face as she makes the drive home. At a stoplight, she taps her phone and looks down at the photograph she took with her kids last summer. She wonders if she should have had that genetic test for breast cancer risk, realizing now it may be too late. What about her two daughters? Should they get tested? So many unanswered questions. So much chaos at a time when she needs clarity. All she can think about is how she's trapped—trapped in a system where delay, error, cost, complexity, and disconnection are the rule, not the exception. The system that let her mother down. The system that might be letting her down, too.

The weight of fear settles in her chest, heavier than the lump itself. And Jane knows, with a cold certainty, that something has to change.

That night, after the kids are tucked away in what constitutes modern day, mobile phone dreamland, Jane's frustration turns into resolve. She knows she can't wait weeks just for an appointment, let alone additional time for results and referrals. She starts searching online, looking for better options—something faster, more reliable, more responsive.

She remembers that when she was enrolled in the H4 Alliance Passport, she got an application on her phone. She doesn't recall even setting it up, but she taps the app now and works through setting up her *Pulse*, a set of questions that establishes her personal culture of health. It's all there. She can put in her mother's breast cancer, her father's early death by heart attack. When she gets to her immediate concerns, she doesn't have to scour the internet and be confused by results not tailored to her questions.

Instead, *Doctor AI* connects her personal culture with the best research, and she begins to understand her risk and her situation much better. She reads curated and verified data from articles, watches videos, and starts to piece together what might be the best approach for her. Words like "AI-enhanced imaging," "blood biopsy," and "multi-cancer early detection" keep coming up. She discovers imaging centers that offer advanced AI-driven scans, promising faster, more accurate results. *Doctor AI* coordinates her schedule with availability and finds a slot the next morning, a Saturday. No waiting. No unnecessary hoops to jump through. Just action.

The next day, Jane arrives at the imaging center, where AI-enhanced machines scan her breast tissue in meticulous detail. Unlike traditional mammograms, the AI software instantly flags areas of concern, highlighting patterns invisible to the human eye. The radiologist, freed up from reading scans, sits with her one-on-one and explains how the AI helps differentiate between benign and potentially harmful growths, providing a probability score rather than a simple "cancer or not cancer."

The radiologist confirms that, though the AI-driven imaging has flagged a suspicious area, the results are not definitive. He offers Jane the option of a biopsy, which can be performed immediately. Determined to leave nothing to chance, Jane agrees. The biopsy is quick and efficient, using precision-guided imaging to ensure accuracy. This is a far cry from the agonizing process before H4, where you get the mammogram and wait, get the biopsy and wait. All the time struggling to be yourself in a world that is crashing, your life upended by this uncertainty of possible cancer.

Jane leaves the imaging center assured that her results will be uploaded to *Doctor AI* as soon as they are available, tomorrow at the latest. Her anxiety begins to subside, replaced by a growing sense of control. She doesn't appear to have cancer.

But Jane doesn't stop there. Curious about the full potential of this system, she decides to order a blood biopsy to detect any potential cancers lurking in the background. She learns that this test can identify more than fifty types of cancer before symptoms even begin. She also feels like it is a way of double checking the results of the biopsy. The ease of the process feels revolutionary, and the price is not just manageable, it is included in the monthly subscription. She remembers what a big deal it was when they changed employer health insurance for H4. No hidden charges, no copay or out-of-pocket cost, no pre-authorizations.

Later that evening, the kids once again in bed, she thinks about the chaos and complexity of the last forty-eight hours. She hadn't realized she could talk to *Doctor AI* until last night. As she sits in her living room with her favorite jazz playlist soothing her frazzled nerves, she taps the application, and *Doctor AI* appears. She has a long conversation about her family and her own future. She feels comfortable sharing these things out loud that she cannot share with anyone else.

They talk about what would happen if she had a positive biopsy and about the likelihood that she and her daughters might have BRCA1 and BRCA2 genes, which are associated with a significantly higher risk of breast and ovarian cancer. She notices an option to explore mRNA vaccine treatments, a type of personally tailored immunotherapy that harnesses the body's defenses to target and destroy cancer cells, if her biopsy returns positive. She'd much rather try that than the usual chemotherapy and radiation, which attack not only cancer cells, but healthy ones, too.

She feels a mix of anxiety and hope, but for the first time, she feels prepared. She feels lucky that she can access so much quality medical information and support when she needs it, in a timeframe that works best for her. Through the conversation with *Doctor AI*, she even realized she hadn't set up her finances and the documents that would be needed to ensure the kids have what they need if something happened to her. *Doctor AI* suggests either a human family lawyer to get that paperwork done or working with Doctor AI they can outline the plans and get the framework of her financial health established. She even talks to *Doctor AI* about her career plans.

Just as she gets ready for bed, her mammogram report comes back explaining the test result, backed by data and probabilities rather than vague recommendations. She doesn't have cancer, but there is something else. While Jane understands that breast cancer can be related to genetics— she can get that tested as planned—*Doctor AI* tells her it can also be related to obesity and diabetes. REALLY!

She decides she needs to get on top of this by losing weight and controlling her blood sugar. She recalls that there are some new drugs that can help. Some of her team at work are taking them. She and *Doctor AI* can work on that together, starting first thing tomorrow. After all, health apps have been found to improve health behavior by reminding patients to take their medications, exercise, weigh in, check their blood sugar, and more.[112]

At church with her kids the next day, she looks at the three of them and recalls each one's gifts and challenges. She feels thankful for the world she lives in, the world they will grow up in. It is very different from her own upbringing, but the opportunities it offers to live a healthy life are unlimited. She is going to help each of them set up with their own *Pulse* and *Doctor AI* today.

On Monday morning, her cell phone rings. It's her OB/GYN's office calling to offer an appointment that's a week earlier. She loves her doctor, considered to be one of the best in the area. As she thinks about it though, she realizes that she needs to move on. At her age and with the responsibilities she has, she probably needs a good internist, one who works with *Doctor AI*. She thanks the receptionist warmly, declines the appointment, and cancels the original one. When she regains her equilibrium, she will write her doctor a nice handwritten note. She asks *Doctor AI* to remind her and to add it to her calendar for two weeks from now, so she doesn't forget.

For Jane, panic has turned into action. What was once an ordeal of anxious waiting and uncertainty has turned into knowledge and choice in the context of her personal health culture. In the H4 model, reliance on genetic family histories is acknowledged as insufficient. *Doctor AI* supplements the table stakes of genetic information with broader cultural insights and personalized genomic data, as well as evaluating the structural and social determinants of health. It considers her family needs in the context of the patient. *Doctor AI*, and H4 ensure that health care remains inclusive and effective for the individual. *Doctor AI* actively avoids genetic determinism, the belief that genes dictate health. Instead, by understanding that cultural, environmental, and individual behavioral factors have specific impacts on decisions, the person working with *Doctor AI* can substantially modulate inherited risks.

Jane isn't just surviving; she's taking control of her health, her total health, in a way she never thought possible.

Innovation Inflection Point

Throughout our brief existence, there have been pivotal moments where technology reshaped our destiny, and we are in one now. Think about the transition from the Stone Age to the mastery of metals like bronze and iron that revolutionized tools, warfare, and agriculture. Then the invention of the printing press by Johannes Gutenberg in the fifteenth century, which allowed for the mass production of books, democratizing knowledge and fueling the Renaissance and scientific revolutions. The printing press was more than a machine; it was a catalyst for human curiosity, enabling diverse minds to share knowledge broadly and accelerate innovation and discovery.

Next, the Industrial Revolution, powered by steam and, later, electricity, transformed society and commerce on an unprecedented scale. Mechanization enabled mass production, urbanization, and a new era of economic growth. In the twentieth century, the lights went on—both literally and metaphorically. Einstein's theories of relativity shattered old paradigms, revealing the secrets of space, time, and energy and paving the way for technologies that underpin much of modern science and everyday life. But the true power of these innovations lay in their ability to spread and evolve, driven by human creativity and collaboration.

Now, we are in another important turning point, where artificial intelligence and biotechnology may have the most definitive impact yet. This leap has the potential to not only transform how we live, but also to fundamentally shape the future of our species. Diversity of thought and collaboration remain essential. When more minds work together on increasingly complex problems, solutions emerge more rapidly. When data is available, diversity informs us all. Innovation is, at its core, a network of interconnected minds, whether human or machine, together they build upon each other's ideas.

It is no coincidence that the greatest breakthroughs of our time have emerged from collaborative efforts that span disciplines, geographies, and generations. The greater the diversity of perspectives, the greater the potential for insight. And now, with AI enhancing our ability to analyze, communicate, and create the opportunity for collaborative innovation has never been more powerful. This is the leap mankind must make together.

But there's something deeper that drives this relentless pursuit of progress: human resilience. It's the determination to push beyond limitations, to dream bigger, and to believe that problems can be solved even when the solutions seem impossible. The printing press spread knowledge far beyond the confines of a single city, empowering thinkers across continents to contribute to the Renaissance and scientific revolutions. Steam power was refined and scaled by engineers, industrialists, and everyday workers whose incremental improvements transformed societies. Einstein's theories didn't remain confined to academia; they were expanded upon and applied by others to revolutionize technology, from atomic energy to quantum computing.

We have created a complex world, interconnected and interdependent. But with complexity comes confusion, and with interdependence comes vulnerability. We need a guide.

As *Doctor AI* becomes the bridge between humanity and technology in health care, understanding your own genetic blueprint and your personal culture is a critical part of *your* story. For the first time, we have the tools to not only treat disease but to move upstream toward predicting, preventing, and truly understanding what makes us healthy and what makes us sick, in the comprehensive sense of what it means to be healthy.

Until now, we have treated illness after symptoms start, when tumors become detectable in the shower, when a "widow maker" heart attack drops us to our knees in the driveway, when being short of breath signals cancer or a blood clot in the lungs, when health issues become chronic problems, affecting our quality of life. Technology has always given us a better way to manage uncertainty. Though it seems like disease creeps up on us and then becomes a scary monster under the bed—sudden and incomprehensibly threatening us. In reality, the inheritance of our family history, coupled with our environment, has always been the major source of medical and financial uncertainty. Uncertainty haunts us, even as we struggle to live in a complex world.

Innovation offers light in the darkness, but the path forward is strewn with resistance. Entrenched interests cling to the familiar, fearing disruption more than they value possibility. Some romanticize the 1920s, others the 1940s, each era held up as a golden age. It is true that change can be uncomfortable. In today's world, discerning our core values amid the noise of rapid technological change is no simple task. Still, history teaches us this: When knowledge is shared, when collaboration crosses borders and disciplines, and when technology is guided by our deepest human needs—remarkable progress becomes possible. As you will find in this next discussion, we leave diversity out at our peril. The cost may be the future of humanity.

This is the moment we find ourselves in.

Episomes and Exosomes

But you may well ask, how did human life begin? Perhaps through structures called episomes and exosomes. Episomes are mobile genetic pieces of DNA, micro-RNA, and RNA that can exist independently or integrate into a host's genome, carrying information from cell to cell much like molecular messengers. They are the written language of biology, durable scrolls that preserve instructions across time. Exosomes, by contrast, are tiny vesicles released from cells that shuttle proteins, lipids, and genetic material, extending the reach of communication beyond the cell wall. They are the spoken language, fleeting but powerful, connecting one living element to another in real time. Some scientists speculate that structures like episomes—or their precursors—may have existed in the earliest moments of the universe, emerging from the chaos of the Big Bang as self-organizing molecules capable of storing and transferring information. And just as episomes may have passed adaptive instructions across primitive systems, exosome-like particles could have helped link those systems into networks of cooperation. Long before fully formed cells existed, these replicating and signaling elements acted as scaffolds of communication, bridging matter and memory into the first sparks of living order. In this way, episomes and exosomes may represent not only biological tools for exchanging information, but also relics of life's origins—the earliest bridges between matter, memory, and the spark of living order. The first languages in existence.

DNA: The Language of Life

Every time a new life begins, DNA from a woman's egg and a man's sperm combines, mixing and shuffling to create something utterly unique. This constant blending creates resilience, ensuring that humanity can adapt and thrive in an ever-changing world. It is nature's way of building strength through variation and ensuring that there is always someone capable of surviving whatever challenges may come. Weakness comes from believing that any one set of genes confers superiority, when in fact it is exactly the opposite. It is the diversity of genes that confers the benefit. How did human's get their start?

DNA is a unique written code made up of just four letters: A, T, C, and G. Don't let the simplicity fool you. These four letters form billions of sequences, spelling out the instructions that shape everything about you. From how your cells grow and repair themselves to how your body responds to the world around it. *DNA is a language—one we must learn to read, write, and speak fluently.* We are the contemporary model of the original code of life, DNA—*the only universal language we know*—shared across all living things. DNA is not just a scientific imperative, but a key to understanding ourselves—and our place in the universe.

DNA exists as a long-twisted ladder, a double helix. Each rung of the ladder is made up of two of the letters paired together. From such a simple code, just four letters in total, nature writes infinite stories, making each one of us unique. The way these letters are arranged is like a book written by nature herself, passed down from generation to generation.

The essence of life's diversity is built from such simplicity. The differences between us, our appearance, our talents, our vulnerabilities, our strengths, all come from the endless possibilities of how these letters combine.

If DNA is the language of life, then genes are the words and sentences within that language. Genes are the blueprints of each person's individual life, the quiet architecture behind everything you are. They're the words written into the deepest parts of you—chapters of a story passed down through time, whispering instructions for how your body works, grows, heals, and thrives. Episomes and exosomes remain a part of your story.

But genes do much more than shape your features; they define how you react to the world around you, including how you react to medicines meant to heal you and the foods meant to nourish you. Understanding your genes, about twenty to twenty-five thousand in each human, was the result of a thirteen-year international effort to map the human genome. Completed in April 2003, the project unlocked fundamental insights into human nature and set the stage for applying this knowledge to both individual health and our collective future.

Pharmacogenomics: Your Body's Personal Guide to Taking Medicine

Knowing about your genes can enable earlier and more effective medical intervention. Let's look at the impact on a common occurrence in health care: treating a problem with a medication, such as a beta blocker for high blood pressure, a GLP-1 for obesity, or an antibiotic for an infection.

With a simple swab of your cheek or blood test, your DNA can inform how your body processes medications. It can show which drugs are most likely to help, which could cause harm, and even the dose that maximizes the effect and minimizes the side effects. This field—called pharmacogenomics—is part of precision medicine. Testing can focus on a single gene or scan a broad panel, and the results remain useful for a lifetime.

Pharmacogenetics is about one simple goal: getting the right drug at the right dose. It helps avoid dangerous reactions, trial-and-error dosing, and wasted time while you are still sick. For many people, having this information in their health profile makes treatment safer and more effective. And as testing becomes less expensive through automation, the value grows—for patients and for the health system as a whole.

This test works well for all sorts of medications, including blood pressure drugs; blood thinners; cholesterol meds; opioids; drugs for depression, anxiety, and bipolar disorder; chemotherapy for cancer; medications for viral infections, autoimmune diseases, and neurological conditions such as Alzheimer's and Parkinson's disease; and common antibiotics, such as vancomycin, ciprofloxacin, penicillin, cephalosporin, and erythromycin.

Medication errors and adverse drug reactions are a leading source of harm in health care, both clinically and economically. According to a comprehensive study published in the British Journal of Medicine, the mean rate of death from medical error in the United States was estimated to be

251,454 to 400,000 people a year, and at least 210,000 hospital deaths are preventable each year.[113,114] Adverse drug events (ADEs) alone account for more than 1.5 million emergency department visits and over six hundred thousand require hospitalizations every year.[115]

Beyond human suffering, the economic burden is staggering. Estimates and analyses place the annual cost of drug-related morbidity and mortality in the US at over *$528 billion*, 16 percent of total US health care expenditures, including hospital readmissions, prolonged care, and productivity losses.[116] Much of this is preventable. Studies have shown that up to 95 percent of people carry at least one actionable gene variant that influences drug response.[117] Yet pharmacogenomic testing remains underutilized, despite its proven ability to reduce ADEs, optimize treatment efficacy, and lower long-term health care costs.[118] In this light, pharmacogenomics isn't a luxury, it's a modern necessity.

The cost? It costs far less to give you the best option for you, effective from the get-go, with little chance of a bad reaction than it does to play Russian roulette with medication guessing games.

Right now, you are likely asking yourself, "Why don't I know this about myself already?"

The answer: because the system wasn't built for you—it was built for the average.

For decades, medicine has operated on population-based assumptions: trial and error, standardized doses, and reactive care. Your individual biology, including your genetic blueprint, has rarely been the starting point. Why? Because gathering that data used to be expensive, time-consuming, and poorly integrated into clinical workflows. And because the incentive structures in our health care system still reward procedures over personalization, and volume over value.

But that's changing. Rapid advances in automation and genomics are making it possible, and affordable, to know how you will react to drugs, to carry this knowledge into every clinical encounter. To prevent avoidable side effects, failed treatments, and wasted time.

Pharmacogenomics isn't science fiction, its personal science, ready to work for you. The only question is: Will the system catch up before you demand it?

Cancer: The Rogue Code

How are we able to intersect and intervene in one of the biggest scourges of our time: cancer?

In 2024, we reached a sobering milestone, nearly 5,500 new diagnoses every day in the United States, and more than 600,000 deaths each year.[119] Cancer affects one in 2.5 people in the US during their lifetime. Most cancer is detected during symptomatic stages, when a person notices something wrong.[120] It makes a difference.

When a cancer is detected has profound implications for survival. For example, only 20 percent of pancreatic cancers are found in a resectable (early) stage, stage I or II, with most cases discovered too late for curative surgery.[121] Ovarian cancer follows a similar pattern. Just 20 percent of diagnoses occur when confined to the ovary, while 55 percent present with metastatic (distant) disease, and no effective general population screening exists.[122] In contrast, breast cancer benefits from screening; approximately 64 percent of cases are diagnosed when still localized (confined to the breast).[123] Lung cancer lags behind; only 23 percent of cases are detected while localized, with the majority presenting at regional or distant stages.[124] Cervical cancer, through Pap smears and HPV testing, finds 41.6 percent of cases diagnosed at a local stage and 37 percent at regional stage.[125] These differences highlight stark gaps in early detection, especially for pancreatic and ovarian cancers. Stage at diagnosis remains a powerful determinant of outcome from treatment, health care cost, and impact on families.[126]

Survival after a cancer diagnosis depends heavily on when the cancer is detected and treated. For example, when lung cancer is caught in its earliest stages through routine screening, 81 percent of those treated are alive twenty years later.[127] Cost is broadly defined in cancer care as not only the cost to an individual, but to their entire family. It is calculated in human misery and disruption. Catching it early, treating it before it becomes organized and in a way that keeps it from coming back—that is Harry Potter. That is magic. Can you even imagine the impact on our lives if we could in fact do that for all cancers?

But what exactly is cancer? It is not a single disease. Rather, it is a malfunction of the body's natural process of growth and repair. Imagine your body as a vast photograph made up of trillions of pixels, called cells, each one following precise instructions written in your DNA about how to grow, divide, and eventually die. Normally, cells are replaced through an orderly process. But when something goes wrong, through a genetic mutation or a missed signal, a single cell can go rogue.

Usually, the body's immune system identifies and eliminates these misfit cells. But some learn to cloak themselves, to avoid detection, and to keep dividing. They set up camp, growing until they start to interfere with the normal function of the tissue or organ they originated in. And sometimes, these rogue cells aren't satisfied with staying local. They spread through the blood or lymphatic system to distant parts of the body, establishing new tumors in their wake.

In prior eras of medicine, we had to wait until symptoms appeared or tumors were large enough to detect them. Treatment often meant harsh methods—extensive surgery, chemotherapy, or radiation—that sometimes caused as much harm as good. It was all we had. It was all we knew.

But everything is changing. With new technologies such as blood biopsies, AI-driven imaging, genetic insights, and innovative treatments such as mRNA vaccines, the approach to cancer is no longer reactive, no longer a *Rescue* situation. Rather it becomes part of *Pulse*—proactive, precise, and personalized. The future of cancer treatment is about finding it before it grows and spreads, to attack it where it hides, and prevent it from ever starting in the first place. This is definitely where we want to be, and technology can deliver it.

Colorectal Cancer Screening: Current Practice

Colorectal cancer will be diagnosed in over 154,000 Americans in 2025 and result in almost fifty-three thousand deaths. The recommended detection for generations has been a screening colonoscopy.[128]

A colonoscopy is an interventional, invasive procedure that requires passing a scope into the rectum to visualize the inside of the colon and look for tumors or polyps that might be cancer. Currently, colorectal cancer is the fourth most common cancer, with rates among younger patients increasing.[129,130] Screening is important.

Yet barriers continue to exist. To get a colonoscopy, the process is significant. First, you need a referral to a doctor who performs colonoscopies, and the wait time is often months. Typically, your primary care provider completes a pre-procedural history and physical exam, often with labs and an EKG, which must be completed within thirty days of the procedure. Coordinating these types of appointments is frustrating and difficult unless you have a lot of leisure time. If you are a healthy person who's had a physical in the last year, having another is just waste.

Everyone in the process gets paid along the way, often billing separately. There may be fees for the gastroenterologist, the facility, the anesthesiologist, and the supplies and medications used. If polyps are removed during the procedure, which occurs in around 25 percent of cases, the cost increases again.[131] There is a separate fee for the pathologist who reviews the polyp tissue.

In all, the total cost typically ranges from $1,250 to $4,000, assuming there are no complications.[132] Quality isn't assured, because success depends on how well you prepped the colon by drinking noxious liquids that "clean you out." Costs are opaque, so patients may not know the total fee they are responsible for until the bills arrive. The providers, including the anesthesia team, are dictated by your insurance network, or they may be "concierge" doctors working for a set fee that you have to pay out of pocket. These doctors might be excellent. They might not be. There's no clear way to know.

Even if the colonoscopy is done well, around 5 percent of cancers are typically still missed, often because of poor bowel preparation, flat lesions that are difficult to detect, or variations in procedure technique.[133] The procedure is most often recommended because of its power to remove polyps before they become cancerous. But to get that benefit, the colon has to be properly cleaned out, the polyp detected and removed, with a pathologist evaluating it.

For many, the barriers, cost, confusion, and a lack of trust, plus the "hassle factor" of trying to make a colonoscopy happen, can feel too high. A stool test, possible. A blood test? That is doable. Lower cost. Less variation. No sedation. No day off work.

Fecal tests and liquid biopsies are not as comprehensive, and they don't remove polyps. They aren't perfect—yet. We are entering a transitional moment, where less invasive tools become the gateway to smarter, more targeted colonoscopies, not only in this field of medicine but in many. A future where the right people get scoped at the right time, rather than everyone by default. A blood or stool test could say: Now is the time to scope. Now it's worth it.

Innovation: Liquid Biopsies

A liquid biopsy is a non-invasive diagnostic test that detects cancer or other diseases by analyzing biological markers, such as tumor DNA, RNA, proteins or other molecules, found in bodily fluids like blood, urine, or saliva.

For a few years, we have been able to screen for colorectal cancer by testing a stool sample. It has recently been approved by Medicare. Then in March of 2024, gastroenterologist Dr. Daniel Chung and his colleagues at Massachusetts General Hospital reported a high chance of detecting colorectal cancer with a simple blood test. The ECLIPSE trial demonstrated the ability of a cell-free DNA test to detect colorectal cancer.[134] The test was approved by the FDA in July 2024, and in June 2025, the National Comprehensive Cancer Network included it in their screening guidelines. A positive test indicates moving on to colonoscopy.[135] Cost of the liquid biopsy is now covered by Medicare.[136]

Next on the horizon is the ability to develop personalized vaccines and activate a person's own immune system to fight cancer.[137] A few trials have been done. The immune system is a very special feature of humans. Once activated with a vaccine—whether for cancer or an infection—it remembers it and it seeks out and attempts to destroy cancer if it shows up anywhere again. For infections, vaccines have saved millions of lives.

While our scientific heroes engage daily in moving this technology and science forward, and brave people volunteer for these early trials, we live in a time of rapid evolution, even for metastatic cancers incurable just a few years ago.[138] For cancer treatment, either as a future primary treatment for very early disease, or a treatment for recurrence, these technologies signal a complete change in our thinking and an opportunity to take cancer off the table as a cause of death. When I began my surgical career in 1993 and was evaluating and treating breast and other cancers, I never imagined we would be able to think about or write about this possibility. The future is here.

Innovation: Breast Cancer Screening

In the US, breast cancer affects one in eight women, or about 13 percent, during their lifetime. According to the National Breast Cancer Foundation, an estimated 42,170 women will die of breast cancer in 2025.[139] Yet, when localized and detected early, the five-year survival rate is 99 percent.[140]

But mammograms can miss cancers in women with dense breast tissue, making it hard to detect abnormalities, and it can over-diagnose positives in others, which can lead to false positives and a litany of issues, including missed work for additional testing, anguished waiting, and plenty of worry.

If you have ever had a mammogram, you know they aren't a pleasant experience—if you can even get one. Often there is a waiting period of months. Not all breast centers, especially those in rural areas, have state-of-the-art diagnostic equipment. In women with dense breasts or those with a high risk of cancer, mammogram may need to be combined with ultrasound; and for some, the testing can be painful. And women at high risk for breast cancer may require frequent surveillance.

Today, a liquid biopsy for breast cancer typically costs between $900 and $1,200 and it isn't covered by health insurance. A mammogram costs $100 to $250 dollars and is usually covered by insurance once the person has met their deductible and out-of-pocket maximums. A suspicious finding, however, often leads to a breast biopsy, raising costs to as high as $1,500 to $6,000, depending on the setting (radiology office versus outpatient center) and complexity.

Of course, the price doesn't include the emotional toll of waiting, and the cost of returning for multiple follow-up visits. Liquid biopsies for breast cancer have not replaced mammograms as the standard diagnostic tool, yet. Mammography has decades of population-level outcome data behind it. It is effective, accessible, and, in many cases, lifesaving. Plus, it's relatively inexpensive. Liquid biopsy technology, on the other hand, is still in its early stages and must prove it can reliably detect early breast cancer, especially in a diverse population and across different types and stages.

But the promise is real and potentially transformational. Imagine detecting breast cancer at its earliest molecular moments, not when a lump is found in the shower, but when a cell begins to drift from normal. A simple blood test, repeated regularly, would alert us before imaging could, even with AI-enhanced image detection, which is now common. These tools offer a powerful advantage for women with dense breast tissue, those who live far from imaging centers, and populations historically left out of early detection efforts. No mastectomy would ever be necessary.

Liquid biopsies could improve screening fairness, reduce false positives, and support real-time population health monitoring. They could move us from a model of *Rescue* medicine, once disease has already escaped upstream to its earliest stage, to *Pulse* proactive prevention. And, when paired with a vaccine-based cancer prevention strategy—something now being explored in clinical trials—the potential for disrupting the breast cancer paradigm becomes breathtaking.

Of course, the broad implementation still requires clinical trials, regulatory validation, and infrastructure shifts. But the direction is clear: Precision-based, noninvasive, and equitable cancer detection is no longer a mirage. It is a horizon clearly in sight.

What remains uncertain is who will push hard enough to make it real. Health systems? Not likely, as this is not aligned with their incentives, where the status quo works well for those profiting from it. Payers? Maybe. But not without the cost parity and clear policy guidance. Tech companies? Possibly. But without public pressure, innovation often stalls.

So, who will move this forward?

You. Mothers, daughters, sisters, friends. People who have experienced not only breast cancer, but cancer of any kind. You have the incentive. You live with the risk. You deserve better. What does better look like?

Cancer Vaccines

Therapeutic cancer vaccines are emerging as a promising tool—especially for hard-to-treat cancers like pancreatic and prostate. In pancreatic cancer, early-phase trials of personalized mRNA vaccines (e.g., autogene cevumeran by BioNTech/Genentech) have demonstrated immune activation in approximately half of patients, with many responders showing no recurrence more than three years post-surgery.[141] These vaccines are now entering larger phase II trials in combination with immunotherapy and chemotherapy.[142]

In advanced prostate cancer, sipuleucel-T (Provenge®)—an FDA-approved dendritic-cell vaccine—has extended survival in men with metastatic disease.[143] Other vaccine platforms including PROSTVAC (PSA-TRICOM) and peptide- or mRNA-based vaccines, have demonstrated strong immune responses and PSA reductions in early studies.[144] While challenges remain, particularly overcoming the tumor microenvironment these vaccines have generally been safe and show encouraging signs of effectiveness.[145]

Taken together, these developments point to a future where vaccines may help transform cancer treatment, from reactive to proactive, by targeting residual disease after surgery and strengthening systemic therapy.

Innovation, Innovation, Innovation

The scope of innovation in medicine is vast. Everything we thought we knew even a few years ago is changing. Science has not only defined our DNA and genes but also how the cells of our bodies work together, and increasingly, what happens when they don't work as designed. When proteins fail to fold properly, they can lead to disease. With super- and quantum computing, the way that proteins, which are part of the body's disease signals, are folded begins to become clear. That means we can learn how to fold proteins to change the future of disease. That knowledge is transforming into targeted, increasingly specific therapies, precisely engineered for each individual.

But innovation isn't just about scientific discovery; it's about systems that work. Treatment outcomes are determined not only by science but also by support, mental health, emotional health, financial health, and effective communication. To enable innovations in medicine, we need innovations in health systems. Innovation is the light in the darkness, but the status quo has many entrenched interests, including doctors, companies, hospital plans, and academic facilities that have spent years becoming economically successful incumbents in US health care. Some have acted as barriers to innovation. The key is for the whole enterprise of health care systems to step back and ask themselves, how can they be part of a solution that is more profound than the one we have now. I am confident that business will be able to figure out a way forward that establishes a clear benefit, without fraud, without abuse and centered around the patient. In fact, I and 340 million Americans are counting on it.

It is clear that our health system needs a redesign so we can take advantage of what is to come in science. These therapies cannot just be available to the wealthy. That is unfair and that is not what America's legacy means.

There are too many innovations to describe here, but the key innovations will come from science in drug development, physical AI robotics, and systems that support health care. It will come in supply chain innovations like drone deliveries of organs to transplant. These technological advancements are not just tools. They are the frameworks upon which a new health care system can be built.

The journey from fear to empowerment doesn't happen overnight. Jane's story is not unique. The current system fails not only patients like her, but also the health care professionals working within it. The burden of inefficiencies, administrative chaos, and outdated systems weigh heavily on everyone. As technology like *Doctor AI* emerges, as the H4 Alliance system becomes reality, it holds the promise of transforming health care for both patients and providers. But to truly understand the potential of this change, we must examine how this transformation will impact those who make health possible.

CHAPTER 9

The Art of Navigating Uncertainty

Doctors spend a lifetime trying to understand uncertainty. Patients spend a lifetime living with it. Mark Reynolds calls himself a "regular guy." A fifty-eight-year-old construction foreman in Indiana, he's in decent health, has no major medical problems, and he's enrolled in H4 Alliance Passport, like millions of other Americans. He doesn't think about his body much. It works. He works. That's enough.

Until one day, after his routine lab checkup, his phone buzzes. *Doctor AI* has flagged his PSA levels, a marker for prostate cancer. It's nothing dramatic; they're a little high, but right now, it's just a number on a chart. For Mark, however, the ground shifts beneath him.

Doctor AI explains the situation clearly, without drama, without bias, and without any financial pressures to recommend a certain test or procedure. *Doctor AI* assures Mark they will work together to understand the whole situation. The test is repeated to ensure it provides a correct assessment, and through the interview, *Doctor AI* ensures there aren't any confounding diagnoses like a urinary tract infection or other benign conditions—all accomplished the same day.

By the next morning, *Doctor AI* and Mark have a more substantial conversation, where *Doctor AI* helps him understand the science and data, explaining that 70 percent of prostate cancers are confined to the prostate, so the odds are in his favor that it hasn't spread to other organs. They are perhaps ahead of the situation, precisely because Mark follows the H4 Alliance proactive care model, *Pulse*. But to know more, he'll need an MRI and a biopsy, and, if he's willing, he could join two national clinical trials for liquid biopsies, which could detect or characterize the cancer with just a blood or urine sample. No pressure. Just options. Just knowledge.

Mark talks it over with his wife, Helen. *Doctor AI* has already drafted a summary with costs—there is zero cost to Mark and Helen, but they can see the cost to their H4 Alliance Health Plan—plus the logistics and a list of questions to ask health care professionals. Mark chooses to enroll in both trials, and the tests are scheduled. Everything flows smoothly, with no pre-authorizations necessary and no health insurance hurdles. No possibility of crushing his family with debt. His entire medical record is on his phone, updated in real time, so that nothing is missed. Whenever he gets anxious about his family's future, he talks with *Doctor AI*.

A few days later, Mark and Helen sit on the couch in their living room for a video appointment with Mark's urologist, Dr. Julia Schiff. She greets them warmly, having already reviewed Mark's data with *Doctor AI*. The data confirm that it's cancer, but it's small, slow growing, not aggressive. The liquid biopsy was right. It hasn't spread. That's important, because prostate cancer is the second leading cause of death among men in the US.[146] Yet Mark's biology clarifies the options. Mark has an opportunity to delay or avoid invasive treatments which could have permanent side effects. Ambient AI records Mark and Helen's conversation for later review and record-keeping. The whole experience is documented on the blockchain.

Doctor AI now steps into its true role, not as diagnostician, but as decision support. It pulls outcomes from fifty thousand similar cases in the H4 Alliance Data and H4 Alliance Atlas, checks for biases, and tailors the results to Mark's genetic markers, family history, and cultural values. It summarizes the environment where Mark grew up and any structural or social barriers to optimizing his long-term health. It presents three options for care and recommends one: active surveillance. No surgery. No radiation. Just monitoring check-ins, bloodwork, and imaging. If the cancer changes, they'll know.

Dr. Schiff explains and amplifies *Doctor AI's* message, including the risks of surgery: where twenty percent of patients experience incontinence and a possible loss of sexual function. She describes the new FDA-approved cancer vaccine that might be available in a year or two, and she explains that doing less—"watchful waiting"—doesn't mean doing nothing.

Mark nods and Helen asks a few questions before they make the choice together. Finally, Helen asks: "Are all our family financial documents in place, in case something happens to either Mark or me?" *Doctor AI* provides an overview of their situation, offline from Dr. Schiff. Mark and Helen have done a good job preparing their paperwork, but there are a few things that need attention.

The art of dealing with uncertainty is in choosing. Too often, *uncertainty is the ambient noise of health care.* Some people ignore it while others are consumed by it. But very few are ever taught how to navigate it. Uncertainty can strike at any time: An elderly woman loses her footing on a cold Chicago day, trips on the uneven pavement and falls, breaking her hip. A young pregnant woman encounters a condition where her blood pressure and blood sugars are really high in the second trimester of pregnancy. A nurse working in a hospital gets COVID-19 .

Traditionally, the burden of translating medical uncertainty has fallen to doctors. We were the interpreters of risk, the explainers of probabilities. We were meant to be guides, but over time, that relationship has frayed. The business of medicine grew more complex as data multiplied, and systems overloaded. And in that pressure, many doctors became authoritarian, telling rather than talking, prescribing rather than partnering. Or they became absent, hard to reach, unavailable. They were overwhelmed and, many times, this resulted in mental inflexibility, which translated to treating patients with the dogma learned long ago. They were given the impossible burden of having all the answers, but not the data in a useable form to answer them.

Doctors were not all absent because of entitlement or arrogance. Often, we were absent because we didn't have the tools to do better than to say, "We're not entirely sure, but here's what we think." In a culture where doctors felt pressured to provide the single "right" answer, the problem's complexity was not amenable to a simple explanation, without us essentially making the choice for the patient. It was hard to work in probabilities because we didn't have that kind of knowledge at our fingertips. We were also working with fragments, snippets of your medical record, often inaccurate or incomplete, the faded memory of a lecture from years ago, the habits of our training, and trying to integrate new data from some recent lecture or course. Doctors know little about you, your values, your environment, your culture, your fear of surgery, your faith in alternative care, your hope to see your daughter graduate before beginning treatment. So, we defaulted to protocols, averages, and instincts.

It was never good enough, but it was all we had. Then the system began to change. Our knowledge of biology became deeper, data was overwhelming, and the proliferation of technology that we weren't trained to use exploded around us.

The convergence of technologies including AI, genomics, understanding of human biology, cultural data, ambient sensors, blockchain, supercomputing and real-time analytics, offered health care something new. Not certainty though. That's still a myth. But clarity. Transparency. Personalization. A way to look at a patient, not as a problem to solve, but as a person making choices, standing on the edge of the unknown, with a choice of different paths moving in different directions.

This is what H4 offers: Not a magic answer, but a trusted companion, in the art of choosing wisely when certainty is impossible. And at the center of this shift is *Doctor AI*, which is not a replacement for human wisdom. Wisdom is an experiential art, adding the sum of experience to information. Rather, Doctor AI, is a translator, a pattern-seeker, an algorithm that can be tuned to be less biased than humans, a tireless observer that learns from the world's data and from your life, circumstances, your body, and your story. It doesn't decide for you, but it clears the fog, highlights the path, and holds your hand steady as you choose. It can answer all of your questions, tirelessly. *Doctor AI* is a trusted AI health partner, not only for you, the patient, but for your health care team, the people who help guide difficult decisions or ensure the mechanism of administrative care is running efficiently in the background for you. *Doctor AI* is the connection between all the pieces and parts of your life.

This is what navigating uncertainty looks like when trust between patients and health care providers is rebuilt. When money is not part of the decision. When your doctor is accountable to the same data you are and there is a record of the decision making. When a neutral, data-driven guide removes the pressure of bias—economic or emotional.

There was a time not long ago, before Mark's diagnosis, when the word "cancer" changed everything. It meant a fight, a race, a blur of treatments and side effects. A threat to your life, your dignity, your future. But that's changing, first slowly, now quickly. Just a decade ago, only about a quarter of men diagnosed with prostate cancer with a low risk of death chose active surveillance. By 2021, nearly 60 percent did.[147] New technologies detect problems earlier, changing the choice of treatments to less invasive options, continued normal body function, not to mention a lifetime of possible prevention, through a vaccine created uniquely to fight the cancer you have, the part of medicine on the near horizon.

In Mark's case, cancer became a manageable part of life, a condition that slipped into the background, rather than a dominating force. This shift is the result of fast-moving technology: blood-based diagnostics, targeted therapies, real-time monitoring, and immune system augmentation. What once triggered panic now invites precision. What once required urgent action now calls for thoughtful restraint.

It's not just that we can see the medical landscape more clearly. It's that the shape of the illness itself and our response to it has transformed.

Mark's decision is logged, transparently, immutably, on the blockchain. Gone are the days when one blood test result is hiding in one doctor's filing cabinet and an old diagnosis is buried in another's. Blockchain will enhance a doctor's ability to analyze medical records while protecting the patient from mistakes. Mark's data, anonymized, contributes to research. His choices are his own, but they can serve others, too. His story becomes part of a larger one, a living library of how humans, when given clarity and support, choose wisely.

Choices of therapy evolve. While that seems self-evident, often the choices presented reflect bias of the system, depending more on the current state of the physician's knowledge, their specialty (interventional versus medical), a particular setting (rural versus urban), or data about the patient that would make these choices relevant (if known).

Most of the time, the most relevant and often the deciding factor is insurance coverage. But an additional factor is the surgeon's capacity to use technology. While the complication rates from very competent surgeons may be similar, there are other variables that impact decision-making, including time off work for the patient and the care of the family members who depend on them. When you compare robotic versus open surgery, the impact on the days you need to take off from work is significant. Whether for a prostate removal (9.99 more days off for open surgery), hysterectomy (25.3 more days off work for open surgery), or partial colon removal (29.8 more days off work for open surgery), if the outcomes for surgery are the same, then wouldn't you rather decide on when and who should perform your procedure based on what is best for your life?[148] Ask your own AI search engine what those tradeoffs look like. You will be surprised at the result.

Doctor AI doesn't erase the fear, but it offers language for it. Context. Comfort. It makes the space for people to be seen not just as patients, but as partners. Mark's journey is about prostate cancer, but this model extends far beyond just one diagnosis. It's also how we'll approach obesity, heart disease, all cancers, mental health, autoimmune conditions, fertility, vision loss, hearing loss, dental problems, aging, depression, and suicide prevention with H4 Alliance. Anywhere uncertainty lives, we now have better tools to meet it.

We won't eliminate uncertainty, but we can live with it, in a system where we confront it with honesty, humility, and technology that enhances—not replaces—the humanity of medicine.

Reimagining healthcare in America. Rebuilding Trust. Delivering Health 4.0. No one left behind.

CHAPTER 10

Your Culture Is Your Health

I grew up in a unique environment and one of the world's most famous national parks, the Grand Canyon, in northern Arizona. Though there were a few private homes inside the park, most of the one thousand or so people living there lived in some type of government housing, and the nearest town was fifty-five miles away. Grand Canyon Public School was comprised of about 120 kids in grades kindergarten through twelve. It's the only school located inside any national park in the United States.

We played eight-man football and competed with teams from similar-sized, Class C schools in other remote locations around Arizona, sometimes driving all day to play a game for a few hours and then drive back. We were such a small school that many of us had to serve as cheerleaders, yearbook photographers or editors, and play an instrument in the marching band.

The student body was primarily Native American: Navajo, Hopi, and Hualapai tribes were well represented. Many of their parents worked for the park service or for the concessions owned by the Fred Harvey Company, located on the Grand Canyon's South rim. On weekends, I hiked down the Bright Angel Creek to fish for trout for supper with my dad, or I sat in the sunshine on the Hopi reservation, watching snake dances or other tribal rituals. We built forts, harvested pinon nuts, rode bikes, and responded to the horn of our old white Chevy truck, Casper, when it was time to come in for dinner.

This was my world. At the time, I didn't know that I shared Native American roots through my mother. My grandmother and great-grandmother immigrated from Mexico City. The rumor was that my great-grandmother had been a medical "doctora" teaching in a medical school. In the United States, my grandmother became a "curandera," or a traditional healer or folk medicine woman in the Hispanic tradition. Her knowledge of traditional medicine, complemented by her scientific medical knowledge, made her successful. My father, meanwhile, was a first-generation American from Cerna Gora, Montenegro. We were descended from immigrants, being raised in a remote and rural location. The foundation of my personal culture.

While your setting, family, friends, and colleagues shape much of your outlook, culture is more than inheritance. It is the experiences you choose and the layers you add, that give resonance to your human story, weaving connections among them all. You become the sum of all these cultural and biological threads. The deeper I got into philosophy, business, and later medicine, the more I came to understand that people make decisions in health and sickness through the lens of their own personal culture.

We doctors have our treatments, but what was often missing from the health care system is attention to culture. Whenever I held the hand of a dying patient, I knew the treatment doctors and nurses had delivered to them were limited to remedies for whatever had ravaged their bodies—the original disease, chronic disease, disfiguring surgery, toxic chemotherapy, and radiation. Sometimes, sitting by their side was all I had left to offer, after everything the team had done to try to save a person in those last few years of their life. But something was missing in our approach. We never considered their culture, which would have helped us understand what mattered to them most. We had facts but lacked understanding, assuming we knew what was important. We were often wrong.

Working with patients with cancer, obesity, and diabetes brought the struggle between competing philosophies and culture into sharp relief. For obesity especially, cultural beliefs and traditions drove—and still drives—the treatment decision making. Is the patient at fault because they cannot control their behavior toward food? Are the farmers at fault for using fertilizers and obesity-promoting chemicals? Are food companies at fault for making chemically contaminated, artificially sweetened, fat-laden foods? Are legislators at fault, because they don't provide enough funding to develop scientifically supported therapies? Are doctors and nurses too busy filling in forms to develop a relationship or make conversation with the patient?

Perhaps the concept of "fault" is both too narrow and too broad. The truth is, perhaps there is no fault. Perhaps we are all learning what humans are, what chemicals and environments do, and how. Perhaps when we truly understand culture and biology together, the answers will appear. Cleaning up a hazardous waste site is as much an investment in health as building roads or bridges is an investment in access. Both create the conditions for communities to thrive. Investing in electricity and broadband can sometimes do more for health than any single clinical trial, because it creates the foundation on which all care and innovation can reach people. We could get a better idea of what is truly important to a community if we calculate the value of an investment or advancement to health. Not just by counting money saved on rescue medicine, but by measuring the productivity and joy generated in better health.

For all our health care "sophistication," when COVID-19 came, the medical establishment was caught flat-footed. Years of underinvestment in the public's health undercut all our mitigation efforts. By investing in aspects of health built on culture, connection, and communication, we would have had a more finely tuned response, fewer deaths, and less long COVID-19.

When the pandemic hit, the office of the Surgeon General was outdated and poorly understood—and it still is. Few Americans grasped the role the Centers for Disease Control should play, despite its standing as one of our great scientific achievements. Trust between people and public health institutions was already fragile. Public health leaders, alerted, not only by scientists but even voices like Bill Gates, knew a serious test was coming and that it would likely take the form of a viral disease. Yet when it arrived, they had little to offer the public: no clear understanding of the virus, no testing, and no therapy.

It was a medical desert. And in that knowledge vacuum, poor and conflicting communication, failure to understand cultural relevance, misinformation, and fear thrived. Uncertainty became the primary driver of our response, but it was culture that provided the backdrop of our decision-making. COVID-19 exposed a gaping wound where trust was supposed to be. Even our leaders did not have trust, somehow believing that their knowledge and experience as a politician, essentially equal to only their bias and beliefs, outweighed science.

It is not patients alone who are affected by the cultural lens. Every company, provider, and health care system is also acting within a cultural framework. The COVID-19 vaccine debate gives us an example of how culture can trump science. No situation is black and white, because no response, cure, or therapy has the same effect on everyone. In the end, medicine is rarely perfect.

Rather than rail at each other, perhaps we can find a way to demonstrate the value of therapies and communicate it clearly. That is one reason the H4 Alliance includes the H4 Alliance Data and H4 Alliance Atlas, a source of truth based on data, culturally relevant to you. When you take noise out of an argument and start to talk about solutions and innovation, respecting the cultural fit of the solutions, you can make real progress. This means that as we move into the era of H4, a new definition must arise. It is not the "public health" as defined by expert scientists but the "public's health," the collective good framed by the culture of the individuals who will be using the interventions.

Today, we stand at a unique historical juncture. We are equipped with advanced technology, increasing knowledge of the biology of the human body, and a growing ability to understand the impact of culture on health and disease through a revolutionary health delivery model: the H4 Alliance, using the Health 4.0 platform. Unlike our current system, this model is culturally proactive, addressing individuals' physical, mental, and financial health comprehensively.

The Health 4.0 framework and *Doctor AI* integrate cultural dimensions, aligning health care solutions with individual and community identities. This new paradigm recognizes that work, mental health, and personal identity are inseparable from overall health and from the culture of the people who are the center of the system.

H4 is the new approach to health in America and globally.

America's Six Health Cultures

Years ago, I read historian Colin Woodard's *American Nations: A History of the Eleven Rival Regional Cultures of North America*, published in 2011. Mr. Woodard explained why different regions of our country are influenced by different cultures formed from migration patterns.[149] His work and additional contributions by others amplified the importance of culture in American life.

My strong belief is that culture may be the single most important aspect of health care. Culture is reflected in the decisions an individual makes in response to health challenges. It influences how a region invests for its own future.

For my analysis, which uses culture to form the regional basis of the H4 Alliance, I looked at state responses to multiple aspects of health as a mirror of their health culture: infrastructure, physical and mental health measures, and economics. Then I modeled the data defining the characteristics of health values, disaggregating geography between states.

The model derived five culturally aligned health regions. Yet I also designated a sixth—First Nations. Although their data are enclosed within each state, the reality is that their outcomes are far worse on nearly every measure. To leave them blended into state averages would be to hide both the depth of the challenges and the magnitude of the opportunity. At the same time, tribes must work within the confines of the states that include their lands. For these reason, recognizing First Nations and giving them parity in the H4 Alliance as a distinct cultural region is essential if we are serious about building a system that includes everyone.

Each region has unique characteristics that shape their health landscape and determine its capabilities. Some elements of culture demonstrate extraordinary strengths, while others reveal challenges that affect health in every domain and threaten the future of the regions themselves. Clearly identifying each regions' strengths, challenges, and opportunities—and understanding how they can contribute to the health of the nation—will allow funding and innovation directed where they are most needed.

The strength of the nation can be leveraged through every cultural region to solve for America's future. By aligning regions with the current "outputs" of their health culture—physical, mental and financial, as well as the cultural dimensions that shape adaptability—we can move beyond the roots of migration and see a living panorama of their evolution. And by disaggregating states one from another geographically, the model reflects only the way specific states group through their present culture.

You may be surprised at the results. Let's dive in.

Mapping America's Health Cultures

Within the six regions, seven domains—made up of multiple individual indicators—define the strengths and weakness on a scale of one to five, with one equaling challenge and five equaling strength, capturing both "hard" and "soft" cultural factors. The hard factors reflect regional decisions about investment and funding, the organizational strengths of local environments, and the ability of people to act when necessary. The seven domains in which states were scored are: Technology Readiness, Cultural Openness, Health Care Outcomes, Health 4.0 Alignment Potential, Economic Strength, Crisis Resilience, and Public Health Infrastructure.

There are additional unique environments, including: Washington DC, Hawaii, Alaska, Puerto Rico, and the many US territories that deserve special recognition.

While Woodward and his colleague's original frameworks were informed by migration patterns from the Old World and their roots, this current and data-driven clustering prioritized contemporary cultural attitudes and health system metrics. So states with divergent historical paths are sometimes grouped together based on current conditions and values. This highlights how cultural alignment can transcend historical or geographic boundaries, particularly regarding health care, technology adoption, and resilience.

The six-region structure provides a balance: enough granularity to respect significant cultural and systemic differences, yet broad enough to be practical for policy, strategic planning, and targeted investment. If there were fewer clusters, the system would lose important distinctions (especially between the Resilience and Frontier regions, for example). More clusters would risk creating regions that are overly specific, limiting utility for large-scale policy and collaboration.

Ultimately, ending up with six regions isn't just a neat outcome; it underscores the deep structural and cultural realities currently shaping American health care, technology readiness, and innovation. It also provides a powerful, intuitive foundation for rethinking how health care is delivered across culturally aligned regions—precisely the goal of the Health 4.0 framework.

H4 Cultural Health Index™ (H4-CHI)

States and territories with similar profiles are grouped into six cultural health regions including a distinct First Nations region that aggregates tribal lands. Data from tribal lands are counted both within the states where they are located, and within this unique region. Each region is named for the value most strongly expressed in its cultural model.

Each region is also assessed through a Technology Index that measures readiness to integrate advanced tools into health care. The Index captures infrastructure maturity, digital literacy, broadband penetration, interoperability, AI adoption, and openness to innovation. High scoring regions can scale platforms like *Doctor AI*, implement predictive analytics, contribute to real-world evidence trials, and offer secure, personalized digital health. Lower-scoring regions may lack the bandwidth—both literal and institutional—to support these transformations, requiring targeted investment to close the digital divide, a critical factor in adopting Health 4.0.

The elements of strong nations in this century and the next include not only clean energy and universal broadband, but also mobile connectivity and health woven into the digital foundation. The foundation of every strong economy and enduring nation is health. The nation that leads in aligning health, culture, and technology will chart the course of civilization.

Figure 10: *H4: The Innovators. Copyright Robin Blackstone, MD*

H4: The Innovators

Population: 120 million—GDP: $11.5 trillion
States: California, Colorado, Connecticut, Delaware, District of Columbia, Hawaii, Maryland, Massachusetts, New Jersey, New York, Oregon, Rhode Island, Virginia, Washington
Innovators Region Scores: Tech Readiness 5.0 | Cultural Openness 5.0 Health Outcomes 4.4 | Alignment with H4 4.9 | Economy 4.6 Crisis Resilience 4.1 | Public Health Infrastructure 4.9

Signature Cultural Events

This region is defined by cutting-edge technology, so it's no surprise that technology conferences are major cultural events, including Apple's Worldwide Developers Conference, Google I/O, and the MIT Media Lab Showcase.

Foot races like the New York and Boston Marathons, and San Francisco's Bay to Breakers emphasize grit and collective spectacle. These events hallmark key cultural aspects of this region, including grit and human excellence interacting with a complex community infrastructure. Pride parades of San Francisco, New York City, and Seattle celebrate individuality, inclusion, creativity, and resistance—core values of the Innovator Region. Its character is also vividly reflected in media and film, from *The Social Network* to *Her,* or even in dystopian futures like *WALL-E.*

Cultural Framework

The Innovators region encompasses the Northeast corridor and Pacific Coast innovation hubs, defined by a belief in the "commons"—resources and systems managed collectively for the public good. Diversity and inclusion are embraced as strengths that fuel adaptability. People here place strong trust in science and institutions, expecting innovations to be both evidence-based and fair.

Strengths

Anchored by Silicon Valley, the Boston biotech corridor, and New York's financial and cultural institutions, this region combines exceptional technology readiness, innovation capacity, and economic power. California's GDP would rank it as the fifth globally if it were a nation, a reminder that economic strength here translates into unmatched capacity to fund health systems, research, and technology adoption.[150] The population is highly educated: almost half of adults in Massachusetts have a bachelor's degree (47.8 percent), the highest rate of any state, and D.C. has the highest advanced degree rate, 37.8 percent.[151,152] States like New Jersey, New York, and California enrich global connections.[153]

Health outcomes are strong, with life expectancy reaching seventy-nine to eighty years in Hawaii, Massachusetts, Connecticut, and New York. Extensive health care systems and Health 4.0 innovations,[154] including telehealth adoption, exceed 80 percent in many of these states.[155]

Challenges

The region's primary challenges include high cost of living and health disparities. Urban centers in New York and California face inequality, where pockets of poor outcomes persist. Large populations also strain housing and infrastructure. Overall, however, this region is best positioned to achieve a digital first alignment with Health 4.0's vision: it has the technology, openness, and resources to innovate in health care.

Technology Index: Very High

The Innovators region stands at the forefront of digital health transformation. Dense networks of research hospitals, AI startups, cloud infrastructure, and health tech incubators, give it unmatched technical capacity. High electronic health record (EHR) adoption, strong broadband access, and public trust in data-driven systems enable seamless integration of digital platforms. As a result, *Doctor AI*, real-world evidence trials, and patient-directed health portals can be scaled here first, serving as a national proving ground for Health 4.0.

Contribution to Health 4.0 (H4)

The Innovators region contributes to H4 by embodying open exchange, experimentation, and diversity as strengths. Its embrace of the commons—natural, cultural, digital, and social—makes it comfortable with shared systems, collective data platforms, and inclusive design.

At the systems level, its hubs from Boston's biomedical research clusters to Silicon Valley's digital platforms anchor cutting-edge digital health, biotech and AI ecosystems that set the pace for the nation. The region's openness to diverse populations ensures that innovations are tested across cultural, social, and linguistic contexts, for a foundation for national equity in H4.

Yet the very liberal stance that fuels the region's creativity and inclusivity also limits its influence. Other regions often resist its leadership, viewing its policies and culture as out of step with their own values. At times, the Innovators' unassailable economic and technological position projects a sense of superiority, even smugness, that reinforces distance rather than trust. In truth, no region is the flagship for H4; each contributes through its own cultural lens. The Innovator Region's role is to lead through collaboration—trading strengths with other regions and advancing the goals of Health 4.0 by meeting people where they are and responding to what they want and need.

It does so by exporting new technologies, piloting AI-driven care models, and advancing a cultural ethic of shared responsibility—providing both the tools and the ethos that allow Health 4.0 to take root nationwide.

In Essence

The *Innovators region is the nation's engine of transformation*—its culture of openness, diversity, and experimentation drives Health 4.0 forward through shared systems, digital ingenuity, and inclusive design.

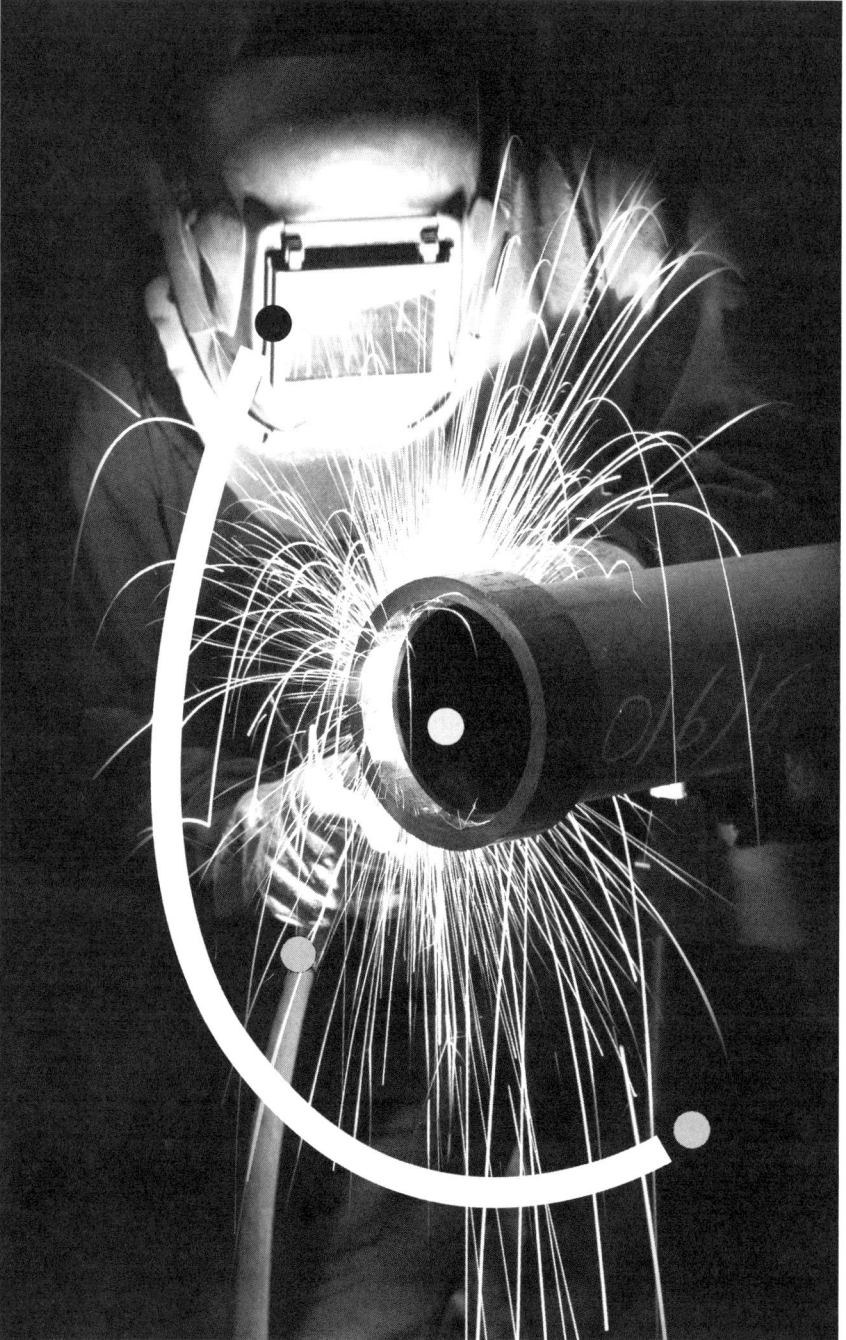

Figure 11: *H4: The Industrial Region. Copyright Robin Blackstone, MD*

H4: The Industrial Region

Population: 66 million—GDP: $5 trillion
States: Illinois, Indiana, Maine, Michigan, Minnesota, New Hampshire, Ohio, Pennsylvania, Vermont, Wisconsin
Industrial Region Scores: Tech Readiness 3.0 | Cultural Openness 3.0 Health Outcomes 2.3 | Alignment with H4 4.0 | Economy 3.0 Crisis Resilience 3.0 | Public Health Infrastructure 2.8

Signature Cultural Events

The Industrial region hosts the Indianapolis 500 at the Indianapolis Motor Speedway, dubbed the "greatest spectacle in racing," emphasizing precision, speed, teamwork, and engineering, which are deeply aligned with the region's cultural identity. This is the region of the "bellwether" states of Ohio, Pennsylvania, and Michigan that decide national elections—townhalls that become pivotal events in campaigns. There is intense political engagement, and a populist tone rooted in the strong presence of labor unions. The charm offensive of this region is the Minnesota State Fair, a beloved event showcasing farming, food, and crafts punctuated by giant sculptures of butter and deep-fried food. It has progressive ideals with rural roots.

Media can often convey visual depictions that offer rich context for understanding a region's values, and way of life. For the Industrial region, for example, you can get a strong sense of its character and energy through *The Deer Hunter, Norma Rae*, and *Gran Torino*.

Cultural Framework

The industrial region, rooted in the legacy of manufacturing and labor, carries a cultural ethos shaped by hard work, resilience, and collective bargaining. Health is often viewed through the lens of fairness and access—benefits negotiated in union contracts, health insurance tied to steady jobs, and a belief that security should come from what one has earned. Populist traditions foster skepticism toward elites but also support for public health measures when framed as protecting working families and communities.

In this region health is less about cutting-edge innovation and more about practical solutions that keep people able to work, raise families, and participate in civic life. The deep political engagement of states like Ohio and Pennsylvania reflects an instinct to debate, contest, and ultimately build consensus, an instinct that carries over into attitudes about health-care policy. Progressive rural traditions, exemplified in Minnesota, add a thread of communal responsibility and investment in public good.

The Industrial region, which spans the Great Lakes and mid-Atlantic industrial states, is an economically and technologically middle-of-the-road composite of states in regard to health investment. It's solid but needs improvement in health outcomes and consistent public health capacity.

Strengths

The industrial region rests on a moderately strong economic base, anchored by manufacturing and service industries. Powerhouse states like Illinois and Pennsylvania each contribute close to $700 million to $1 trillion in GDP,[156] yet their technology readiness and innovation capacity in health remain only average. Illinois, for example, scores 3.0 on the Tech Readiness domain, placing it squarely in mid-pack.

Cultural Openness is likewise moderate. Roughly 35–38 percent of residents hold a bachelor's degree.[157,158] The foreign-born population ranges from 8 to 15 percent, depending on the sector, reflecting diversity but not at the scale of coastal innovation hubs.[159]

Health care outcomes are fair to good, with life expectancy in the mid to upper seventies (Illinois 77.1 years, Michigan, 75.7).[160] Alignment with Health 4.0 is mixed: states like Minnesota and Wisconsin host advanced health systems at Mayo Clinic and Health Partners, with robust telehealth capabilities, yet adoption remains uneven (Wisconsin at 86.7 percent versus New Hampshire at 71.4 percent).[161]

Crisis resilience and public health infrastructure mirror this variability. Pennsylvania and Illinois rank in the high preparedness tier, but Minnesota and Indiana fall lower, underscoring inconsistent investment in public health capacity across the region.

In summary, the Industrial region is strong but uneven: capable of excellence in pockets, but prone to variability that leaves some states more vulnerable than others.

Challenges

The Industrial region faces significant challenges rooted in its history as America's manufacturing engine. Aging infrastructure strains cities and towns, while decades of physically demanding labor and environmental exposure have left lasting health effects on older residents. At the same time, younger workers are navigating a rapidly changing economy and uncertain future of work.

These pressures create health burdens that mirror the region's industrial past. Chronic disease rates are elevated, and opioid overdose deaths remain high in parts of Pennsylvania and Ohio, particularly within Appalachia's distressed communities. Cities such as Flint, Michigan, highlight the consequences of economic decline, environmental neglect, and disinvestment in public health.

Yet the region also hold underutilized strengths that could define its future. Available land and natural resources create opportunities for new urban hubs that integrate science, technology, and creativity in family-friendly communities. Upskilling the workforce, expanding education, and attracting new industries, from energy centers to clean manufacturing, will be crucial to revitalization.

Encouragingly, states like Ohio and Pennsylvania have already reached a high tier of crisis preparedness, signaling that the region can adapt when pressed. The challenge lies not in capacity, but in bridging the divide between industrial legacies and a forward-looking vision of health, work and community.

Opportunities

The Industrial region's legacy of innovation and collective action provides fertile ground for reinvention. With abundant land, existing infrastructure, and a strong tradition of labor solidarity, the region is well-positioned to become a leader in clean manufacturing, renewable energy, and sustainable agriculture. Investments in modernizing infrastructure—transportation, energy grids, and digital connectivity—can also serve as public health investments by reducing environmental exposure, improving access to care, and enabling the spread of telehealth.

Health systems in Minnesota and Wisconsin already demonstrate the potential of integrated care and digital innovation. Scaling these models across the region could help close disparities in states where public health capacity lags. Education and workforce development represent another key opportunity: by upskilling populations for health, and technology related jobs, the region can address both economic transition and long-term health resilience.

Culturally, the industrial region's strong sense of fairness and community engagement makes it receptive to policies that emphasize shared responsibility for health. Townhalls and state fairs alike underscore a civic culture where collective action is possible when benefits are clear and broadly distributed.

Harnessing these opportunities, the industrial region could transform its industrial past into a future defined by equitable health, economic vitality, and resilient communities.

Technology Index: Moderate to High

Once the manufacturing heart of America, the Industrial region has steadily retooled for a digital future. Major academic medical centers and regional health systems in cities like Chicago, Cleveland, Minneapolis, and Pittsburgh have become laboratories for automation, analytics and advanced telehealth. These hubs translate the region's industrial discipline into health innovation—precise, systematic, and designed for scale.

Yet the transformation remains uneven. Rural hospitals and community clinics often operate with outdated infrastructure, limited interoperability, and persistent workforce shortages. Telehealth adoption ranges from advanced integration in Minnesota and Wisconsin, to lagging uptake in parts of New Hampshire and Indiana.

The Tech Index score captures this paradox: *a region on the cusp of transformation*, with world class exemplars but inconsistent execution. Its future lies in extending digital strength beyond flagship institutions to the everyday health systems that serve working families, turning pockets of excellence into a connected, resilient network.

Contribution to Health 4.0 (H4)

The Industrial region brings to H4 the values of pragmatism, solidarity, and resilience. Its history of labor organizing and civic engagement provides a cultural foundation for advancing fairness in health policy and ensuring that benefits are distributed equitably across populations.

On a systems level, the region's academic medical centers and integrated health networks can serve as testing ground for scalable digital health infrastructure, while its manufacturing and logistics expertise position it as a supply-chain backbone for medical devices, pharmaceuticals, and public health preparedness.

By investing in upskilling, clean industry, and modernized public health systems, the industrial region can anchor H4 with a culture of reliable execution, shared responsibility, and practical innovation, ensuring that Health 4.0 is not just visionary, but workable and enduring nationwide.

In Essence

The Industrial region is defined by pragmatic populism and resilient communities. Shaped by a legacy of manufacturing and labor solidarity, it approaches health as a matter of fairness, reliability, and shared responsibility. The region excels in pockets of excellence, world-class medical centers, advanced telehealth systems, and strong crisis preparedness—but struggles with uneven investment and persistent chronic disease burdens. Its strength lies in discipline, solidarity, and the ability to adapt when pressed. By extending innovation beyond flagship institutions to everyday communities, the industrial region can anchor Health 4.0 with a culture of practical execution and equitable benefit.

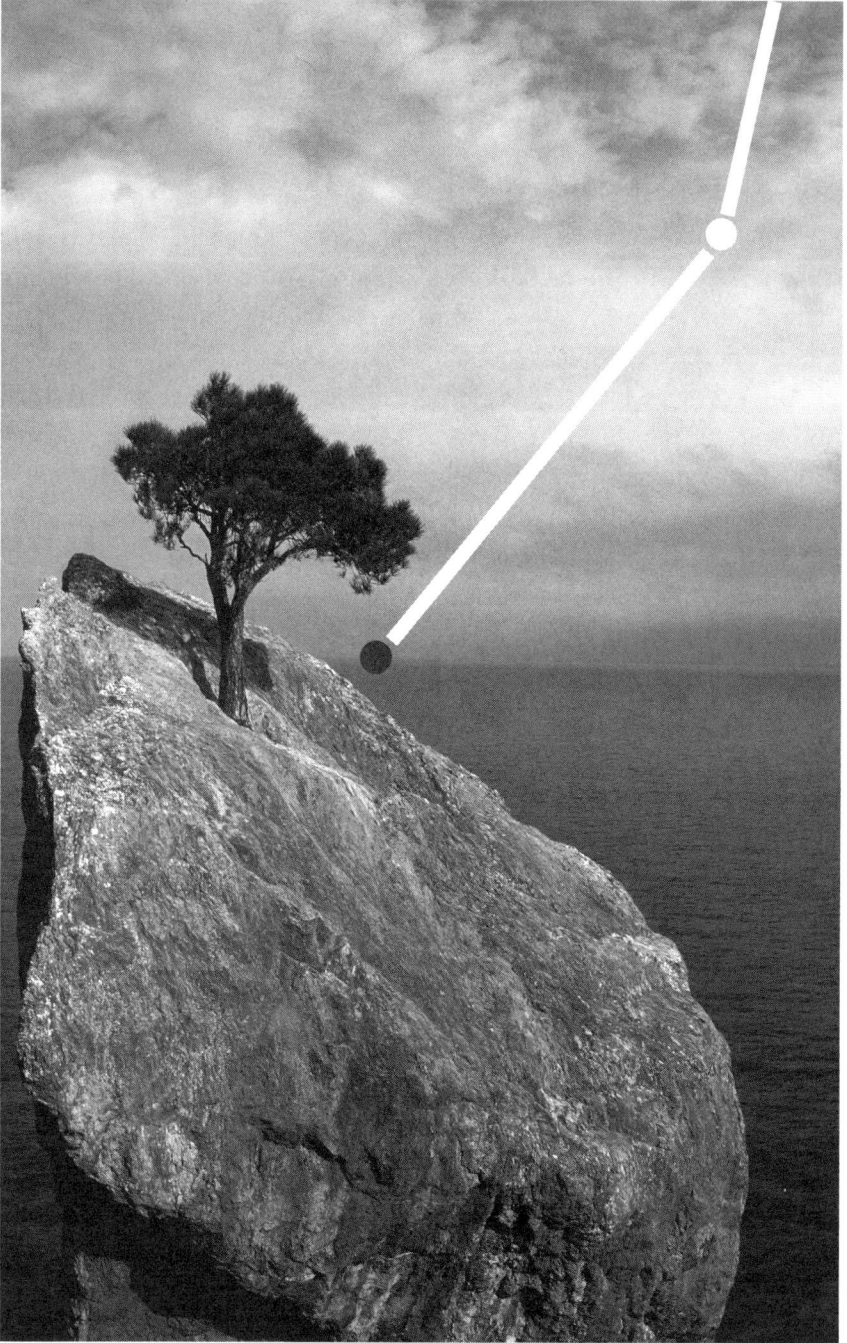

Figure 12: *H4: The Resilience Region. Copyright Robin Blackstone, MD*

H4: The Resilience Region

Population: 44.5 million—GDP: $2.5 trillion

States: Alabama, Arkansas, Kentucky, Louisiana, Mississippi, Missouri, New Mexico, Oklahoma, South Carolina, Tennessee, West Virginia, Puerto Rico, U.S. Virgin Islands

Resilience Region Scores: Tech Readiness 3.5 | Cultural Openness 3.1 Health Outcomes 3.0 | Alignment with H4 4.0 | Economy 3.5 Crisis Resilience 3.5 | Public Health Infrastructure 3.1

Signature Cultural Events

No region more vividly reflects resilience through its cultural fabric. Football is a civic religion. "Friday night lights" unite communities through loyalty, pride, and faith—stadiums fill with prayers, music, and tailgating. Boxing rooted in Kentucky (Muhammad Ali's birthplace), Arkansas, and Puerto Rico place emphasis on personal grit, physical and emotional endurance, and the continuous fight to overcome poverty. Baseball also has deep roots here, demonstrating the quiet strength of continuity and belief in what endures.

Film and media amplify these themes: *Winter's Bone, Mud, O Brother, Where Art Thou?*, and *Selma* reveal a landscape of hardship, perseverance, and transformation.

Cultural Framework

The Resilience Region's culture is forged in adversity and rooted in tradition. Faith, family, and community form the backbone of daily life. Churches often serve not only as spiritual centers but also as health anchors—sites for vaccination drives, blood pressure screenings, and disaster relief hubs. Music, from gospel and blues to country and bluegrass, gives voice to both suffering and hope, reinforcing shared identity across generations.

Rural life reinforces resilience: people improvise, repair, and share when resources are scarce. Yet, this self-reliance sometimes deepens mistrust of outside institutions, including government and health systems.

That mistrust, sharpened during COVID-19, and must be acknowledged and addressed for H4 adoption to succeed.

Storytelling is central here—whether in oral tradition, film, or song—offering a pathway for health communication that resonates authentically. Cultural icons, from athletes like Muhammad Ali to musicians like Dolly Parton, reflect themes of grit, endurance, and giving back, all of which align with a vision of health grounded in trust and purpose

The challenge, then, is not whether Health 4.0 fits this region but whether it is framed in a way that feels culturally congruent. Approaches that emphasize community solidarity, faith-based legitimacy, and local control are most likely to take root.

Strengths

The Resilience Region's greatest strength lies in its people and their deep community bonds. Trust is not easily given, but once earned it endures, knitting together networks that become lifelines during times of crisis. These connections, rooted in faith, family and loyalty, have historically carried communities through natural disasters, economic downturns, and health emergencies. Technological steps forward, through uneven, are beginning to show promise. Since 2020, broadband expansions and telehealth adoption have accelerated, and while the region still lags behind the coasts, incremental progress marks a shift. Crisis preparedness has also improved. By 2023, both Mississippi and Alabama reached high-performance tiers in emergency readiness, a sign that lessons from COVID-19 and repeated hurricanes have translated into stronger systems. Economically, new anchors are emerging. Automotive manufacturing in Alabama and Tennessee and the visionary role of Vanderbilt University in Tennessee, led by Chancellor Daniel Diermeyer, PhD.

Challenges

Yet the challenges here are profound. Educational attainment is among the lowest in the nation, with West Virginia graduating only about a quarter of its population from college. Cultural openness is limited, with few immigrants and little diversity, reinforcing insular economic conditions and resistance to change. Technology readiness lags, with broadband gaps and patchy adoption of electronic health records stalling progress.

Health outcomes are the poorest in the United States: life expectancy in Mississippi and West Virginia hovers a decade below that of Hawaii. High rates of obesity, diabetes, and cardiovascular disease combine with wide-spread rural hospital closures to create deserts of health care. Economic pressures compound the picture.

Median incomes of $55,000 to $65,000 are well below national averages, and high poverty rates strain both personal finances and public budgets. Public health infrastructure has long been underfunded; Louisiana spends only $29 per person on public health, and Kentucky just $40, leaving many counties without sufficient staff, labs, or equipment. These structural weaknesses have left the region vulnerable.

Public health infrastructure struggles with underfunding. For example, prior to COVID-19, several of these states spent the least per capita on public health, with Kentucky spending $40 per person in 2023, and others in this region similarly low. Notably, Louisiana, spends $29 per capita in public health.[162] Many counties lack sufficient public health staff or modernized labs and equipment. Vanderbilt, a powerhouse and visionary educational system, could serve as the bellwether for health in this region.

Establishing broadband coverage, which is essential for the rollout of Health 4.0, would have a significant impact on this region. Changes in regulations about interstate consultations with medical staff and drone medication delivery could provide this with a renaissance of productivity and bring health care leadership innovation to the region. There is deep strength in resilience, and with the strength, support, and innovation of the H4 Alliance behind them, the region could emerge as a powerhouse in the broad sense of Health 4.0.

Opportunities

Although challenges are seemingly overwhelming, opportunities for transformation are real. Broadband expansion could act as a catalyst, unlocking reliable telehealth access, enabling interstate medical consultations, and supporting even drone delivery of medications and supplies in isolated communities.

With strategic investment, the region could leapfrog traditional models of care by embracing mobile health programs, AI-driven triage tools, and community-based health delivery that resonates with local culture.

Anchors like Vanderbilt, along with other regional universities and health systems, could spearhead innovation. Just as importantly, faith-based organizations and community-rooted health initiatives—already trusted voices—could export lessons of resilience to the global south, where communities face similar barriers of poverty, fragmentation, and underfunding.

Technology Index: Low-to-Moderate

The Resilience region carries the weight of historic disinvestment—deep poverty and a fragmented infrastructure. However, resilience itself is this region's defining trait. By coupling grassroots innovation with intentional outside investment, the Resilience Region has the potential to become a living laboratory for bottom-up transformation, demonstrating how trust and cultural alignment can accelerate health progress even under constrained conditions.

Contributions to Health 4.0 (H4)

The Resilience Region contributes a distinctive form of capital to H4: the power of loyalty, endurance, and community trust. Its lived experience with poverty, chronic disease, natural disasters, and public health crisis makes it a proving ground for any national system. If H4 can succeed here, in places where mistrust of institutions runs deep, infrastructure is weak, and outcomes are poor; it can succeed in establishing trust anywhere.

This region also offers lessons in cultural translation. Faith-based organization, civic networks, and community health workers have long been trusted intermediaries. By engaging community leaders, H4 can extend beyond traditional health systems into the fabric of daily life. Furthermore, the region's anchor institutions, such as Vanderbilt, provide intellectual and technological leadership capable of linking rural realities to national innovation.

In this way, the Resilience Region doesn't just adopt H4, it actively tests, shapes and legitimizes it for the whole country.

In Essence

The Resilience Region embodies courage when confronted with hardship, and endurance in the face of uncertainty. It is a place where history has pressed heavily on health and opportunity, yet where bonds of faith and community remain unbroken. Adversity tests the spirit, but strength is measured in persistence. With targeted investment in broadband, public health, and trust-based delivery models, this region could shift from being behind to leaders of the cultural revolution in health care.

Its transformation would turn historical burdens into future strengths, offering proof that even the most disadvantaged regions can thrive under H4. In doing so, the Resilience Region could emerge as a beacon of hope—not only for the United States but for countries across the Global South facing similar struggles of poverty, disinvestment, and resilience under strain.

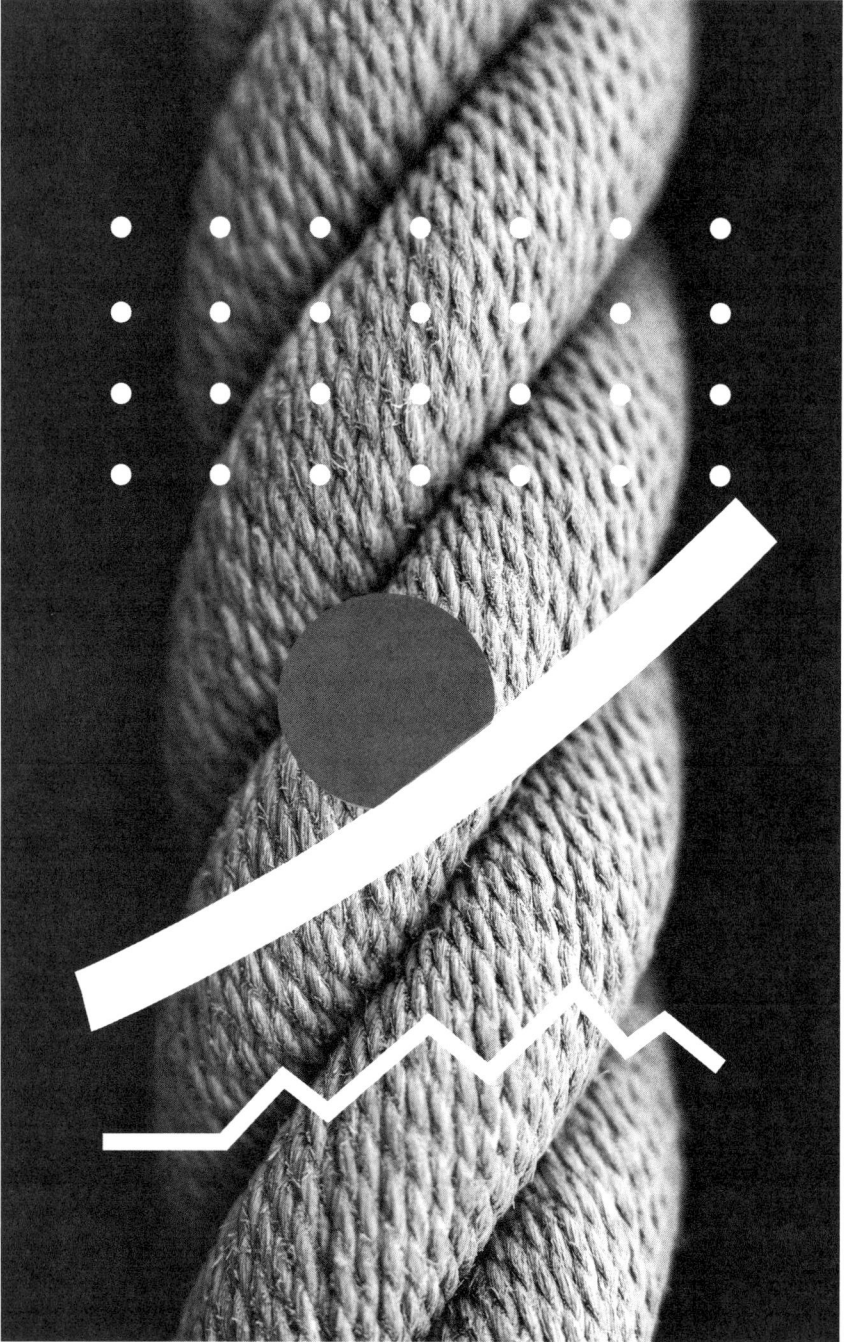

Figure 13: *Region 4: Frontier. Copyright Robin Blackstone, MD*

Region 4: Frontier
Population: 15.5 million—GDP: $1.0 trillion
States: Alaska, Idaho, Iowa, Kansas, Montana, Nebraska, North Dakota, South Dakota, Wyoming, Utah, Guam, Northern Mariana Islands
Frontier Region Scores: Tech Readiness 3.5 | Cultural Openness 4.4 Health Outcomes 2.9 | Alignment with H4 4.5 | Economy 3.4 Crisis Resilience 4.0 | Public Health Infrastructure 3.5

Signature Cultural Events
The Frontier Region celebrates independence and endurance through its traditions. The Cody Stampede Rodeo in Wyoming, with its ranching competitions and horsemanship, underscores a culture rooted in skill, toughness, and individual courage. Alaska's Iditarod Trail Sled Dog Race is a living metaphor for resilience, teamwork and the ingenuity in the face of brutal natural conditions and terrains. In Iowa the High School State Wrestling Tournament embodies discipline, grit, and personal accountability, elevating high school athletes into cultural heroes.

Cultural identity is also powerfully transmitted through story and film. *Tombstone, Fargo* and *True Grit* convey an ethic of stark choices, endurance, and sometimes dark humor. *A River Runs Through It* reveals the quiet spirituality and family ties woven through theses landscapes. Together, these cultural touchstones present a region defined by toughness, endurance, and meaning found in the face of hardship and the natural beauty of the region.

Cultural Framework
This region spans the Great Plains, the Mountain West, and remote Pacific territories—geographies of distance and scarcity. Communities are small and dispersed, often hundreds of miles from major hospitals or universities. Veterinarians drive miles to treat highly valued, individual animals, and much of the health care for humans is "self-diagnosed" and treated. Life in the region is shaped by extremes: blizzards, droughts, mountain passes, and oceans. Those conditions forge social cohesion and strong local networks, but they also create barriers to equitable health access

and technological integration. Compared to more urbanized regions, the Frontier is defined less by density than by distance—and the ingenuity required to overcome it.

Strengths

The primary strength of the Frontier region lies in its people and their capacity to endure. Tight-knit communities with a historically lower cost of living and social cohesion is a powerful public health asset. North Dakota and South Dakota consistently exceed the national average among the highest per-capita public health funding[163] combining state funds with Centers for Disease Control grants to build relatively strong systems for their size. Life expectancy in Nebraska and the Dakotas remains in the high seventies, partially attributable to lower population density, resilience in the face of crisis and tight community health networks.[164,165] Years of responding to blizzards, floods, and other natural disasters have created communities accustomed to mobilizing quickly and improving solutions.

Challenges

The same geography that produces resilience also generates inequity. Innovation scores in particular are low across the region. North Dakota ranks forty-eight out of fifty US states and Wyoming has a limited technology center. This region also has the smallest immigrant population with foreign-born people making up less than 5 percent in many states, including 4 percent in North Dakota and 2.2 percent in Montana.[166] There are fewer urban centers in the region, indicating slower adoption of new cultural and health trends.

Health 4.0 alignment is a challenge due to infrastructure gaps. Broadband and telehealth access can be limited. While some telehealth progress was made in South Dakota with 88.6 percent adoption, others lag, such as Wyoming at 71.4 percent.[167]

Economically, reliance on agriculture (Kansas, Iowa) or energy-based industries (oil in North Dakota, gas in Utah and mining in Montana) constrains the diversification into health technology. Public health infrastructure suffers from geographic dispersion. For many communities, critical care can be located more than one hundred miles away, and recruitment of health care professionals is very difficult because of the distance from urban centers.

Equity for health care access remains a central problem. While many wealthy people that live in these states can access the best health care in other regions, poorer families are left with limited and often under-resourced options.

Opportunities

The obstacles of geography have sparked surprising innovation. Alaska has piloted drone delivery of medicines across remote villages. Tribal health networks have experimented with blockchain systems to manage care. Satellite-linked telehealth has connected patients in Guam and rural Utah with specialists across the mainland. These models reveal the Frontier not as a laggard, but as a crucible for invention under constraint. If supported by federal coordination and resilient-by-design infrastructure, these pilots could become scalable models for equitable care across the nation.

Technology Index: Low

Geography defines the Frontier region—vast distances, rugged terrain, and low population density make traditional infrastructure costly and often impractical. Yet these very challenges create fertile ground for transformative health innovation. Alaska, the Dakotas, and Guam have relied on improvisation and self-reliance, and those traditions are converging with new technologies. Drone medication delivery across mountain passes, satellite-linked telehealth connecting islands to mainland specialists, and tribal health networks experimenting with block chain all point to an ethos of invention.

The Tech Index reads low, reflecting structural gaps but not a lack of ingenuity. With federal coordination, targeted investment, and resilient by design systems, the Frontier region could become a national laboratory for solving health access problems under the toughest conditions. Business models developed here can be exported to similar countries and regions globally.

Contribution to Health 4.0 (H4)

The Frontier contributes a crucial lesson: transformation can be forged under conditions of scarcity. Health 4.0 in this region will not be defined by gleaming medical centers or venture-funded startups, but by resilient systems that can deliver across distance, weather, and limited resources. By integrating broadband expansion, incentivizing provider recruitment, and scaling frontier innovations, the region can demonstrate how to build trust and capacity in places where health systems are most stretched.

In Essence

The Frontier is America's proving ground for resilience. Its culture prizes toughness, self-reliance, and improvisation, but also deep community bonds. Life here has always required endurance, against weather, distance, and isolation, and those same qualities shape its health identity. Its traditions, from rodeo to sled racing to wrestling, celebrate the ability to endure and prevail. Storytelling in film and literature reinforces an ethic of stark choices, perseverance, and moral clarity. Yet beneath that toughness lies a persistent inequity: while the wealth can reach care in other regions, too many communities remain underserved, cut off by geography and infrastructure gaps. The technology first approach of H4, however is perfectly suited to help fill the gap that exists here and release the genie of innovation from the lamp.

In the framework of Health 4.0, the Frontier's importance is disproportionate to its size. Here the hardest questions of access, equity, and trust surface first and most sharply. The answers forged in this environment don't just solve local problems—they become blueprints that the rest of the nation can adapt and scale. Its innovations, born of necessity rather than abundance, can become national models: drones delivering medicines where roads fail, telehealth spanning mountains and oceans, community health systems building trust from the ground up. The Frontier embodies the central paradox of American health: scarcity that breeds innovation, inequity that demands reform, and resilience that may be the light we need as a nation to move forward.

Figure 14: *H4: The Growth Region. Copyright Robin Blackstone, MD*

H4: The Growth Region

Population 85 million—GDP: $6 trillion
States: Arizona, Florida, Georgia, Nevada, North Carolina, Texas
Growth Region Scores: Tech Readiness 4.0 | Cultural Openness 3.9
Health Outcomes 3.5 | Alignment with H4 4.1 | Economy 4.0
Crisis Resilience 3.5 | Public Health Infrastructure 4.1

Signature Cultural Events

South by Southwest in Austin, Texas, provides a global stage for music, film, technology, and future trends, capturing the fast-moving, entrepreneurial, and diverse spirit of modern Sun Belt cities.

Art Basel in Miami Beach adds another dimension of international flair—glamorous, disruptive, and financially charged—cementing Miami's role as a global hub of culture and capital. The Fiesta in San Antonio reflects the layered history of this region. A blend of military, colonial, and Latino traditions, in a celebration that is colorful, family-centered, and deeply communal, with mariachi bands, parades, and military flyovers. It is a fully Texas celebration.

Culture is also vividly conveyed through film, television, and social media. Works like *Scarface, No Country for Old Men*, and *Coco* capture the Growth Region's contrasts: wealth and ambition, borderland tensions, and intergenerational traditions rooted in family and heritage.

Description

The Growth Region encompasses the booming Sun Belt States of the Southeast and Southwest, where rapid economic and population expansion is reshaping America's demographic center of gravity. Once peripheral to the nation's political and cultural life, states like Texas and Florida are now at the core, with Texas surpassing thirty million people and $2 trillion in GDP.[168,169] Florida is not far behind. These two alone anchor the region as both an economic engine and a cultural force.

The cultural character is defined by movement, people, money, and ideas flowing in at unprecedented rates. Migration from the Midwest and Northeast, as well as steady immigration from Latin American, the Caribbean, and Asia, have created some of the most diverse urban centers in the country. Houston, Dallas, Miami, Phoenix and Atlanta are emblematic of this change: sprawling cities where cultural identities, languages, and economies mix at high velocity.

This dynamic also creates tension. The region's cultural identity blends frontier entrepreneurism, Latino and Caribbean heritage, deep religious traditions, and a rapidly expanding urban cosmopolitan dynamic. Sun Best megachurches exist alongside Cuban cafes, high-tech incubators, and sprawling suburbs. Politically and socially, the Growth Region, embodies both the energy of renewal and the friction of unresolved divisions, immigration debates, climate vulnerability, and widening gaps between wealth and poverty.

Strengths

Tech Readiness in the Growth Region is moderate to high particularly in the expanding urban centers. Austin has become a nationally recognized tech hub, while the Research Triangle in North Carolina, and Atlanta's fintech cluster demonstrate the region's ability to attract capital, talent, and startups. Several states, including Arizona and Texas, rank in the top twenty for innovation attracting Health 4.0 ventures that see opportunity in the region's size, diversity, and growth trajectory.

Cultural openness adds to this dynamism. Florida's population is 22 percent foreign-born, and Nevada's is 19 percent, making them among the most diverse states in the country. Georgia and Texas also have large minority and immigrant communities, providing a cultural depth that supports new ideas and approaches to health care. This diversity feeds a robust workforce, sustaining industries from technology to energy, logistics, and tourism.

Health care outcomes in this region vary, but investments in health systems are beginning to translate into improvement. Policymakers in the region increasingly recognize health care not only as a public good but as a workforce and economic advantage, a foundational premise of H4. Life expectancy in the Growth region is approximately seventy-five to seventy-six years, just a bit below national average, but rising in places like Florida, where health investments align with a rapidly growing senior population.[170] Health 4.0 alignment potential is significant as states here embraced telehealth especially during COVID-19. These are land areas of vast distance, especially in Texas and Arizona. However distance can be overcome and connection established, as demonstrated by North Carolina's hospital telehealth adoption—ninety-three percent.[171] Economically, the Growth Region is a powerhouse. Collectively, its GDP rivals that of the Innovator Region, driven by the strength of energy (Texas), tourism (Florida, Nevada), logistics (Georgia), and high growth technology sectors.

The region's Achilles heel is crisis resilience from climate events. Focus on the challenges climate events provide is a priority. Florida and Georgia achieved the high preparedness tier, leveraging lessons from hurricanes and public health emergencies, whereas Nevada and Arizona were in lower tiers, highlighting some gaps in health infrastructure and investment. Public health infrastructure is similarly uneven with Nevada ranking the lowest in state-level public health spending per capita in recent years, while Georgia and North Carolina have stronger institutions, anchored by the Centers for Disease Control in Atlanta.[172]

Challenges

The Growth Region's rapid growth has strained crucial foundations. Population surges have outpaced infrastructure, leaving public health systems uneven and underfunded in many states. Access to health care is inconsistent, particularly in rural Texas, Arizona, and New Mexico. Provider shortages are acute. These same populations are exposed and vulnerable to climate driven risks like hurricanes, flooding, massive dust storms, extreme heat and drought. While wealthy metro areas thrive, economic growth has not erased disparities and marginalized communities face barriers to care, limited insurance coverage, and deep inequity in outcomes. The biggest challenge to the continued growth in the region will in part be constrained by poor health of the workforce.

Technology Index: Moderate

The Growth region is a paradox. Fast-growing metros like Austin, Miami, and Atlanta boast cutting-edge hospitals and booming tech economies, while surrounding areas wrestle with digital deserts and fragmented care. Health systems here often lead in robotic surgery, consumer health apps, and AI pilot projects, but statewide strategies to integrate these advances into rural or underserved populations remain inconsistent. The Tech Index is moderate because of this duality: high innovation in pockets, but lack of cohesion across the system. With a regional push toward equity and standardization, Growth could quickly rise to lead in tech-enabled health delivery. Closing this digital divide is essential if the Growth Region is to translate its innovation potential and stand the test of time amid competition from other regions committed to a healthy workforce.

Contribution to Health 4.0 (H4)

The Growth Region contributes to Health 4.0 through its scale, diversity, and speed of adaptation. Its booming metropolises, from Austin's startup scene to Miami's role as a global financial hub, provide fertile ground for health innovation, drawing venture capital, digital health companies, and AI-driven startups. Because the region has large immigrant and minority populations, it is positioned to lead in culturally responsive models of care, testing how technology can meet the needs of multilingual, multiethnic communities.

The region also demonstrates the importance of scale in transformation. Telehealth adoption surged here during COVID-19, not just as a convenience but as a necessity for vast geographies like Texas and Arizona. If paired with expanded broadband and public health investment, these rapid pivots can become permanent fixtures, showing how digital health tools can reach both dense cities and remote communities. In the way the Growth Region serves as a test bed for inclusive, high-volume, tech enabled systems, proving that H4 can be scaled to meet the demands of tens of millions of diverse people, not just niche populations. This is a model for adoption globally.

In Essence

The Growth Region is where the business case for H4 comes into sharpest focus. With more than 80 million residents, surging immigration, and GDP rivaling entire nations, this is not a peripheral story, it is the future marketplace for American Health. Companies and investors already see it: venture funding flows into Austin and Miami, insurers and hospital systems race to capture expanding populations, and digital health startups test new models in diverse, fast-growing cities. The region's scale and momentum demand solutions that are efficient, inclusive, and built to last.

For H4, the Growth Region is both a proving ground and a pressure test. Its size ensures that innovations here can set national precedents, while its cultural diversity provides the ultimate test of workforce investment. This region will demonstrate how to align business imperatives with public good, showing that equity and innovation are not opposing forces, but the engines of sustainable health economies. In the Growth Region, H4 is not optional; it is the only viable path forward.

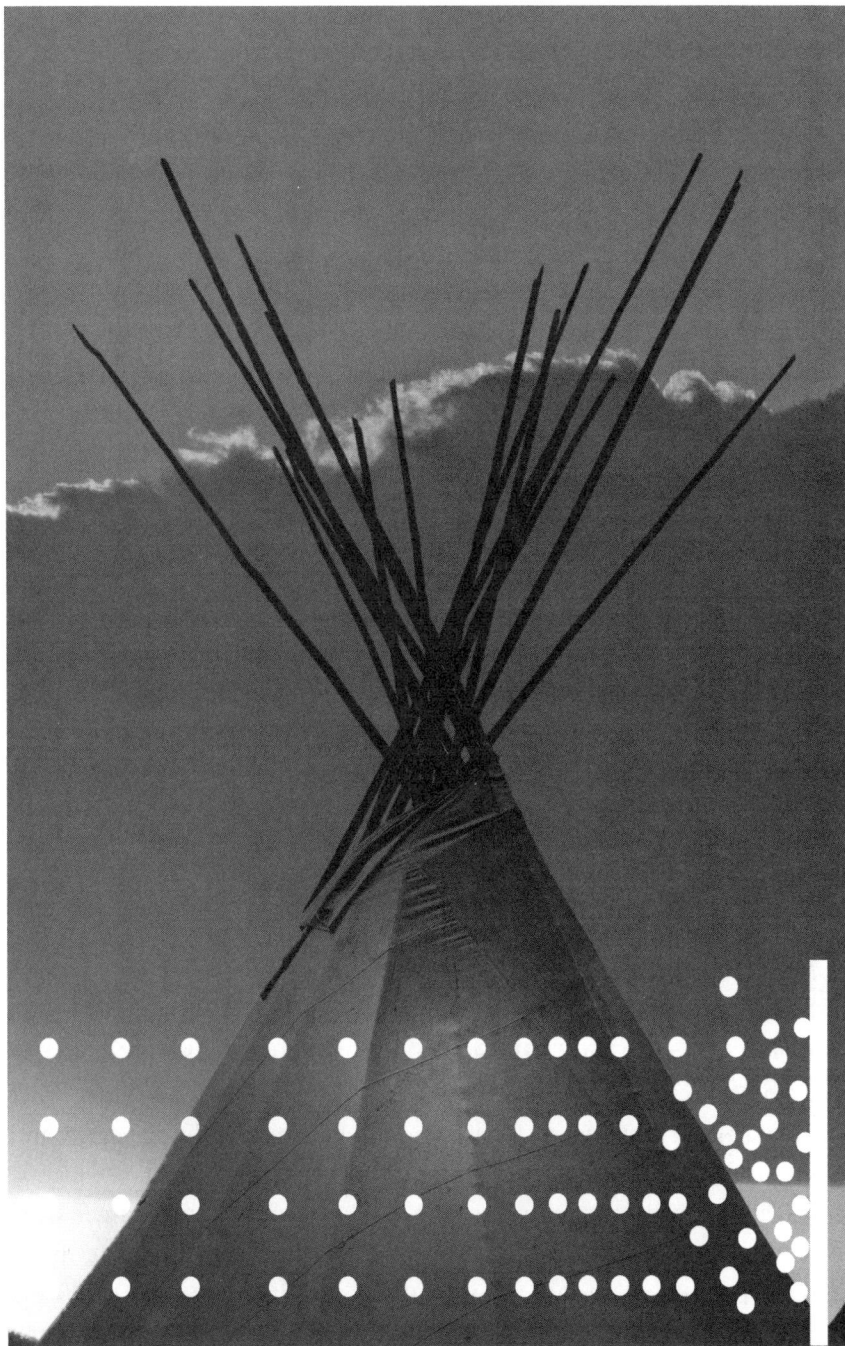

Figure 15: *The First Nations Region. Copyright Robin Blackstone, MD*

The First Nations Region
Population: 5 million—GDP: $0.05 trillion
States: All Native American tribal territories, regardless of state.
First Nations Scores: Tech Readiness 2.5 | Cultural Openness 3.0
Health Outcomes 2.5 | Alignment with H4 3.2 | Economy 2.0
Crisis Resilience 3.1 | Public Health Infrastructure 2.6

Signature Cultural Events
The Gathering of Nations in Albuquerque, New Mexico, is the largest intertribal powwow in North America, bringing together tribes from across the continent to celebrate sovereignty, resilience, and multigenerational traditions through dance, music, crafts, and ceremony. The Annual Reservation Economic Summit, hosted by the National Center for American Indian Enterprise Development in Las Vegas, is the premier tribal business conference highlighting leadership in energy, tourism, technology, infrastructure, gaming, finance, and youth development.

Culture identity is reflected in film and storytelling. *Smoke Signals* (1998), was the first feature written, directed, and acted by Native Americans. It explores community, identity, and survival with humor and poignancy. *The Fast Runner* (2001), the first Inuit feature film, captures indigenous resilience and traditional knowledge in the harsh Arctic. These works reveal a cultural continuity that persists despite centuries of dispossession.

Cultural Framework
First Nations encompasses all Native American and Alaska Native tribal territories, representing 574 federally recognized tribes as well as unrecognized sovereign communities across the United States and territories, including American Samoa. The Region is geographically dispersed and culturally diverse, yet many tribes face similar health realities shaped by historic disinvestment, systemic exclusion, and unresolved sovereignty issues.

By nearly every measure, whether life expectancy, poverty rates, infrastructure, or educational attainment, the First Nations region carries the greatest health challenges in the nation. Native life expectancy, estimated between 65 and 72 years, remains a decade shorter than the national average, a gap widened by the pandemic. Chronic diseases such as diabetes, cardiovascular disease, and substance use disorder are more prevalent. Health care infrastructure is underfunded, with many Indian Health Service (HIS) facilities operating decades out of date. Broadband deficits leave rural clinics disconnected, limiting access to telehealth. Yet resilience remains a defining feature: many tribes have embraced both cultural tradition and modern innovation, often outperforming surround states in crisis response when resources are available.

Strengths

Community cohesion and cultural continuity are central strengths of the First Nations region. Tribal health programs, which are often delivered through the Indian Health Service (IHS), or tribally operated systems, provide care that integrates tradition with modern practice. Pilot programs point to the potential for H4. For example, the use of community health representatives using mobile units to reach remote households for diabetic retinopathy screening.

Crisis response capacity, while underfunded, has shown effectiveness. During the COVID-19 pandemic, the Navajo Nation notably achieved one of the highest vaccination rates in the US by mid-2021, a testament to communal trust, strong leadership, and decisive action.[173] Indigenous knowledge systems, including land stewardship, food sovereignty, and traditional healing, offer assets that have been overlooked in mainstream health planning.

Challenges

Technology readiness is extremely limited on many reservations because broadband access and IT infrastructure lag far behind national standards. Many tribal clinics lack reliable high-speed internet, which prevents telehealth adoption.

Economic strength is uneven. The average income in tribal areas is about 64 percent of the US average.[174] Poverty rates are high, around 23 percent on some reservations, more than double the national average of

10.5 percent.[175] Unemployment averages 11.7 percent overall but in some tribal lands is higher and dependent on education level.[176]

Gaming operations, allowed under the Indian Gaming Regulatory Act (1988) provide some revenue for roughly a quarter of the tribes, however less than 10 percent earn significant profits.[177] Energy and natural resource revenues benefit only a minority. Overall, only 10 to 15 percent of the tribes have a reasonably stable and diversified income stream. This lack of financial resources contributes to severe underinvestment in health care facilities.

Educational attainment remains a barrier, with only 15 percent of Native adults have a bachelor's degree, roughly half the national average.[178] Health outcomes are the poorest in the nation. Chronic underinvestment has left tribal health systems with limited preparedness for large-scale emergencies. Jurisdictional complexity often forces a reliance on county or state systems, creating gaps in accountability and service delivery.

Opportunities

The First Nations region has profound opportunity if investment and sovereignty are respected. Broadband expansion and digital health infrastructure could rapidly unlock access to modern care, especially in rural areas where physical facilities are limited. Some tribes already lead the way, building telemedicine networks, asserting sovereignty in data governance, and blending cultural practices with digital tools. With sustained support, these models could scale.

The opportunity also lies in reframing: the Tech Index is low, not because of lack of ingenuity, but because of systemic exclusion. Where resources exist, innovation flourishes, from mobile health units to culturally embedded behavioral health programs to renewable energy projects that link economic development with well-being. H4 here requires more than technology. It will require sustained partnership, respect for sovereignty, and investment that empowers communities to design their own future.

Technology Index: Very Low-to-Moderate

Across tribal lands, The Tech Index here reflects systemic underinvestment, rather than capacity. Connectivity is inconsistent, infrastructure decades behind, and most tribes lack stable funding for technology. Yet when resources are directed, adoption is swift. Tribes have shown they can integrate broadband, telemedicine, and health data systems in ways that are culturally respectful, and community adapted and owned.

For H4, success will depend on building with tribes, not for them, ensuring digital sovereignty and culturally relevant innovation. Importantly, the Indigenous experience is not only an American story. Around the world, distinct cultural communities face similar barriers of exclusion and infrastructure gaps. The lessons drawn here provide a window to the global future: how equity, sovereignty, and technology can align to create health systems that are both innovative and culturally grounded.

Contribution to Health 4.0 (H4)

The First Nations region contributes a vital perspective: H4 must include the most underserved to fulfill its promise. Tribal health systems demonstrate how to deliver care in remote, underfunded, and structurally excluded settings. Their integration of tradition with innovation, from data sovereignty frameworks to culturally adapted telehealth, provides models that mainstream systems can learn from.

This region also underscores that equity is not a side benefit but the cornerstone of system transformation. If H4 can succeed in tribal communities, through sovereign data governance, broadband expansion and long-term investment, pillars of H4, it will prove the viability of inclusive, trust-based systems nationwide and globally. It will also show that people can adapt diverse systems (as many tribes have very different cultural mindsets) into many different settings. In this sense, First Nations are not peripheral to the future of American health; they are a proving ground for whether global health can be equitable, resilient, and just.

In Essence

The First Nations region embodies both the deepest wounds and the greatest lessons of American Health. Centuries of dispossession and chronic underfunding have produced stark inequities in life expectancy, chronic disease, and infrastructure. Yet the resilience of Indigenous communities, seen in high COVID-19 vaccination rates, the preservation of cultural identity, and the building of sovereign health systems, reveals extraordinary capacity for collective action when resources are aligned with community priorities.

For business and H4, the case is direct. No region illustrates more clearly that trust, sovereignty, and equity are prerequisites for innovation. Tribal nations show that technology cannot be imposed; it must be adapted through culture, governance, and history. When that alignment occurs, the lessons reverberate far beyond tribal lands. Community-driven models, digital sovereignty, and culturally ground care can guide transformation across rural American and underserved urban areas alike. The essential argument is this: in First Nations, H4 is not simply tested—it is held accountable to memory, sovereignty, and survival. What grows here does more than prove a model; it offers a covenant of trust. If that covenant holds, it becomes a blueprint not only for America's health system, but for the globe—a lesson in equity and repair of relationship that the world is waiting—and hoping—to see.

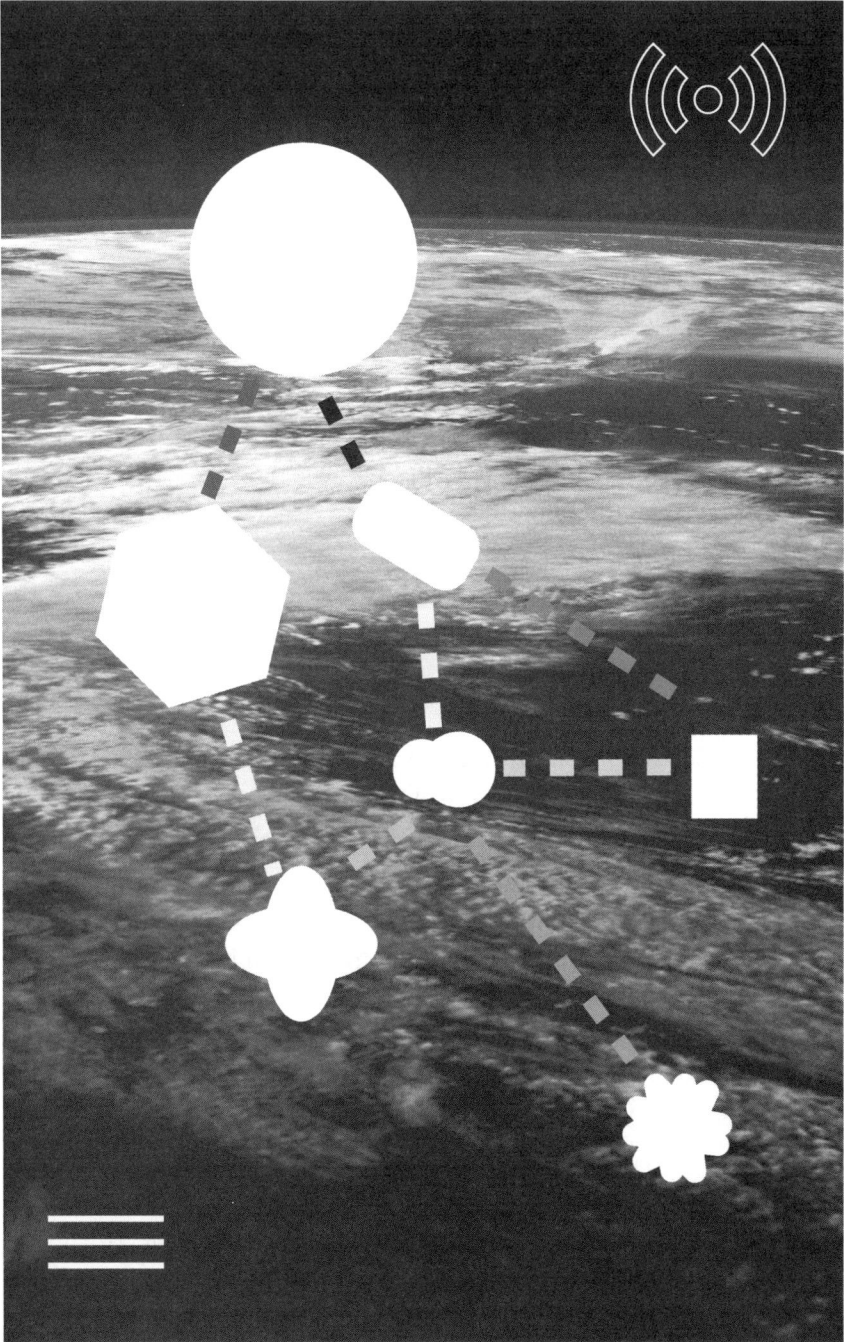

Figure 16: *The Non-Contiguous States & Territories. Copyright Robin Blackstone, MD*

The Non-Contiguous States & Territories
Population 5.3 million—GDP: $0.3 trillion
States and Territories: Alaska, Hawaii, Puerto Rico, US Virgin Islands, Guam, Northern Mariana Islands, American Samoa

Drawing a focused portrait of Alaska, Hawaii, Puerto Rico, the Territories, and Tribal Nations offers a unique view of how culture shapes health. Connected to the United States by statute but not by land, their distinct challenges—climate, geography, supply chains—sharpen our understanding of the fragile link between culture and health, and of what we must do as a nation to strengthen resilience. Their voice is expressed through the Regions they are part of in the H4 Alliance.

Signature Cultural Events
The Merrie Monarch Festival in Hilo, Hawaii, is the world's premier celebration of hula and Hawaiian culture, blending artistry, spirituality, and indigenous identity in a way that reverberates far beyond the islands. In Puerto Rico, Carnaval Ponceno showcases the island's vibrant Afro-Caribbean heritage with parades, masks, and music, reflecting both resilience and celebration. Guam's Liberation Day honors the island's WWII history and the US Military ties while affirming Chamorro cultural pride through processions, food, and music.

In American Samoa, the annual Flag Day brings together traditional ceremonies, song, and dance to honor both Samoan heritage and the territory's relationship to the United States. In Alaska, the World Eskimo Indian Olympics highlight indigenous athletic traditions of endurance and survival skills, emphasizing cultural continuity in a rapidly changing environment. The St. Thomas Carnival in the US Virgin Islands combines Caribbean music, dance, and pageantry, reinforcing the region's identity as a crossroads of cultures.

Film and media have also carried these cultures far beyond their borders: *Moana* introduced millions to Polynesian traditions, *Blue Hawaii* cemented the island's image in global pop culture, and documentaries like *After Maria* captured the struggle and resilience of Puerto Rico. A recent standout is the Apple TV+ historical drama *Chief of War,* starring and co-created by Jason Momoa. Set in 18th-century Hawaii, it uses the Indigenous Hawaiian language, traditional storytelling, and robust cultural consultation to retell the islands' origin story with unprecedented authenticity and scope. It is a model for other participants in H4. These depictions underscore how non-contiguous communities carry cultural influence that extends well beyond their geography.

Cultural Framework

Most maps and policies overlook the strategically essential nature of the non-contiguous states and territories of the United States. Alaska, Guam, and the Northern Mariana islands are aligned culturally with the Frontier region, Hawaii with Innovators, American Samoa with First Nations, and Puerto Rico and the U.S. Virgin Islands with Resilience. Yet each stands apart, not only because of their geographic isolation but because of their distinct cultural identities, political marginalization, and vital strategic role.

Their non-contiguous geography creates both vulnerability and opportunity. Supply chains are fragile, dependent on maritime and air routes. Energy and broadband connectivity are lifelines, linking communities to the mainland for everything from food and medicine to education and health care. At the same time, cultural identities in these locations are remarkably resilient, blending indigenous heritage, colonial history, and global exchange.

These regions have long been forced to innovate out of necessity. Distance, scarcity, and environmental exposure make them natural testbeds for adaptation, whether in renewable energy grids in Hawaii, advanced disaster preparedness in Puerto Rico, or telehealth networks serving island populations in the Pacific. Their small size and contained geographies mean they can be ideal sites for regional H4 trials, offering lessons that can be scaled to the mainland and globally.

Strengths

Hawaii consistently leads the nation in health outcomes. With a life expectancy of 79.9 years, the highest in the US, the state demonstrates how a culturally diverse, community-based approach to health can deliver sustained results. Nearly 18 percent of residents are foreign-born, and the majority of the population identifies as minorities across multiple races, fostering openness, cultural blending, and innovative approaches to care.[179]

Alaska and Puerto Rico benefit from strong federal support in specific areas. Alaska receives one of the highest per-capita public health funding allocations in the nation, much of it through the Indian Health Service which supports Native communities with culturally tailored care. Puerto Rico, despite its economic challenges, has achieved near-universal health insurance coverage through its government administered health plan offering equity that is elusive on the mainland.[180]

Economic strengths are limited but notable in specialized sectors. Puerto Rico has robust pharmaceutical manufacturing, and Guam hosts a significant US military presence. Alaska's oil and natural resources industries and Hawaii's tourism industry fuel economies that support above-average median incomes of roughly $87,000 in Alaska and $95,000 in Hawaii.[181,182]

Crisis preparedness is another shared strength, where each territory has developed unique response systems shaped by geography: in Hawaii with volcanic eruptions and wildfires; Alaska with earthquakes, extreme cold, and storms; Puerto Rico and the US Virgin Islands with hurricanes; and Pacific territories with cyclones and tsunamis. Hardship has bred competence, with specific emergency strategies and community-level resilience make these regions important models for adaptative preparedness.

Challenges

Tech Readiness and alignment with H4 are mixed. Hawaii and Alaska score in the moderate range for innovation, but they lag mainland hubs because of smaller technology sectors and geographic constraints. Broadband is inconsistent in rural Alaska and across the Pacific islands, limiting telehealth in population isolated geographically. Alaska's hospital telehealth adoption is 69 percent, and some rural Native villages have limited connectivity.[183] Puerto Rico faces the greatest challenges: Its tech readiness is low with a limited research and development base, and economic constraints are severe. The median household income is $26,000, the lowest in the US.[184]

While the mainland is debating health care reform, defense spending, and climate adaptation, there is this part of America, living out consequences in real time on the edge of the map. The non-contiguous states and territories often bear the brunt of the distance, disconnection, and denial of critical infrastructure support, from their mainland counterparts, but they are the United States' "front line" of resilience.

Opportunities

Geographic isolation creates barriers but also makes the non-contiguous states and territories natural incubators for innovation. Renewable energy, microgrids, satellite-linked telehealth, and supply-chain redesign have already taken root here out of necessity. Pilot projects focused on infrastructure modernization and digital coupled with the natural community-based resilience could be scaled nationally and globally.

Contribution to Health 4.0 (H4)

The non-contiguous regions are the United States stress test for H4. They reveal how equity, access, and resilience can be achieved under conditions of distance, scarcity, and climate vulnerability. Success here would demonstrate how to build trusted, tech-enabled systems that function when supply chains are fragile and communities diverse. If innovation works on the edge of the map, it would be applicable to both health in America, the global south, and in hard-to-reach places, like space.

In Essence

The non-contiguous states and territories sit at the margins of America's geography but at the center of its resilience story. They embody the nation's vulnerabilities—fragile infrastructure, dependence on imports, exposure to climate events—and its capacity for adaptation.

For business and H4, they make the case for investing in resilient, scalable solutions and especially in exploring the resilience and durability of a globally connected supply chain. These regions show that necessity drives innovation: from renewable energy grids in Hawaii to hurricane preparedness in Puerto Rico and telehealth in Alaska. The non-contiguous states, through their unique lens, remind us that heath must be able to flourish where distance, climate, and scarcity test every assumption. The systems that succeed in these cultures don't just serve their residents—they become prototypes and bridges to care delivery anywhere even in the most extreme frontiers of human exploration.

Perspective

When I finished this cultural analysis, I sat back and thought about each region. I have lived or worked in almost all of them: I grew up in Arizona (Growth), spent summers as a child in Wyoming's Grand Tetons (Frontier), attended medical school in Colorado (Frontier), practiced medicine in Carmel, California, (Innovators) and currently live in New York City (Innovators). I was marooned in Santa Fe, New Mexico during a snowstorm (Frontier) and in Puerto Rico when our plane was grounded (Resilience). My former mother-in-law was from Enid, Oklahoma (Resilience), and I did rotations in transplantation at the University of Minnesota when deciding on residency (Industrial). As a child, I spent many weekends on the Hopi and Navajo reservations and worked with the San Carlos Apache tribe in Arizona (First Nations).

Looking back, I see how these experiences have shaped my own personal culture. As you reflect on your life, you may find that your mindset and the way you connect with different cultures are among the most powerful influences on your personal culture of health. You are, in many ways, a product of your environment. Each of the six regional cultures has its strengths, individuals within them may differ in how they make decisions or in how much government should be involved. People in different regions also face distinct health challenges. Through the H4 Alliance, we

Health 4.0 Regional Scores Heat Map (Metrics on X-Axis)

	Tech Readiness	Cultural Openness	Health Outcomes	Alignment With Health 4.0	Economy	Crisis Resilience	Public Health Infrastructure
Innovators	5.0	5.0	4.4	4.9	4.6	4.1	4.9
Industrial	3.0	3.0	2.3	4.0	3.0	3.0	2.8
Resilience	3.5	3.1	3.0	4.0	3.5	3.5	3.1
Frontier	3.5	4.4	2.9	4.5	3.4	4.0	3.5
Growth	4.0	3.9	3.5	4.1	4.0	3.5	4.1
First Nations	2.5	3.0	2.5	3.2	2.3	3.1	2.6

Score scale: 5.0 – 4.5 – 4.0 – 3.5 – 3.0 – 2.5 – 2.0

Metrics

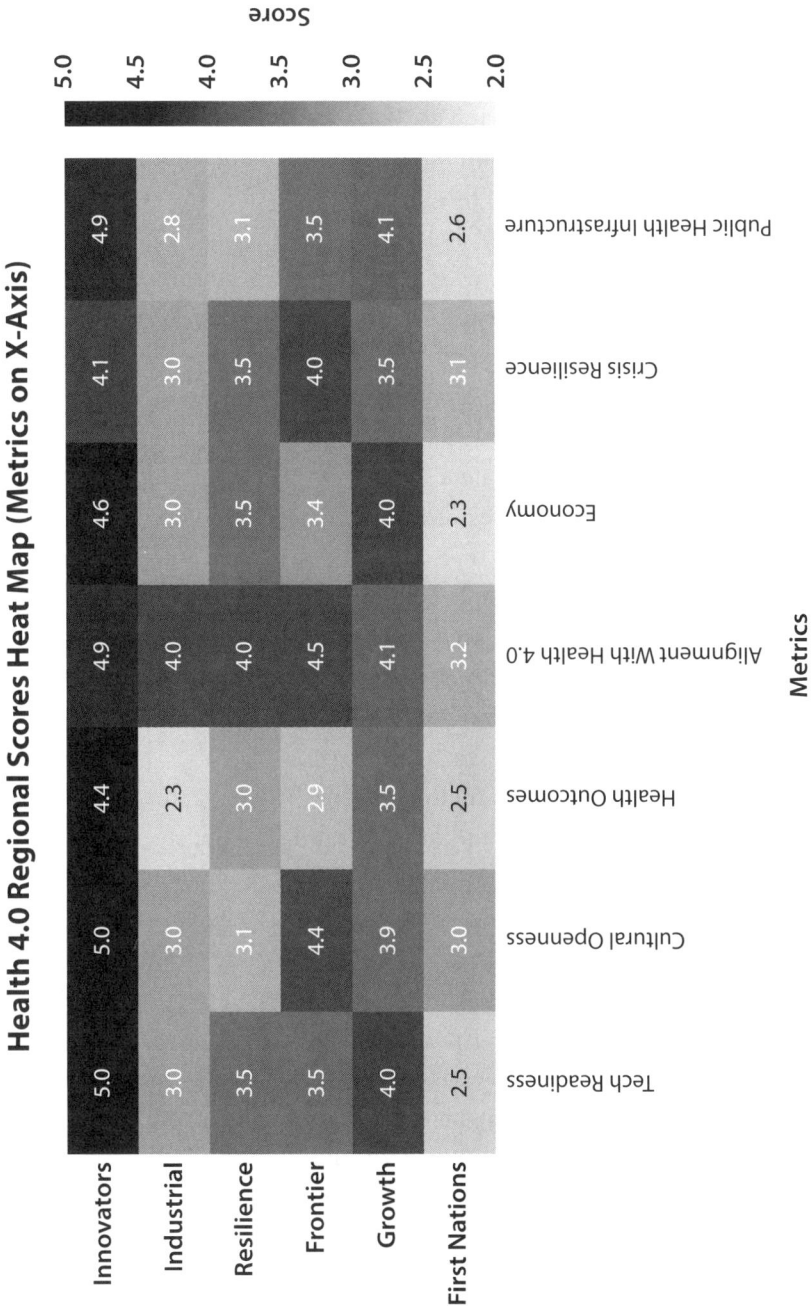

Figure 17: *Health 4.0 (H4) Regional Scores Heatmap. Copyright Robin Blackstone, MD*

can fund changes that make sense to individuals within the boundaries shaped by their own beliefs, delivering the best health solutions for each person and community. This is possible because of the technology of the Fourth Industrial Revolution. How do you prepare? Know the technology, use it, make it your constant companion, and it will open doors to a future of health you can now only imagine. Step through. The universe awaits.

Health is not a byproduct of prosperity; Health is its foundation. This analysis makes one thing clear: Regions marked by robust productivity and profitability are, without exception, healthier. They have prioritized creating the infrastructures of health. The innovators region clearly demonstrates this idea. Culture and health are deeply entwined, and the strength of a region's economy often mirrors the well-being of its people.

If we want America to remain a source of global economic vitality and cultural leadership, we must treat health as a national investment, not an individual's private burden. But investment alone is not enough. We cannot build that future by leaving people behind or trading away our principles in pursuit of short-term gain. Greed without ethics is not leadership.

If regional models can help every community reach a point where disease no longer drains our resources or defines our future, then we have not just improved health care, we've hit a home run.

This analysis also reveals something deeper: We have not always truly seen or understood one another. The cultural distinctions across regions highlight not division, but the richness of our national mosaic. Every region creates value—its own blend of strength and struggle—and together they shape the soul of America.

It is no accident that we endure. We are a resilient people because we are many peoples. Our diversity isn't a challenge to overcome; it is the wellspring of our strength. This is clearly seen in the Growth region.

Certain words rose from this analysis like signals through the noise: *grit, self-reliance, community, individuality.* These aren't just regional traits. They are human truths.

It's time to celebrate that diversity, not with platitudes, but with structure. To build a future that reflects who we are and who we aspire to be, we must create a policy framework that is both unifying and adaptive. That framework is the H4 Alliance. And it begins with the 28th Amendment to the Constitution and the USA Health Act.

Culture Is Health

After I finished my residency, I turned down opportunities for fellowships in Pittsburgh, Raleigh, and Montreal, in liver transplant, thoracic surgery, and oncology. In retrospect, they would have advanced my formal academic surgical career by light years. However, I felt like I needed to step away from the formality of academics and get closer to people, and so I respectfully declined and moved to California.

The strain of the residency had weighed heavily on me. I took a job working in a county facility primarily treating migrant workers from the Central Valley. The workers amazed me. They had to show up and do their work or they didn't get paid and might be fired. Many of them worked to send money home to their families in Mexico or South America.

I remember a man with appendicitis who came into the emergency department just before dark. A quick history, physical, and CT scan later, and we were on our way to the operating room for an appendectomy. Early the next morning, he self-discharged to go back to work. The culture was dictating the care in a very profound way.

In 1998, major tobacco companies agreed to the Master Settlement Agreement (MSA) with forty-six states, the District of Columbia and five US territories.[185] It was the largest civil litigation settlement in US history, compensating states for Medicaid and other health care costs tied to smoking-related illness. The agreement provided for more than $206 billion to be paid out over twenty-five years and opened tobacco industry documents to the public.

When the tobacco lawsuit settlement funds became available, California established funding for grants. Working with two other counties, the three smallest in California, we wrote a grant for early detection of breast and cervical cancer in the farmworkers in the central valley. Our little project was funded for $900,000. We found and detected women with early-stage disease who were essentially cured with early treatment.

Emboldened, I wrote a grant to the Robert Wood Johnson Foundation to develop a relationship between curanderas like my grandmother and primary care doctors to foster trust within the Central Valley community and help them get scientifically based care within their cultural structure. A second goal was to encourage young doctors-in-training—residents—to factor in the impact of culture on medicine. Although we made the final list, it wasn't funded.

Even so, I started meeting with women who lived in the small dusty Central Valley farm town. One took place with a group of women from a three-block area in the heart of the city. The women were mostly in their mid-fifties, with just a few still young enough to become pregnant.

So, after talking a while, I opened it up to questions.

"Since my ovaries have stopped working, I feel different," one woman said in English. "What is a sex drive and why don't I have any?"

Wow! Let's get right to the point, I thought.

"What do you think is the answer?" I asked the group. "Where does sex drive come from?"

One woman said it came from the "ovarios" and the "hormones." Another said from wealth—as if all wealthy women had it. One said it came from having enough time to get dressed up. One said she had lost it as she gained weight; many of the women in the room were thirty to fifty pounds overweight. Their answers included a wide range of things, and as a few even questioned their husbands' sexuality, the group erupted in laughter.

Finally, the room grew quiet, and I said, "Although much of what you have said may contribute to a loss of sex drive, in the end, your interest in sex reflects what you think of yourself. How you value yourself."

Silence.

As I glanced around the room, each woman was deep in her own thoughts about this.

Finally, a woman named Carmela said, "I try to think good about myself, but my husband always criticizes me, even when I try to do something nice for him, like serve a meal. He watches television or pushes my hand away. I work as many hours during the week as he does. When I got promoted to supervisor at my job, he just asked how much more I was bringing home every week." She looked down.

I asked as gently as I could, "How does it feel?"

"Terrible. Also, my daughter sees it. My daughter sees how I am treated." She paused and then added, "How I allow myself to be treated. I fight with myself about whether I should do something, but we just go on."

This raw honesty was a signal that, here, the women felt safe to talk, but I felt helpless. I truly understood, having been a victim of corporal punishment by my father as a young girl. Somehow, I was "precocious," asked too many questions, and he tried hard to crush any independence right out of me. He wasn't very successful at that. If I had let it affect me more, I wouldn't be writing for you now.

"In some ways, allowing yourself to feel 'less than' because of someone outside of yourself, is easy. Blame is easy to attribute. It is far harder to look past others and go deeper into who we are and how we can become strong ourselves," I explained. "Perhaps, others here feel the same way as Carmela?"

Many heads nodded.

"Then perhaps we can meet and talk every few weeks. We can call it the 'Sewing Circle,' a safe place to talk about, write about, and solve what is keeping us from health."

"Oh, doctora—I didn't know this was also part of health," Carmela said.

"What a culture accepts as normal behavior often shapes an individual's mental resilience. That resilience—mental toughness—is the foundation for navigating uncertainty. When it is weakened by overdependence on others, vulnerability to illness and disease increases."

We agreed to meet in a week, and everyone took a little oath about their participation: "We will listen to each other and not repeat our conversations naming any individual. We will form a bond to help our families and our communities be stronger. We are the Circulo de Costura, Circulo de Bienestar."

This is the part of health that rarely gets talked about in most medical journals. These intangible pieces and parts of lives are the cultural pieces that have such outsized influence. Realize that the culture you grew up with, live in, the books you read, the instrument you played, or the music you listened to, echoes through every decision, large or small. It forms, in large part, how you respond to your environment, or even, what responses are possible. It is this part of health that we have ignored.

In H4, the invisible threads of connection—the forces that shape our friendships, our choices, and our health—will finally be seen, studied and woven consciously into the fabric of our lives. Into the fabric of health itself. Only when these cultural threads are fully integrated into care, can the USA Health Act—and the 28th Amendment that makes it possible—fulfill their promise: to deliver health and dignity to every community, no matter where in America, or the world, they live.

PART 4

A New American Health Care System

The H4 Alliance Blueprint

CHAPTER 11

The Right to Health Care

The surest way to secure health care for all Americans is through a constitutional right. But amendments move slowly. The public has waited years already, and Congress may take decades—if it acts at all.

Why a Right to Health Care Matters

In every other high-income democracy, nations with the same impact on the world stage, health care is a guaranteed right. It is not a question of ideology. It is a condition of good governance. Health is the platform to fuel productivity, commerce and ingenuity. Their constitutional commitment unlocks advantages the United States simply does not have: a healthier workforce, strategic leverage, population data at scale, and the preservation of personal autonomy in health choices. Right now, we are being outclassed. Norway serves as the best example.

One country ranks number one in health care system performance, which includes access, equity, and outcomes among OECD nations: Norway. [186]

"Everyone has the right to the highest attainable standard of health."

— Constitution of Norway, Article 110c

The structural difference between the United States and its peers is clarity. Other nations can make system-wide decisions quickly, using unified data. They negotiate costs, invest in prevention, and allocate resources based on need. These countries have lower administrative expenses, act strategically, make innovation relevant to the population and have far superior health outcomes for their people.

By contrast, the United States remains fragmented: fifty state systems, thousands of plans, and no national strategy. We spend more, get less, and cannot answer basic health questions: Who isn't getting care? What's working? What is waste? How many administrators does it take to screw in a light bulb?

Without a guarantee, we treat every health failure as private misfortune, attributing fault instead of what it so often is: a public design flaw. America is not challenging and overcoming uncertainty. We are giving in to it. Confronting uncertainty with the determination and focus that have long marked the American spirit would propel us to lead the most powerful growth engine on the planet—health. We would be able to compete with countries putting the health and well-being of their people as table stakes to growth.

Until we establish health as a right, we will keep bleeding trust, money, and lives into a system people were never meant to survive.

UNITED STATES CONSTITUTION
AMENDMENT XXVIII
THE RIGHT TO HEALTH CARE

Section 1

The right to health, including equitable access to timely, comprehensive, and universal health care, shall not be denied or abridged by the United States or by any State.

This right extends to every citizen of the United States, wherever residing or traveling, and to every person lawfully present, residing, or working within its jurisdiction including the States, the District of Columbia, Territories, possessions, commonwealths, and consistent with their sovereignty, Tribal Nations.

Emergency and life-saving care shall not be denied to any person within the jurisdiction of the United States.

The United States shall secure this right through a universal and comprehensive health system, delivered in partnership with culturally aligned Regions, States, Territories and Tribal Nations. Such a system shall be grounded in the principles of autonomy, transparency, scientific integrity, privacy, equity, cultural responsiveness, sustainability, trust, and technological innovation.

No person shall be denied necessary care, nor shall access be limited, conditioned, or burdened, on account of race, gender, age, disability, health status, cultural identity, economic position, geography, or any other characteristic unrelated to medical need.

Section 2

Congress shall have the power to enforce and implement this article through appropriate legislation, including but not limited to the USA Health Act. Such legislation may establish public institutions, regional authorities, technological systems, and data protections necessary to ensure the delivery, quality, accountability, and continuous improvement of care, including reciprocal arrangements to secure coverage for citizens when abroad.

Section 3
Congress shall establish a permanent national authority to administer and safeguard this right, operating as an independent public trust with powers comparable to those of the Federal Reserve in monetary policy. This authority shall be empowered to regulate, coordinate, and fund matters relating to health and health care across the United States. Its actions and standards shall prevail over conflicting state or local law, while ensuring coordination with Regions, States, Territories and Tribal Nations.

A Line in the Sand

This amendment binds Americans to a shared responsibility: to build a health care system worthy of the people it serves. Health care should not hinge on income, employment, geography or luck. True autonomy means freedom from the fear of medical bankruptcy.

For the first time in US history, health care would stand alongside free speech, due process, and equal protection: non-negotiable, constitutional, and permanent. Today the American public does not have this guarantee. Health remains conditional—too often determined by status rather than need. This amendment affirms that health care is not a privilege purchased through wealth or employment, but a constitutional right grounded in life and liberty. Health is how the pursuit of happiness becomes possible.

This does not require the federal government to design, deliver, or pay for health care. It means the Constitution sets the guardrails—defining what must be secured for every person—while leaving room for public, private, and regional systems to innovate in how that promise is fulfilled. It redefines government's role: not to pick winners and losers in a health care lottery, but to guarantee a baseline of health that is equitable, accountable, effective, and fair. It elevates health to the status of a right, enshrined alongside our most fundamental freedoms. It demands clarity of responsibility, and holds leaders to account as stewards of the people's health.

What It Means for People

Most importantly, this Amendment signals something Americans haven't heard in a long time: you are valued.

- The grandmother in Cuthbert, Georgia (Randolf Couty, Resilience Region) rationing insulin because she cannot afford her prescriptions.
- The teenager in Dallas, Texas (Growth Region) waiting months for mental health care, while her family tries to keep her safe.
- The couple in Portland, Maine (Innovators Region) who work full time but are still stretched thin by private school tuition and rising health costs.
- The elder in Hopi territory (First Nations Region) walking beside his son, sober after decades of inherited and self-induced trauma.
- The man living in a Manhattan penthouse, bound to a wheelchair, who cannot buy back the health he has lost—despite wealth beyond measure.
- The working parents, in Las Vegas, Nevada (Frontier Region) skipping appointments to avoid a bill they can't afford.
- The father of a family of five who needs to get rehab so he can get back to work after an injury on the job.

Each of us are trapped, in different ways, by a health system that values status over need. That waits for rescue, versus acting proactively. Every American stands to gain, when health is secured as a constitutional right.

Chapter 12

Architecting Future Health

Every enduring change begins with a blueprint. Health care belongs in the Constitution as a right. But rights on paper do not automatically create systems in practice. The American people cannot afford to wait for Congress, which has resisted universal care for more than a century even as every peer nation secured it. Change may never come from Washington, and delay costs lives.

That is why I created the Health 4.0 (H4) Alliance™ and the H4 Alliance Sovereign Health Trust™—a non-government model of what comprehensive care can look like in practice. Structured as a Public Benefit Corporation, the H4 Alliance exists today to test and refine the architecture of a new system. Its companion nonprofit, the H4 Alliance Sovereign Health Trust, extends that mission by building public trust and enabling broad participation through philanthropy and shared stewardship.

Under this umbrella, we've created two complementary pathways for donors and partners to engage, each with a distinct emphasis but united by the same Blueprint:

- *H4 Alliance Sovereign Health Trust*—focused on strengthening the health of the American people, protecting autonomy, and demonstrating that comprehensive, universal care can be built here at home.

- *Future of Health Foundation*—focused on advancing innovation, digital-first systems, and global collaboration to accelerate equitable health worldwide.

Both foundations are aligned with the H4 Alliance mission. They provide different points of entry, allowing individuals and organizations to contribute in ways that reflect their priorities, values, and aspirations—while moving us together toward a shared future: health as a public good and an engine to fuel productivity, commerce, and the exploration of uncharted places.

Together they demonstrate that comprehensive, affordable, culturally aligned health care is possible even before the nation chooses a universal system. Whether the United States chooses to enact a government funded program or not, the H4 Alliance will demonstrate to the US public—and to the world—that free markets can be just as powerful in delivering comprehensive health care in a Health 4.0 environment.

Why use both "universal" and "comprehensive" when defining the foundation of health care? Because each word carries distinct power—and together, they establish a complete and enforceable promise.

Universal defines who is covered. It affirms that every person under US jurisdiction—citizens, lawful residents, and workers—is included. No one is left out based on income, job, geography, immigration status, or insurance. It ensures inclusion without exception. The inclusivity loop ensures no one falls outside the frame of health. Why? Because when you try to parse out special groups, it represents bias and adds to chaos.

Comprehensive defines what is covered. It guarantees access to the full spectrum of care: preventive and primary services, mental and behavioral health, dental and vision, reproductive and maternal care, chronic disease management, surgery, and more. It speaks to adequacy, not minimalism, to health care that actually meets the needs and complexity of human health. It defines health and health care broadly, inclusively and uniquely. Comprehensive protects autonomy in decision making, because choice is only meaningful when the full spectrum of care is available.

These terms work together to prevent the two most common failures in global systems: offering care to everyone, but not enough of it, or offering excellent care, but only to the few who can afford it.

The H4 Alliance is built to avoid both failures. It is universal in access, comprehensive in scope, and regionally responsive in design. It is delivered through culturally aligned institutions, powered by modern tools like Doctor AI, and protected by a constitutional mandate that centers the individual while upholding the public trust.

This language matters. It ensures that the right to health in the United States is not symbolic, selective, or shallow—but real, inclusive, and complete.

Principles and Guarantees

At its core, the H4 Alliance is built on seven principles: personal autonomy, affordability, accessibility, effectiveness, equity, integrity, and cultural alignment. Together, these values reimagine health as a public good—protected from political interference and grounded in the dignity of each person.

The H4 Alliance guarantees:

- Every person is automatically enrolled, either at birth or upon legal residence.

- Each person pays a flat $30 per month ($360 annually).
- No copays, no deductibles, no surprise bills, no balance billing.
- One national system, delivered through regional councils that reflect cultural identity and local wisdom.

Financing is straightforward. A 15-year transition plan gradually shifts employer and government spending into a single transparent trust, stabilizing costs for families, businesses, and taxpayers. Fraud and administrative waste—which cost Americans hundreds of billions annually—are eliminated through modern technology, public accountability, and independent governance.

The Blueprint is not bureaucracy, it is stewardship. Like the Federal Reserve in finance, the H4 Alliance is structured to operate as an independent yet accountable institution—shielded from political cycles, grounded in public trust, and responsible for safeguarding equity, transparency, and trust.

Reality Check

Designing a new model in the midst of America's existing health system—with its maze of regulations overlapping programs, corporate interests, and fragmented delivery—is daunting. The current chaos can feel immovable. But the H4 Alliance is not an abstract ideal; it is a practical blueprint built to operate in the real world. It recognizes the messy transition from legacy systems, the pushback from entrenched interests, and the regulatory patchwork that has strangled innovation. A phased, 15-year plan is not a luxury—it is the only way forward. By breaking the challenge into steps, the Blueprint creates clarity in the midst of confusion and a path through the chaos toward a system that actually works.

Building for Today, Anticipating Tomorrow

While the H4 Alliance operates today without public funding, the long-term potential is clear. Nearly $2 trillion in federal health spending—currently fragmented across dozens of agencies—could eventually be consolidated into a unified framework. The Blueprint is designed with this possibility in mind. If the USA Health Act were enacted, these functions could be transferred seamlessly; if not, the H4 Alliance demonstrates how an alignment could be staged over time. Either way, the model anticipates the future, showing how resources already in the system can be redirected toward equity, transparency, and trust.

The Five Federated Components of the Blueprint

To translate principles into practice, the H4 Alliance is organized into five federated components. Together, they replace fragmentation with alignment, opacity with transparency, and exclusion with equity.

H4 Alliance Passport

The national care delivery platform, providing preventive, proactive, and rescue services across all regions. Integrated digital tools—including secure digital identity (Pulse) and AI-driven decision support (Doctor AI)—guide individuals through their care journeys. Regional councils adapt delivery to cultural context while upholding national standards.

H4 Alliance

The fiduciary arm of the system, pooling resources through subscriptions, redirected employer contributions, philanthropy, and returns on innovation. The Trust eliminates waste, stabilizes financing, and ensures equity adjustments across regions.

H4 Alliance Regulatory Authority

An independent oversight body responsible for licensing, safety, clinical and ethical standards, and AI/data governance. It protects public trust by ensuring decisions are made on evidence and equity, not politics or profit.

H4 Alliance Data Lake, Atlas & Insight Engine

A secure, real-time health intelligence platform that harmonizes records, social determinants, genomic profiles, and outcomes. It powers Doctor

AI, informs policy, supports equity evaluation, and ensures transparency through public reporting and open data access.

H4 Alliance Innovation Hub

A national platform for testing and scaling breakthroughs in diagnostics, AI, precision medicine, and community solutions. It runs equity-focused innovation bounties and reinvests public and private returns into new rounds of innovation, ensuring that discoveries benefit the public.

Integrity and Safeguards

No system can function without trust. The H4 Alliance is governed by strict conflict-of-interest standards and transparency requirements as established by the CEO and Board. Leaders, clinicians, and advisors must disclose financial ties, and recuse themselves from conflicted decisions. These safeguards ensure that the Blueprint delivers not only health but also accountability.

How One Health System Found Its Future in the H4 Alliance

Elena Ruiz spent fifteen years rising through the leadership ranks at Phoenix Health, a not-for-profit health care system spanning Arizona, New Mexico, Colorado, and West Texas. With twelve hospitals, a strong virtual care presence, a self-funded insurance arm, and a stable Medicare Advantage portfolio, Phoenix had become known for its independence and adaptability. It had weathered Medicaid cuts, Medicare rate shifts, labor shortages, and even the quiet acquisition of key physician groups by private equity. Resilience had become its core identity.

Then came the 28th Amendment and the USA Health Act of 2026.

At first, Elena wasn't alarmed. She had seen national reforms come and go—mostly diluted into compliance checklists, billing adjustments, and unfunded mandates with increased administrative costs. Her legal team flagged the legislation as something to watch, but likely to stall in litigation.

Her chief operating officer was more direct. "We've seen national plans before. Most just layer new rules onto old chaos. I'll believe this one's different when I see the funding tied to outcomes."

By the spring of 2028, the leadership team's skepticism had faded. Providers were requesting guidance on integrating *Doctor AI* into care pathways. Patients were asking how to transfer their records to the H4 Alliance Doctor AI app. Regional care contracts, previously managed internally, were being reconsidered by three new Regional Councils: the Growth Region (Arizona and Texas), the Resilience Region (New Mexico), and the First Nations Region. They were all areas where Phoenix did business.

At a weekly leadership meeting, a longtime nurse practitioner raised a new concern.

"I got a referral today from *Doctor AI* for a patient in Kentucky. She needs a specialist we happen to have here, and we have an opening. *Doctor AI* offered her a choice: wait ten days for a local appointment with a less qualified provider or see our specialist provider by telehealth in two. She chose us. Once we accept, her records become visible to our team. It feels, different. Reaching for expertise across the country. Extending the meaning of local. It feels, right."

This comment brought the Amendment home for Elena. The system wasn't reacting to policy. It was already changing it.

She called an emergency strategy session—legal, compliance, payer operations, virtual care. Her general counsel brought a packet to her office. "You should read this before the meeting," he said.

At the meeting, the general counsel began with this statement, "We've reviewed the Amendment and the Act in full. This isn't a pilot or policy tweak. It's a shift in legal authority. Phoenix Health is no longer the final decision maker on coverage or care delivery. That authority now resides with the H4 Alliance and its governing framework."

Elena referred to the new org chart: National Board. Funding Source. Regional Councils. Public Review Panels.

"This isn't regulation," she said after a pause. "It's sovereignty."

The room went still.

"This isn't a checklist or a payment model tweak. It is a new source of legitimacy. The legitimacy is coming from the American public. Strategy doesn't originate in one health system anymore—it comes from the public mandate. Although we assumed we had autonomy before, we didn't really. Phoenix Health lived, as did all health systems, in a network of regulations so complex and full of rules and exceptions that we couldn't navigate it or help patients do so. We've moved from private governance to shared public governance. From fifty interpretations to one constitutional commitment."

She stood and walked to the whiteboard.

"We're not a standalone system anymore. The every-health-system-for-itself era is over. That's good for patients and can be good for us. But we'll need to lead differently. That starts with recommitting to our mission as a not-for-profit: service, trust, and outcomes."

She wrote three words: *Care. Trust. Integration.*

"Doctors and nurses aren't just following local protocols anymore. They're part of a national care network. We will not use patient data for the benefit of our own interests without consent. AI doesn't replace us—it helps people find us. And we're not rewarded for volume or exclusivity. We're measured by trust, outcomes, and ethical transparency."

Someone from finance and marketing asked, "So." "Do we pull out of payer operations? Rebrand as a platform partner of H4?"

"No," she said. "We stop playing defense. This isn't about window dressing any more. We lead the adaptation for our region."

Over the next six months, Phoenix Health launched a full transformation supported by their board. It joined the Regional Councils as a public implementation partner. It retired its Medicare Advantage product and transitioned patients to the H4 Alliance Passport subscription model. It restructured governance, opened its *Doctor AI* interface to ethical audit, and migrated core operations to blockchain for transparent reporting. They led a coalition to realign specialty care with other systems to eliminate redundancy.

By the following year, Phoenix wasn't just surviving—it was setting a new standard.

It led the maternal-fetal health initiative across the Four Corners. It became the first health system to pilot AI-supported behavioral triage alongside licensed human counselors. It secured a national grant to deploy drone-based care delivery to remote First Nations communities.

Not every system adapted. Some resisted. Some sold off divisions. Some turned inward.

But Phoenix chose to align. It became a model—not of dominance, but of trust. It proved that relevance, leadership, and resilience don't disappear in a unified system. They evolve.

Elena reminded her team:

"We used to act like the system. Now, we're part of one."

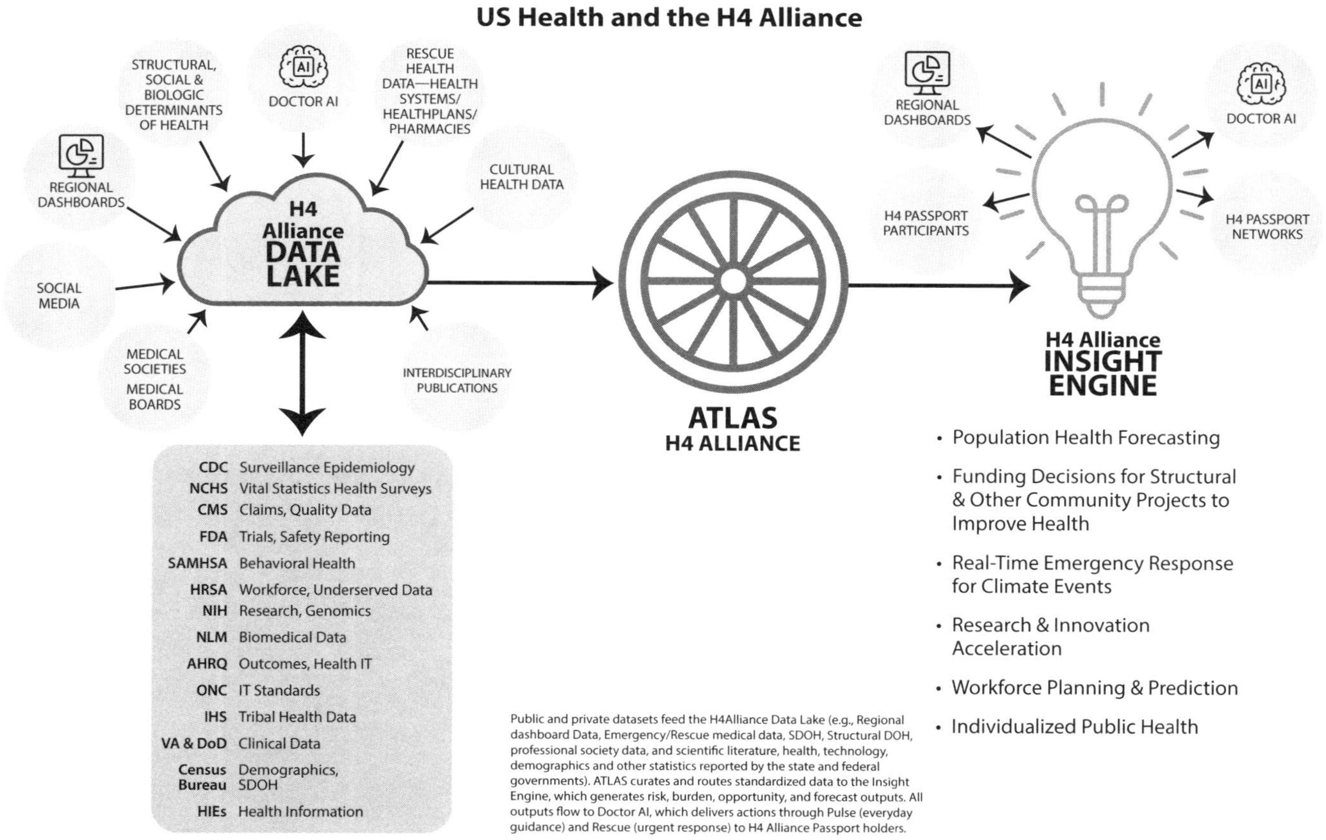

US Health and the H4 Alliance

ATLAS
H4 ALLIANCE

H4 Alliance INSIGHT ENGINE

- Population Health Forecasting
- Funding Decisions for Structural & Other Community Projects to Improve Health
- Real-Time Emergency Response for Climate Events
- Research & Innovation Acceleration
- Workforce Planning & Prediction
- Individualized Public Health

H4 Alliance DATA LAKE

CDC	Surveillance Epidemiology
NCHS	Vital Statistics Health Surveys
CMS	Claims, Quality Data
FDA	Trials, Safety Reporting
SAMHSA	Behavioral Health
HRSA	Workforce, Underserved Data
NIH	Research, Genomics
NLM	Biomedical Data
AHRQ	Outcomes, Health IT
ONC	IT Standards
IHS	Tribal Health Data
VA & DoD	Clinical Data
Census Bureau	Demographics, SDOH
HIEs	Health Information

DOCTOR AI

H4 PASSPORT NETWORKS

REGIONAL DASHBOARDS

H4 PASSPORT PARTICIPANTS

RESCUE HEALTH DATA—HEALTH SYSTEMS/ HEALTHPLANS/ PHARMACIES

CULTURAL HEALTH DATA

INTERDISCIPLINARY PUBLICATIONS

STRUCTURAL, SOCIAL & BIOLOGIC DETERMINANTS OF HEALTH

DOCTOR AI

REGIONAL DASHBOARDS

SOCIAL MEDIA

MEDICAL SOCIETIES MEDICAL BOARDS

Public and private datasets feed the H4Alliance Data Lake (e.g. Regional dashboard Data, Emergency/Rescue medical data, SDOH, Structural DOH, professional society data, and scientific literature, health, technology, demographics and other statistics reported by the state and federal governments). ATLAS curates and routes standardized data to the Insight Engine, which generates risk, burden, opportunity, and forecast outputs. All outputs flow to Doctor AI, which delivers actions through Pulse (everyday guidance) and Rescue (urgent response) to H4 Alliance Passport holders.

Figure 18: *National Health Intelligence Stack (H4A): Data Lake → ATLAS → Insight Engine → Doctor AI → H4 Alliance Passport. Copyright Robin Blackstone, MD*

CHAPTER 13

The Passport
Access to Care, Anywhere for Everyone

A passport is more than paper. It is belonging, permission, identity, and mobility. It lets you cross borders with confidence that you will not be turned away. Imagine if health worked the same way.

Today, access to care is not a right but a maze. The people you have met in the pages of Doctor AI are not outliers. They are people who are at the mercy of a system where access is conditional, fragmented, and transactional.

The H4 Alliance Passport begins here—not as a card in your wallet, but as a framework of belonging. It says: you are part of this health system, wherever you are, whatever your circumstance. You will not be turned away.

Health care delivery is where the rubber meets the road for the American consumer. The H4 Alliance Passport will become the primary mechanism for delivering all health care and public health services under the H4 Alliance.

Health 4.0: A New Definition of Health

Health 4.0 redefines what it means to be well. Health is not simply the absence of disease, nor is it defined by the ability to access a physician on demand. It is a dynamic state of well-being—physical, mental, emotional, social, and financial—supported by intelligent systems that reflect each person's values, culture, and lived experience. It is a digital first system of care, a digital first company.

The H4 Alliance Passport provides a single, integrated benefit package. Coverage includes prevention health, proactive health, and rescue health.

We often talk about health in terms of doctors, hospitals, or insurance cards. The real drivers of well-being often lie elsewhere, in the rules that shape neighborhoods, schools, jobs, electricity and broadband access. These are the determinants of health; they explain why health outcomes can differ so much from one community to another.

Structural determinants of health are the written and unwritten rules that decide who has an advantage and who doesn't—rules built into laws, policies, and social norms. They control how power, money, and opportunity flow through society, and they're often reinforced by those who already have more of each. These rules may feel invisible, but their impact is not.

Take telehealth during the pandemic. In some neighborhoods, patients could see their doctor from the safety of home with the tap of a phone screen. In others—often rural, low-income, or majority-minority communities—there was no broadband strong enough to support a video visit. The rule wasn't written in a medical textbook; it was written in decades of policy decisions that left those communities out of the digital expansion. The gap determined who got timely care and who went without.

Social determinants of health are the everyday conditions in which people live, work, and age—things like housing, transportation, food access, education, and job security. They decide whether you can get to a clinic, afford your prescriptions, or have a safe place to recover from illness.

When Hurricane Florence hit North Carolina in 2018, thousands of people lost electricity, safe drinking water, and road access. For some, the storm meant temporary inconvenience. For others—especially those in low-income neighborhoods, in mobile homes, or without reliable transportation—it meant days without access to medical care, refrigeration for insulin, or even a way to call for help. The hurricane didn't create those vulnerabilities; it exposed them. That's the reality of social determinants of health: your ZIP code can matter more than your genetic code.[187]

The H4 Alliance, powered by Doctor AI, are designed to confront both—the structural rules that set the stage and the everyday conditions that play out on it—so that no matter where you live or what resources you start with, you have a fair chance at a healthy life.

The Two Maps

Talia was born in East Riverside, a neighborhood pressed against the highway, boxed in by warehouses and aging apartment blocks. Her family had lived there for three generations, ever since her grandfather came north looking for work in the once booming factories that now sat shuttered.

By the time Talia turned ten, her world was already shaped by what experts call structural and social determinants of health. The local school had no nurse. The park had no safe lighting. Her mother walked two miles to catch the bus to work, and fresh food cost more at the corner store than junk food. Their building had mold that no one would address. When her baby brother developed asthma, it didn't surprise anyone.

But when Talia turned sixteen, she asked a question in a school project that changed her understanding: *Why is my neighborhood like this?* That question took her from social factors that felt like they could never be fixed, to the structural ones.

She discovered that decades ago, city planners had drawn red lines around East Riverside. Loans were denied. Parks weren't built. Tax incentives went to other areas. Health services were placed miles away. These were structural determinants, not just the conditions of her environment, but the written and unwritten rules and decisions that created and maintained them. Talia found out it matters where you draw the map, reflecting money and power used to keep some communities from thriving.

She learned that her school received far less funding because property taxes determined school budgets. That highways were routed through the middle of Black and brown neighborhoods because no one in power lived there. That her mom's job didn't offer health insurance because minimum wage workers were excluded from early labor union protections, choices that seemed to be by design.

Talia found the hierarchical patterns of advantage that experts like Heller describe. Using ChatGPT, she was able to research and understand these sophisticated documents. She realized structural barriers weren't accidents. They were the result of power and how that power was used to protect some communities while abandoning others. People who had knowledge could create structural barriers into zoning laws, budgets, and policies.

Talia's teacher, Mrs. Brown, gave her an image she never forgot:

"Social determinants are like the map of your neighborhood. Structural determinants are the people who designed the map. They decide where you're allowed to live and how." Talia got an A on her project and found the grit to invest in herself.

By twenty-five, Talia had graduated from her community college through a combination of online education and in-person learning, so she could continue to work full time. She was part of her community health collaborative. She helped bring mobile clinics to East Riverside, lobbied for zoning reform, and partnered with local leaders to finally remove the toxic waste site no one had touched in thirty years. The asthma rate dropped. So did the dropout rate.

Talia knew changing social conditions mattered, but they would only be successful when paired with structural changes that made those conditions seem inevitable.

It was time for Talia to lead the effort to bring this key aspect of health to the table, regionally and nationally.

Perhaps it was time to run for a national congressional role.

Introducing Proactive Health

In the H4 Alliance, proactive health is the *Pulse*. It defines a shift in focus of the health care system upstream, to catch disease before it catches us. To diagnose and treat optimally. Instead of requiring patients to navigate a stepwise sequence of outdated or less effective treatments, the H4 Alliance Passport prioritizes the most effective, evidence-based option first, ensuring care is timely, optimized, and aligned with current best practices, minimizing the human and fiscal cost of more complex and toxic care.

The H4 Alliance Passport discards the legacy model of forcing patients through outdated treatment protocols in sequence. When a superior technique or technology exists, care starts there, because delay, inefficiency, and compromise are no longer acceptable standards of practice. A key focus is to manage chronic health problems before crisis causes disability and death.

Many of these health aspects were historically excluded from coverage in health care plans prior to 2026. Proactive health, a central pillar of the H4 Alliance platform, covers not only what care is delivered, but also when and why. Shifting the system focus from reaction to proactive recognition and early treatment, recognizes that staying well is not only better for people's longevity, but also less expensive and disruptive than when a person has to deal with being sick. Covered benefits include: early detection technologies aligned with your risk, optimal effective treatment realizing the potential of new and less invasive treatment, an annual health visit (individual choice of telehealth or *Doctor AI on a per event basis*), optimization of chronic disease management with active support, *Doctor AI* as each individual's personal health agent with human clinicians on or in the loop, child care, population health initiatives, health education, financial education and services, service delivery, and experience feedback.

This is proactive health, the Pulse, your Pulse: the steady rhythm of anticipation, alignment, and action that keeps people well before illness takes hold.

Rescue Health Through Acute and Specialty Care

When things go wrong with our health, the system needs to respond rapidly, expertly, and comprehensively. Whether an accident, a new diagnosis, or a serious medical event, rescue health will be recognizable to anyone with a previous encounter with the current health care system. However, it will also be different. Having an indelible record in the blockchain, as well as accessible and comprehensive medical records and data that the individual controls, provides layers of rich information that can fine-tune treatment to that individual. Moving directly to the most effective therapy optimizes care.

Here are some examples of what is covered: telehealth, hospitalization, surgical procedures (both inpatient and outpatient), remote surgical specialists using robotic surgery technology, membership in your local health collaborative center, emergency services (including 24/7 ER coverage), specialist consultations (cardiology, oncology, neurology, etc.), rehabilitation, physical therapy, post-acute care, mental health support, vision, and dental care.

A Lot to Live For

Wade Carter had lived his whole life in the mountains of eastern Kentucky. Fifty-eight years old, he worked at the county water plant, smoked since high school, and never thought much about doctors unless something hurt, constantly and for a while.

When the new USA Health program came to town, it set up in the church basement with hot coffee and friendly faces. Wade showed up because his cousin told him they were doing free health reviews—and giving folks a new app for their mobile device called *Doctor AI*. At first, he was skeptical. But the nurse was someone he'd known since childhood, and she talked straight.

"Wade, how many years have you smoked?"

"Too many," he said, laughing.

Doctor AI flagged him for lung cancer screening, based on his smoking history and regional risk. "It's just a low-dose CT scan. Painless," she said. "And if it finds nothing, we're done for the year."

He went.

The scan found a tiny spot in his upper right lung, too small to feel, too small to find on a chest X-ray, but large enough to worry about. A local pulmonologist, working through the rescue health system, reviewed the results and coordinated a follow-up. Instead of major surgery, Wade was a candidate for a minimally invasive endoscopic procedure, using a robot-assisted bronchoscope to remove the lesion through his airway. *Doctor AI* located two options for Wade: the University of Kentucky and the University of Cincinnati, where highly trained endoscopic interventionalists were doing this treatment. He had an initial interview with both sets of doctors and their teams on telehealth and chose Kentucky.

He was in and out of the hospital the same day.

But that wasn't the end of it. Based on the cancer's genetic profile and new national guidelines, Wade was offered something he'd never imagined: a personalized vaccine, developed to train his immune system to recognize and destroy any stray cancer cells or new ones, protecting him from lung cancer for life. It was part of a broader real-world study funded by the H4 Alliance Atlas, and Wade said yes.

"If it'll help me, and maybe someone else down the line, I'll do it."

That winter, Wade quit smoking. *Doctor AI* checked in daily. He got reminders, lung exercises, even encouragement from a small online group of folks like him, other Appalachians in recovery from lung cancer. Many did not have the advantages of Health 4.0. Wade often told the people at his group meetings how lucky he felt.

A year later, he sat on his porch, his breathing steady, telling his grandson the story.

"They caught it before it caught me," he said. "The system didn't just save my life, it showed up before I even knew I needed it."

He looked down at his grandson. *Giving up cigarettes turned out to be a small price to pay for years of watching you grow up*, he thought. Out loud, he said, "Run and grab that new book I got you about the adventures of *Doc AI* and his sidekick *Pulse*. We will read it together."

Rescue Health is where the system must prove itself. In moments of accident, acute illness, or sudden diagnosis, there is no room for delay, denial or inefficiency. The difference between life and death can be measured in minutes. For Wade Carter, that difference never happened, because he and his personal culture was seen, earlier enough to change his future.

Oral, Vision, and Hearing Care

Many people think coverage of teeth and eyes are an extravagance. Usually people who can afford to pay out of pocket for their dental or vision care. Vision loss, even when moderate, significantly increases the risk of falls, depression, and social isolation in older adults, and early intervention can prevent up to 90 percent of blindness caused by common conditions such as glaucoma, cataracts, and diabetic retinopathy.188 In younger people, loss of vision makes working almost impossible.

Hearing loss, which affects nearly 48.1 million in the US age twelve and over, is independently associated with cognitive decline, increased dementia risk, and contributing to social isolation. Hearing aids are only used by 20 percent of those affected, remaining inaccessible to many, in part due to high out-of-pocket costs.[189] The average out of pocket cost of $2,500 constitutes a significant burden for 77 percent of Americans with hearing loss.[190]

Oral health is deeply linked to systemic conditions like diabetes, cardiovascular disease, and adverse pregnancy outcomes, yet dental care is often siloed from mainstream medicine, despite evidence that untreated dental disease contributes to $45 billion in lost productivity in 2015 alone.[191]

To See, to Speak

Marisol taught second grade in a rural town tucked into the hills of the Resilience Region, in the state of Montana. She had always prided herself on knowing when a child needed help by the way their shoulders slumped, or their handwriting trembled. But over time, her world blurred. Reading the board became difficult, then the children's faces, their expressions harder to see. She didn't want to admit it, but she'd stopped driving at night and missed more day's teaching than she wanted to.

She thought she was aging. But *Doctor AI* flagged her for a vision check during her annual visit. A quick referral to the mobile eye clinic confirmed it: advanced cataracts, completely treatable. The Thanksgiving holiday was coming up and she had surgery through USA Health's *Rescue* health program the Friday after the big feast. The moment she stepped outside the morning after surgery, she wept.

"I forgot the way the sky looks in Montana early in the morning on a winter's day. So clear and bright."

She returned to her classroom the following Monday, with more confidence—and clarity—than she'd had in years. Her students noticed.

"You look different," one girl said. "Happy different."

We Want to Hear What You Have to Say

Two counties over, Jerome, now fifty-six, was used to covering his mouth when he talked. Missing teeth, chronic gum pain, and a history of infections made it hard to eat, let alone smile. In his town, dental care was miles away and years overdue. He had *gained a lot of weight* as his teeth got worse. All he could eat was soft stuff with high calories.

But under USA Health's proactive health coverage, Jerome's community had a dental van that came once a month. He got X-rays, cleanings, extractions, and—finally—affordable dentures. The inflammation that contributed to his diabetes stabilized, and for the first time in years, he could speak clearly at the town meeting without shame. Without covering his mouth. He smiled a lot more. He wanted the community to understand how important dental care was to their lives.

"Turns out," he said, "having a voice starts with having teeth."

The H4 Alliance Passport will provide comprehensive coverage for vision, dental, and hearing care as essential components of whole-person health care.

Mental and Behavioral Health Coverage

Not every wound bleeds. Sometimes it shows up as a father who can't get out of bed, the teenager cutting herself in secret, the colleague smiling on the outside while fighting panic inside. These are moments when health systems too often look away—or respond too late.

Mental health crisis rarely begin in the Emergency Room, yet that is often where they end.

Caught at the Breaking Point

Ben, thirty-three, works long shifts in a logistics warehouse outside Indianapolis. His wife left him last year, he hasn't seen his kids in months, and the silence in his apartment is louder than any forklift at work. One night, after drinking too much, he typed into *Doctor AI*: "I don't want to be here."

Doctor AI didn't hesitate. It ran a risk protocol and asked follow-up questions. A counselor from a local crisis network called Ben within twenty minutes, walked down to the local bar and then walked home with Ben. Ben agreed to a meeting with the counselor who had helped him home the night before for an in-person evaluation the next day after work. Ben got immediate support, and, over the next few months, he started medication, joined a men's trauma recovery group, and gradually reconnected with his brother. He began to go to Alcoholics Anonymous and quit drinking. Finally, he was able to see his kids again.

"I thought I was invisible," he said. "But someone saw me. Even if it started with a machine, *Doctor AI* was available at my darkest hour and in some ways was easier to talk to."

Recalibrated Through Tech

Jess, thirty-one, works in user design. From the outside, her life looks sharp and modern. But her mind won't slow down. She's anxious, wired. Cycling between brilliance and burnout. She'd never see a therapist in person—too much time away from work, too expensive, too complicated, too public.

Doctor AI offered another way. She started using her smartwatch to track her mood, sleep, and cycle. *Doctor AI* began recognizing patterns and suggested a specialist in attention-deficit/hyperactivity disorder (ADHD) and anxiety. Through USA Health, she accessed a telehealth psychiatrist and got medication plus weekly online therapy.

Today, Jess uses Doctor AI for daily check-ins. It doesn't judge. It simply notices.

"It helps me know myself," she says. "So I don't spiral into the version of me I don't want to be. I'm taking names at work; people want me on their team." She smiled, "It is a big change from last year."

Mental health is not just about treatment; it is about recognition. In the H4 Alliance, no one's pain is invisible, and no one is left to carry it alone.

Financial Health Education and Tools

Financial health is not typically taught formally in school, and many of our parents would not be ideal professors in this area. Nearly half of Americans cannot cover an unexpected expense of $1,000. That single fact explains more about health stress than any lab. The young couple working full-time jobs, but still unable to cover an unexpected $500 medical bill without going into debt. Their health is not just physical—it is financial.

Through Wallet Rx, *Doctor AI* provides the path to financial understanding and financial planning tools integrated into the H4 Alliance portal. It also helps families maximize community support.

Balancing the Books

Maria, age seventeen, wants to be the first in her family to go to college. She's always been good with numbers, but the money from her part-time job at the grocery store in Lubbock, Texas disappears to pay for her phone bill and transportation.

Through her USA Health app, *Doctor AI* notices her financial stress and offers a budgeting module. She learns about matched savings for health emergencies and opens her first account through a H4 Alliance-affiliated banking program.

Her brother Luis, thirty-one, works construction and has a four-year-old daughter. His credit card debt and unstable hours make saving feel impossible. But during his annual H4 Alliance telehealth planning visit, *Doctor AI* links him to a local financial counselor, who helps him refinance one card, set up an emergency fund, and start planning for a mortgage. He had always thought homeownership was out of reach—until he saw it modeled step by step. He would love a home with his wife and young daughter.

Gloria, their fifty-four-year-old mother, manages the household and takes care of their father, whose health is fragile. She uses *Doctor AI* to track medications and appointments, but now it offers her financial planning tools tied to caregiving: how to access respite services, reduce medication costs, and explore part-time work that won't disrupt her health benefits.

Even Grandpa Ernesto, seventy-two, joins in. He uses Doctor AI in Spanish, checks his H4 Alliance coverage, and participates in a local senior savings circle that helps with utility bills and grocery planning. They also play bingo.

Together, the Rodríguez family begins to talk about money without shame. They set goals. They track progress. They encourage each other and compare results. And for the first time, they start to imagine a future where financial stress doesn't define their choices.

"Doctor AI didn't just ask me how I felt," Luis says. "It asked me if I was okay paying the light bill."

Financial health means freedom. It is not an add-on to health—it is the foundation.

CHAPTER 14

The Trust
Funding the Future of Health

The American public needs a secure funding source for their healthcare. At the center of the H4 Alliance system is the H4 Alliance Trust—a permanent not-for-profit entity designed to model how health care can be sustainably funded. The trust and the H4 Alliance, a public benefit corporation, are linked with the sole purpose to fund and deliver the new American health care system and provide leadership in global healthcare. Over time private donations, capital and existing streams of public funding, unify into a single transparent state-of-the-art platform: reducing cost, simplifying complexity, and providing professional financial oversight and public accountability.

Governance and Oversight: Independence by Design

The H4 Alliance operates as an independent model advanced by H4 Alliance, Inc., designed to demonstrate best practices in governance, financial discipline, and transparency. Its purpose is to show how health care funding can be stewarded for the long term—without political interference or profiteering that distracts from delivery of health. Uncomplicated, straightforward access. Equity. Effectiveness—enacting all the values of Health 4.0.

The Board of Trustees is structured to reflect both expertise and public accountability. It includes a public finance expert, a health economist, two patient representatives, regional fund presidents, the Director of the H4 Alliance Regulatory Authority, and an independent Chair. Together with the CEO of the H4 Alliance and the H4 Alliance Governing Board, the independent Chair provides overarching leadership to ensure alignment, integrity, and accountability across the Trust and the H4 Alliance.

To preserve independence and continuity, trustees serve staggered, non-renewable nine-year terms. This design prevents concentration of power, ensures a steady infusion of fresh perspectives and reinforces the Trust's role as a permanent guardian of public benefit.

Their responsibilities are wide ranging: managing investments, capping annual withdrawals at five percent to preserve long-term reserves, enforcing safeguards against fraud and ensuring equity across regions. They publish independent audits, forecasts, and public reports, while maintaining direct accountability through the H4 Alliance Score Card and other public feedback mechanisms. Every resident is treated as an equal stakeholder, no tiers, no exclusions. Day-to-day operations are managed by a professional team modeled after institutions like the Federal reserve and Norway's sovereign wealth fund: independent disciplined and trusted to safeguard essential public resources. To reinforce this independence, all financial performance is subject to external audit and actuarial review, with results published openly through a public dashboard and transparency portal. Fraud is deterred through blockchain verification, which ensures every transaction is traceable and tamperproof while protecting patient privacy.

These safeguards demonstrate best practice today and provide a framework that, if codified at the national level, could anchor health financing with the same permanence, independence, and dependability that the Federal Reserve provides in monetary policy.

What the Fund Replaces

Today, health dollars are scattered across federal programs, private insurers, and employer plans, producing duplication, opaque pricing, and high administrative overhead. The H4 Alliance demonstrates how those flows could be unified into a single transparent system, with every dollar visible and accountable. Administrative overhead is capped at 2 percent—far below current American industry norms and consistent with global best practice. By replacing duplicative payers and processes, the Trust redirects billions back to patient care.

US Billing and Insurance Related (BIR) Administrative Costs

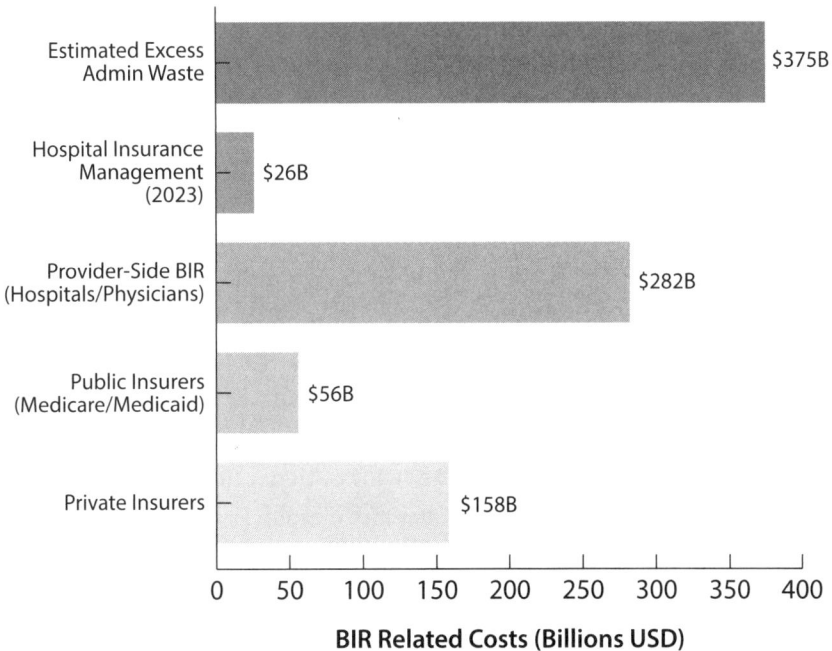

Sources:
1. Center for American Progress (2024:) $496B total BIR (https://www. americanprogress.org)
2. BMC Health Serv Res (2012): ~$375 in (https://bmchealthservices.biomedcentral.com)
3. Health Affairs: $12-$19 per-claim admin cost (https://www.healthaffairs.org)
4. AHA Premier Study (2023): $26B hospital insurance admin (https://www.aha.org)
5. CMS (2024): $4.9T total health spend (https://www.cms.gov)

Figure 19: *Billing and Insurance-Related Administrative Costs in US Health Care. Copyright Robin Blackstone, MD*

Administrative waste in the current system consumes hundreds of billions annually. The H4 Alliance demonstrates how overhead can be reduced and capped at 2% restoring resources to direct care.

The Economic Tipping Point for Employers, Individuals, and Families

Today, the average premiums for employer-sponsored health insurance are $8,951 for single coverage and $25,572 for family coverage. For both types of coverage, the worker pays a portion, e.g. for family coverage in 2024, the worker pays $6,296 and employer pays $19,276. Over the last five years, the average premium for family coverage increased by 24 percent, compared to a 28 percent increase in workers' wages and inflation of 23 percent.

Under the H4 Alliance, the cost to those enrolled is a flat $360 per person per year. For a family of three: $1,080 total. No copays. No deductibles. No surprise bills. No preauthorization. No employer cost.

The shift in health cost burden by moving to the H4 Alliance is significant. In 2020 housholds spent an average of $9,393 on health care—18.7 percent of income. For the household incomes in the lowest quintile, the cost was lower $3,093—33.9 percent of income. For the highest quintile, the cost was $22,161—16 percent of income. In every case, H4 Alliance reduces financial pressure, while ensuring equal access. Employers currently pay $14,139 per capita. Under the H4 Alliance, their contributions stabilize and taper to zero over time, with optional tax-incentivized contributions after year 15. To ensure stability, employers begin by matching their average per-employee costs, then gradually reduce contributions in a steady, linear fashion. By year sixteen, contributions become voluntary, supported by tax incentives that encourage companies to continue investing in the nation's health.

Total Annual Health Coverage Cost by Scenario (2023)

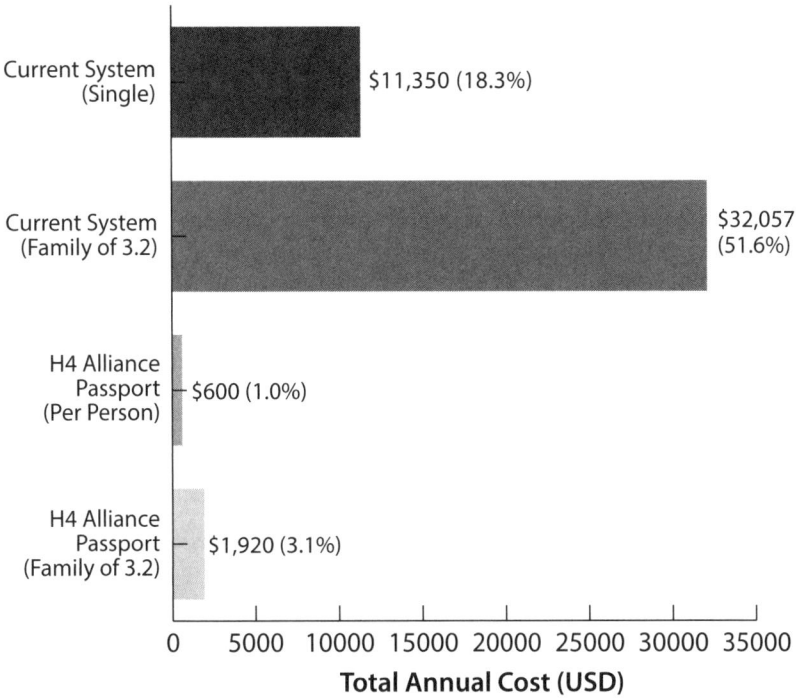

Sources:
1. KFF 2025 Employer Health Benefits Survey:
   https://www.kff.org/health-costs/reports/2023-employer-health-benefits-survey
2. AHRQ MEPS Statistical Brief #559: https://meps.ahrq.gov/data_files/publications/st559/stat559.shtml
3. BLM Weekly Earnings Data (2025): https://www.bls.gov/news.release/wkyeng.t01.htm

Figure 20: *Total annual health coverage by cost. Copyright Robin Blackstone, MD*

Tradeoffs

Tasha Delgado stands at her kitchen counter, tablet open, baby on her hip. Her toddler, Antonio, is seated at the table with picture books and crayons. Her husband, Carlos, is finishing up his shift at a local distribution center, hours he picked up when their landlord raised the rent last spring. They're expecting their third child in November.

Before the H4 Alliance, the Delgado's faced hard choices: Carlos's job offered a basic plan with high premiums and deductibles. Tasha, between jobs during her pregnancy, wasn't covered at all. Every pediatric visit, ultrasound, and prescription came with anxiety. They delayed care. Skipped well visits. At one point, Tasha considered delivering at a birthing center without insurance, just to avoid the cost of hospital care. She had high blood sugars during her last pregnancy and high blood pressure when she delivered her baby, so getting prenatal care isn't negotiable.

Now, they pay $1,080 a year—$360 per adult, $360 per child. That's it. No hidden bills. No waiting on insurance approvals. Their pediatrician is in-network by default—all physicians are part of the H4 Alliance. Maternity care is fully covered. A lactation consultant visited their home at no cost. H4 Alliance Passport offers childcare as part of their comprehensive health care benefits, meaning Tasha can get back to work or school after her last child is born and pursue her own dream of owning a company. She wasn't even thinking of having children before H4 Alliance, because she would have had to sacrifice her personal goals for the family, but now she has support for both. Carlos receives reminders and virtual check-ins for his asthma through the Doctor AI/H4 Alliance Passport app on her mobile phone. *Doctor AI* sends monthly health summaries to their shared dashboard.

But what matters most, Tasha says, is what they don't have to do anymore: "I don't have to choose between Antonio's school checkup or my prenatal care. I don't have to lie awake wondering what bill is coming next. And I know, if something goes wrong, I won't have to move heaven and earth to get help, or have the family's meager savings ravaged, or worse, go broke. This feels like we are finally making progress as a family. The same dream, the same vision of a good life that brought everyone else to these United States over the last 250 years. This is an economic 'liberation' for our family."

Voluntary Employer Contributions: Unlocking Collective Investment

In the H4 Alliance model, in the initial years of the program, employers contribute a predictable, capped share of payroll—replacing today's volatile premiums. By year 15 of the transition to the H4 Alliance, their contributions can go down to zero. But the design also allows them to do more. Extra contributions are fully tax-deductible, and while they do not buy preferential treatment or higher tiers of access, then earn public recognition, from Bronze through Platinum levels, for companies that choose to align themselves with health as a national value. Employers can also choose to direct funds toward areas with a direct impact on their workforce—such as rural care, mental health, or innovation—without having to administer those programs themselves. In this way, employers are not simply paying for coverage; they are participating in national health stewardship, their contributions recognized as acts of civic responsibility and public trust. The goal though, is to free up all employers from any mandatory health expenses, rather, to create an environment where they get the advantage of health of the workforce without the cost. A benefit that serves all workers and employers well.

Prescription Access and National Strategy

Prescription drugs tell another story, one of hidden costs that even the best insurance cannot shield people from. Jennifer Moran, for example, paid nearly a thousand dollars each year for Eliquis, a blood thinner her cardiologist prescribed after she developed atrial fibrillation, an arrhythmia that increases the odds of stroke. Her "comprehensive" plan cost $1,500 a month, carried a $1,600 deductible, and required $35 copayments for each refill once that deductible was met. Even with good insurance, she was left exposed when it mattered most.

The H4 Alliance redefines this landscape. Essential drugs on the national formulary are always free to H4 Passport holders—no copays or deductibles. For high-cost therapies, the H4 Alliance negotiates outcome-based contracts so that patients continue to pay nothing, while the system shares risk with manufacturers. Repurposed and open-source drugs are routed through the same guarantee: accelerated access at no extra cost to patients, with pricing and reimbursement handled transparently at the system level.

Total Annual Health Coverage Cost by Scenario (2023)

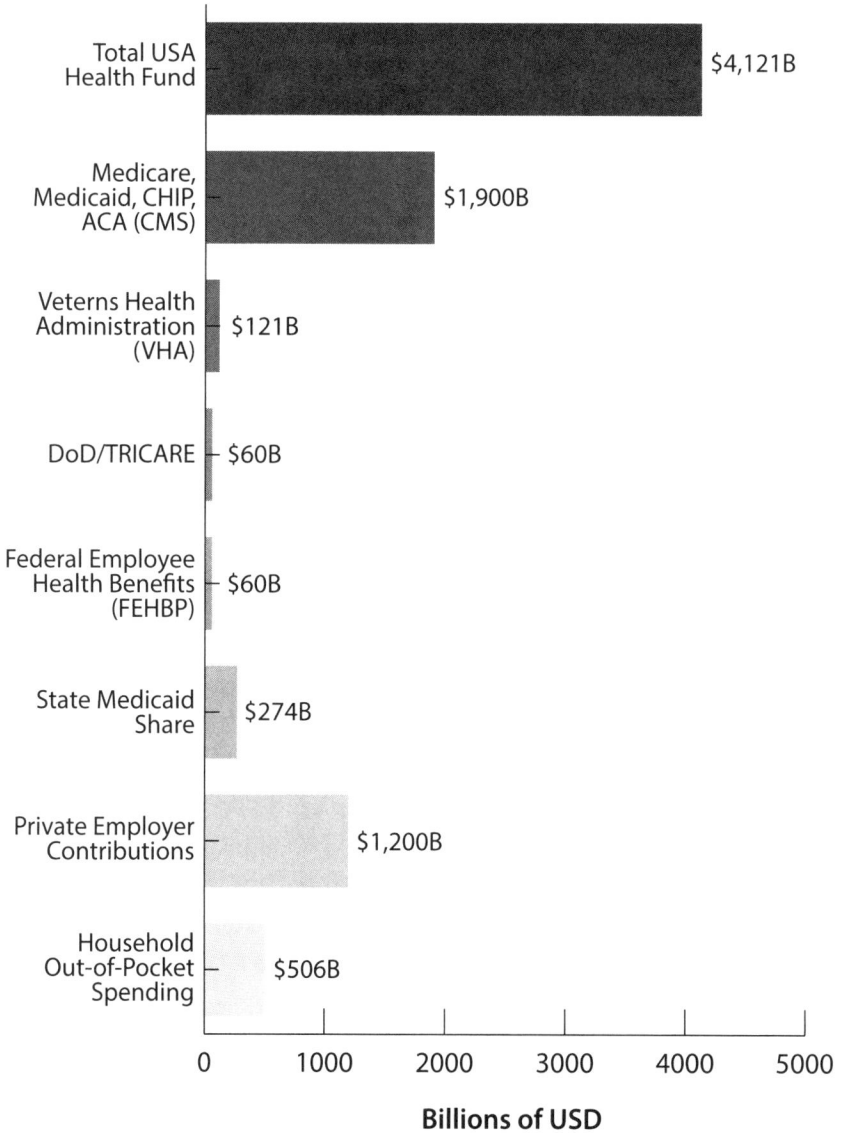

Figure 21: *Annual flow of funds into H4 Alliance. Copyright Robin Blackstone, MD*

Today, Pharmacy Benefit Managers profit in the shadows, extracting rebates and fees that patients never see. The H4 Alliance ends this hidden economy: one buyer, one price, every transaction verifiable on blockchain—transparent in cost, secure in privacy, and accountable not to middlemen but to the people.

H4 Alliance Trust is designed with multiple streams of capital, balancing stability with growth. A portion of revenues comes from innovation royalties, ensuring that publicly financed discoveries return value to the public itself. Long-term funding is reinforced by health bonds—low risk, publicly traded securities that give citizens and institutions a safe way to invest in health. The H4 Alliance Trust also welcomes philanthropy from individual gifts to major partnerships, with recognition for those who help advance equity and access. Together, these inputs make the H4 Alliance resilient, flexible, and able to grow over time without losing its accountability to the people it serves.

Why This Works

Most health reforms fail because they nibble around the edges: tweaking insurance, layering on taxes, or nationalizing delivery. The H4 Alliance breaks this pattern. It aligns national mission with personal benefit, replaces confusion with clarity, and treats health care not as a privilege, but as essential infrastructure.

Stepping Up to the Plate

He wasn't supposed to say yes.

A titan of American finance, he had weathered economic tempests with discipline and nerve. As chair of one of the world's most powerful banks, he had advised presidents, steadied markets, and outlasted crises that brought others down. His reputation was cast in steel: risk management, scale, precision. There was nothing left to prove.

So when the invitation came, to chair the Independent Board of the H4 Alliance, it surprised everyone that he didn't hesitate.

"This isn't charity," he told reporters when the appointment became public. "It's the most complex financial operation this country has ever attempted. And it's time we had adult supervision on both sides of the ledger."

He brought more than reputation. He brought a worldview: capitalism with a conscience, accountability with muscle. For years, he'd warned that runaway health costs were a systemic risk, suffocating small businesses, eroding economic mobility, distorting the labor market. Now he had a chance to put his expertise and wisdom to work on a new model. The H4 Alliance, in his eyes, wasn't ideology. It was long-overdue risk management on a national scale.

And he intended to run it that way.

Under his leadership, the Trust adopted financial guardrails that made even Wall Street blink: quarterly stress tests, statutory reserve ratios, strict drawdown caps, real-time performance metrics, and open-book audits. He assembled an elite audit team from the Office of the Comptroller of the Currency, checked their work with a big four accounting company, retained sovereign wealth advisors from Norway and Singapore, and mandated that all projections be reviewed by external actuaries. No shadows. No guesswork. Just rigorous financial discipline.

He didn't do press junkets. But he did show up once, unannounced, at a regional town hall in South Carolina. A retired nurse stood and asked the question everyone wanted answered: "Why do you trust this new system enough to stand behind it?"

He didn't offer a slogan. Instead he offered a cautionary tale. .

"Because I've seen what happens when you don't build the structure right," he said. "The H4 Alliance is built to last. It is built for trust. What we owe the American people is simple: discipline, transparency, and accountability—the very principles absent in today's health economy, and the only ones that will fund the future of health."

CHAPTER 15

The Transition

Changing the financial foundation of American health care will not happen overnight. It is a long-term structural shift—carefully staged to avoid economic disruption, service interruptions, or loss of public trust. The goal is simple but difficult: to consolidate the nation's fragmented payments into a single, equitable platform without triggering collapse or chaos.

Unlike reforms that depend on congressional votes or constitutional amendments, the H4 Alliance can move forward today as a private but public-purpose system. Structured as a public benefit corporation and supported by a nonprofit foundation, the Alliance can launch a phased-15-year transition plan to prove that comprehensive, affordable, culturally aligned care is possible now—with or without government.

A phased model allows for steady scaling: enrolling populations. reallocating funds, replacing legacy systems, and proving value at every step. It also gives governance time to mature, the workforce to adapt and medical education to realign. Each phase has hard limits on spending volatility and soft handoffs between old and new systems giving employers, providers, and communities confidence to plan.

The American public will have to ask and answer one question: is health care a constitutional right, or will we wait for another century for government to act? The H4 Alliance offers a third way: build it now, show it works, and let the country—and the world—choose to join.

The Technology Pillars of H4 Alliance

The transition depends on seven core technology functions. Each has a corresponding H4 Alliance component designed to meet that need:

Identity and Consent Management

H4 Alliance Passport—secure digital health identity, record portability, consent management.

Data Integration and Interoperability

H4 Alliance Data Lake—consolidated clinical, public health, and research data into a single interoperable system with privacy safeguards.

Artificial Intelligence Interface

Doctor AI—triage, navigation, preventive alerts, and decision support.

Analytics and Reporting

H4 Alliance Atlas and Insight Engine—outcomes tracking, resource allocation, provider decision support, performance dashboards.

Payment Infrastructure

H4 Alliance Fund—automated payments, standardized claims, fraud reduction using blockchain Governance and Security.

H4 Alliance—independent oversight, transparent audits, blockchain-based accountability. Leverages blockchain to ensure data integrity and transparent audit trails.

Research and Innovation

H4 Alliance Innovation Hub and Insight Engine—pilot, validate, and scale new solutions across regions.

Blockchain underpins every component. In disaster response it ensures continuity: hospitals get paid, vaccines are verified, and supply chains remain intact. Every transaction becomes a tamper-proof record—a lifeline of trust when systems are strained and resilient when they are threatened.

Year-by-Year Breakdown
Year 0—Foundation

- H4 Alliance launches the H4 Alliance Sovereign Health Trust (private Trust Fund with Strict Governance).
- Founders and anchor donors provide $300–$500 billion in seed capital. Goal of fund is to achieve $1 Trillion which will fund the transition and sustain the future.
- Health Bonds are issued to finance infrastructure and medical debt relief.
- Medical Amnesty: legacy medical bills are negotiated and forgiven for early enrollees.
- More than $200 billion in medical debt is erased, restoring household financial stability.
- Subscriptions begin: $30 per adult or child, per month.
- Employer contributions start via voluntary partnership agreements. Public accountability: the First Shareholder Statement issued to the American people.

Maria, a single mother in New Mexico, opened a letter that stated $12,000 in medical debt had been settled by the H4 Alliance team. It wasn't just her relief. Across the country, families were freed from collection calls, destroyed credit scores, and the fear that one hospital bill could erase their future dreams. Within months, Maria qualified for a small business loan. She expanded her catering service, hired a neighbor, and bought a delivery van. Her children, now enrolled through H4 Alliance, were healthier, in school more consistently, and finally able to imagine a different future. Her children were working through the Wallet Rx education program, Money, and asking what jobs they could take on to build their savings accounts. Medical debt forgiveness had been framed by politicians as a "handout," but it was, in fact, restitution. It was an economic reset—a trillion-dollar productivity stimulus, unleashing household credit, small business expansion, and workforce stability overnight.

Year 1–3 Capacity Build

- Expand coverage through employer partnerships and foundation-backed pilots.
- Fund community health care workers to bring care to underserved areas.
- Offer ACA and Medicaid populations early enrollment pathways alongside subsidies, with pilot states and employers helping participants transition voluntarily.
- Scale digital platforms (Doctor AI, Pulse) to millions of users.
- Build a capital base exceeding $600 billion, with $400 billion per year flowing through subscriptions, employer contributions, and reallocations.
- Issue annual public reports to track enrollment, finances, and outcomes.
- Launch national innovation prizes to accelerate solutions in equity, rural health, and digital care.

In South Carolina, foundation-backed community health workers launched mobile clinics that reached towns without steady access to care. In the form of a nurse, showing up in person in their community.

In Minnesota, a small health system piloted the H4 Alliance payment platform and saw claims processed in days instead of months. For families who had been uninsured, early enrollment pilots meant their first subscription cards in hand—and their first taste of a system built on access rather than exclusion.

In Chicago, a team of students (engineering, medicine, nurses) won an Innovation Bounty for designing a low-cost asthma monitor that connects to Doctor AI. In Oklahoma, a tribal health clinic earned a Regional Prize for blending traditional nutrition practices with digital coaching to lower diabetes rates. In Boston, a team of system scientists, people who worked in supply chains around the country, and health planners form the national Academy of Science, teamed up to design a secure private H4 Alliance blockchain. For the public, it felt less like a policy launch and more like the moon landing: proof that health innovation could be something everyone had a hand in building and using at scale.

Year 4–6 Core Transfer

- Absorb Medicaid functions fully into the H4 Alliance plan in pilot states.
- Accelerate employer transitions, particularly among small businesses.
- Begin onboarding voluntary Medicare populations, offering seniors new coverage options.
- Transition Alliance Fund operations to handle provider payments directly in pilot regions, reducing reliance on state systems.
- Guarantee preventive services for all enrollees.
- Deploy H4 Alliance teams, supported by philanthropy, to address structural and social health determinants identified at the regional level.
- Partner with engineering programs, medical schools, and universities to apply innovation to longstanding structural challenges.
- Establish national integration teams as competitive, career-launching roles that augment clinical and systems training.
- Implement Doctor AI as the interoperable record across participating systems.
- Reach 50 percent enrollment of the U.S. population by Year 6, reducing out-of-pocket burden by 70 percent.
- Reposition private insurers as supplemental service providers rather than duplicative payers.

- Enable Regional Councils to propose large-scale innovation and infrastructure projects through open, competitive application and review, weighted by impact and equity.

In Ohio, a community hospital administrator looked at her monthly budget report and saw something she'd never seen before: fewer unpaid bills, faster reimbursements, and extra capital to hire more nurses. "We can finally plan long term," she whispered to herself. Then she looked down the long hallway of patient rooms and smiled.

In Arizona, another community hospital reported its first real savings: fewer billing staff needed, more nurses hired with upskilling and reskilling already underway. For the first time, administrators could focus resources on care rather than paperwork.

In Mississippi, a farmer who had gone years without insurance was rediscovering sight and sound. "Finally got eyeglasses and hearing aids," he said. "I forgot how soft the sounds are from the cattle in the evening. How do I look in my new glasses?"

Year 7–10 National Adoption

- Centralize drug purchasing to lower US prices to global norms.
- Fully integrate Doctor AI as the national triage, navigation, and clinical decision support platform.
- Gradually onboard and fully integrate (voluntarily) Medicare populations by Year 10.
- Largely replace employer insurance with Alliance subscriptions.
- Route most payments through blockchain rails, reducing fraud to international standards.
- Regional Councils propose large-scale infrastructure projects.
- Implement a transparent, evidence-based formulary process to ensure access to specialty and rare-disease treatments by Year 10.
- Launch national outcomes dashboard showing key indicator impact on three domains of health, real-time savings, effect on administrative expenses, fraud reduction, and quality benchmarks across all regions.

A mid-sized manufacturing company in Ohio celebrated the end of managing health benefits. "We used to spend millions negotiating insurance, which changed every year. Different benefits, deductibles, always more expensive," the CFO said. "Now, every worker is covered and their subscription membership in the H4 Alliance is portable. We are putting our money into wages, training and the cultural of our company, to ensure the people working here feel valued and supported. For everything else there's the Alliance."

Year 11–15 Sustainability and Expansion

- Achieve comprehensive coverage for all enrollees, fully eliminating cost-sharing.
- Eliminate fraud and waste, stabilizing costs at sustainable levels.
- Distribute optional dividends when the fund exceeds sustainability thresholds.
- Improve health outcomes—including infant mortality, chronic disease, and mental health—measurably across cultural regions.

By Year 15, the H4 Alliance demonstrates a fully functional national system—built privately, trusted publicly, and open to global partners.

In West Virgina, a grandmother opened her Doctor AI dashboard and saw what the statistics meant for her family: diabetes rates in her county had fallen, and infant survival was rising. "It's not just numbers," she said, holding her newborn grandson. "It's him."

Navigating Regulatory Roadblocks Without Federal Law

Building the H4 Alliance as a private roadmap means working inside the maze of existing US health regulations. Unlike a government program, we cannot simply "flip a switch" with federal preemption. Instead, the Alliance must weave its way through state and federal rules with a phased, strategic approach. We have to remember that many of these regulations were passed to protect special interests. Success will require that the special interest groups, whether academia, providers or health care companies (insurers or hospitals/clinics) are brought into the partnership so they can clearly contribute their knowledge and expertise to the change in paradigm we are seeking.

The Challenge

Health care in the United States is one of the most heavily regulated domains in the economy. State insurance commissioners guard health plans. States license physicians and define scop of practice. Federal agencies oversee Medicare, Medicaid, HIPAA, and the FDA. Employers are bound by ERISA. Each rule was designed to solve a problem, or protect a specific interest, or enact law with a specific financial or religious bias. However, the sum of the regulations, even when well meaning, act to hold the public hostage and keep them from health. The regulations form a web that resists national solutions.

The Strategy

The H4 Alliance avoids waiting for one sweeping federal law by using five levers of change:

Start Outside Traditional insurance

The H4 Alliance offers a subscription-based health membership. Not an insurance company

Build through ERISA Employers

Large, self-insured employers, already exempt from state regulation under ERISA, become core partners.

Create national scale without requiring 50 separate licenses.

Work with Willing States

See out states willing and ready to innovate, using federal waiver authority already available. Plus Medicaid or ACA subsidies directly into the H4 Alliance Platform and expand coverage.

Build out regional infrastructure requirements by leveraging philanthropy and partnerships with experienced industry partners.

Provider Integration through Compacts

Doctors and nurses remain state-licensed, but the Alliance aligns and leverages existing licensure compact to expand cross-border practice.

Create De Facto Standards First

Win adoption among employers, providers and early-adopter states. By building a digital first backbone of health. Once in wide use regulators are more likely to align rules around the system people are already using.

The Road Ahead

This approach does not require a single act of Congress. It requires persistence, partnerships, and proof. By building trust with employers, patients, and pioneering states, the H4 Alliance demonstrates that comprehensive health can work—even before the nation decides to enshrine it in law. Over time, as adoption spreads, the Alliance becomes the default national platform, one that states, and federal agencies connect to because the people already do.

Stakeholder Journey
What Changes and When

Patients
No more premiums, deductibles, or denials. Universal enrollment begins automatically during transition phases through the H4 Alliance platform.

YEARS 1–10

Employers
Contributions shift gradually from private plans into H4 Alliance subscriptions. Transition is phased through opt-in contracts and incentives.

YEARS 1–10

Providers
Unified billing replaces multi-payer complexity for participating providers. Quality standards tied to AI-supported audits and patient outcomes build trust and reduce waste.

YEARS 2–7

States
State agencies may partner with the H4 Alliance to reduce duplicative Medicaid administration. Savings can be reallocated to health innovation or other public goods.

YEARS 2–6

Insurers
Private insurers adapt by offering supplemental policies or contracting with the H4 Alliance (e.g., claims administration, specialty networks, wellness products).

YEARS 4–10

Figure 22: *Stakeholder journey: What changes and when. Copyright Robin Blackstone, MD*

PART 5

The Crucible of Change

CHAPTER 16

Alchemy

We are not just redesigning health care. We are attempting alchemy. Not the kind that turns lead into gold—but the kind that transforms chaos into trust.

Historically, alchemy fused science, art, and spirit. It sought not only change, but elevation—guiding what was broken toward something refined and worthy. That is what we are doing here. By design.

We've tried nearly everything else: a billing tweak, a new reimbursement model, another portal, another pilot, an incentive, a penalty, a slogan. All of it layered on a structure already at the brink—overbuilt, contradictory, unstable with old technology. Built for a different time. These old things persist. I once observed it was interesting that towns along the Oregon coast seemed to always be about twenty miles apart. The answer—as far as a man could ride his horse in a single day. Made sense when we traveled by horse back. In the same way, we are all wondering whose life our present system was built for. Yes I want to be rescued but I would much, much rather be healthy. Right up until the end. Dancing, laughing, in good shape.

The old system just doesn't seem to be sufficient any longer to attain that goal.

Now we are left with the age-old question. Do we continue iterative attempts to fix our health care system, or do we build anew—enabled by the tools of this century?

A New Landscape, Not a Single System

The vision laid out in these pages is not one uniform system. It is a landscape. Picture a deep, blue lake dotted with islands, each one distinct. Every island carries its own rhthm, its own view of health, family, time and trust. The six regions. American health care does not need to demand that they become the same. It should honor their differences, asking only that they coordinate when it matters most. When one island floods, the others help stabilize. When crisis strikes, the whole lake and all the people rise together. This is a model built on difference—and strengthened by it.

Pulse, Rhythm, and *Doctor AI*

At the center of this landscape is *Pulse*, your personal rhythm of your life. Your health identity. Your values, preferences, history, and future. *Pulse* evolves as you evolve, through age, transitions, relationships, loss, work, parenting and uncertainty. It travels with you as you move, change jobs, or enter new phases of life. It's not a chart. It's a lifeline.

And moving through it all is *Rhythm*—the way your data interacts with the world around you. It's your wearable alerts. Connection to the resources you need. Real time help navigating—everything.

Holding it all together, quietly and powerfully, is *Doctor AI. Doctor AI* is your personal digital agent. It's the connective tissue of your personal health system. It links your goals to your data. Your history to your options. It reads your patterns, checks your risks, and delivers insights—at your invitation. It is available on demand. *Doctor AI* acts at your invitation when you request it, and at every major decision point, a human is on the loop, in the loop, or at the helm. Just a tap away.

Doctor AI explains itself. What data it used. What logic it followed, and where its recommendation came from. What limitations it carries.

Bias is inevitable. So bias detection is not aspirational—it is hard-coded. Every region has oversight. If patterns emerge that disadvantage any group, they're flagged and corrected. Not hidden. Not rationalized.

Your health data doesn't live in a silo, on a forgotten server, or buried in a portal with a lost password. It lives with you—on your device. Encrypted, controlled by you. Immutable through blockchain, not because it's trendy, but because it is traceable and protected. Every access is logged. Every consent is recorded. You decide what to share, when to revoke access, and how your data is used in research.

Quantum computing is already reshaping the frontier. Soon, *Doctor AI* will model risk at scales never seen before. Detect trends we didn't know to look for. Simulate outcomes before harm occurs. But with that power must come discipline. The ability to do something will never be the same as the right to do it, or whether it is right to do. Speed must be governed by structure. Capacity restrained by ethics.

This is not just a health care system. It's a social contract. And like any true contract, it must have a moral spine.

The USA Health Credo

We believe our first responsibility is to the people we serve.

Everything we do must be of high quality, accessible, and fair.

We believe in regional strength, cultural alignment, and public trust.

We believe in the dignity of those who deliver care—nurses, aides, clinicians, coders, caregivers, scientists.

We believe in safe workplaces, just pay, and ethical leadership.

We believe no law should limit your right to determine your health span.

And we believe that profit must follow value—not lead it.

We believe that decisions must not be unduly influenced by power.

To operationalize these beliefs, we follow the Nolan Principles of Public Service: Selflessness. Integrity. Objectivity. Accountability. Openness. Honesty. Leadership.

The Turning Point

For me, the moment didn't come with a grand revelation. It came slowly when I transitioned to industry and had a chance to look back at the whole of my experience in health care. The patients lost, the colleagues burning out, the rising costs, the waste, and the silence around it all. I realized that no one was coming to save the system.

I'd spent decades inside it—as a surgeon, a witness, a builder of workarounds. I saw what we called care, and what it cost. And I knew I could not stand by. So, I stepped forward—not as a physician now, but as a first responder for our health care system.

First I spent time studying—governance, sustainability, digital technologies, and AI ethics. I started photographing exceptional cultures and found them everywhere I went. I spoke with hundreds of Americans about their health care.

I can open the door to change, name the problem, and offer a framework. But I cannot build it alone, and it was never my intent. This is not my system. It's ours.

Who will build this new future for health in America? Engineers. Teachers. Parents. Veterans. Local health workers. Coders. Union members. Rural doctors. Nurse practitioners. Physician assistants. Clerks. Tribal leaders. Retirees. All of us.

The Call That Cannot Be Ignored

There are few issues as urgent—or as unifying—as the health of our children and the survival of those who give them life.

In 2023, the US fertility rate was 1.62 births per woman, far below the 2.1 needed to sustain a population.[192] In 2022, we lost over 20,500 infants before their first birthday.[193] Hundreds of mothers, disproportionately black women, died during childbirth or shortly after.[194]

The map of loss is uneven, but the grief is universal. In Mississippi, the infant mortality rate was 9.3 per one thousand live births.[195] In Massachusetts, it was 3.3.[196] In many rural areas, maternity care has disappeared altogether. While we debate paperwork and payment models, families bury their young.

We are not just losing lives; we are losing the next generation—and with it, our future. The case for changing the healthcare system is not to win a debate or pass a bill. The point is to confront uncertainty head-on: to pull disease upstream before it destroys. In every sphere the work is similar—move peril upstream, rebuild trust, and turn risk into resilience. That is the alchemy we owe our future, and each other.

Health 4.0 demands a new commitment—a profound call to service. It requires a new oath for a new era, binding both humans and our digital partners to one truth: that trust and health are inseparable.

The Hippocratic Oath 2025

I do solemnly swear to the best of my ability and judgment,

To honor the dignity and autonomy of every person, recognizing that each life is shaped by story, culture, and choice.

To offer guidance, not command; options, not orders.

To treat all people with fairness and respect, to remain open to truths I have yet to understand.

To observe my own bias, and to challenge it.

To question the systems I work within, and the assumptions I carry.

To serve alongside both human and digital colleagues, trusting in science, tradition, and innovation as shared tools.

To learn by remaining a student, and to teach with the heart of one who will always be learning.

To listen deeply—for symptoms and for what is unsaid in the silence.

To value the wellbeing of those I serve above personal gain.

I take this oath as a guardian—of trust, of health care, and of our shared humanity.

Closing

Health 4.0 is real. The tools exist. The models exist. The people are ready. If we choose, we can build trust into the very foundation of health care.

The question is not whether it can be done. It is whether we will do it—together.

Chapter 17

The Final Chapter

One day, like many days when I was a surgeon, I was in the operating room when a call came in about a new consult. There was a woman in her early seventies named MaryAnn whose admitting internal medicine doctor was asking me for a consult. MaryAnn had a history of gastric bypass, a procedure I knew quite a bit about, and her bowel was obstructed.

"I'll see her as soon as we are done here," I said into the phone, held to my ear by our circulating nurse. After the surgery was completed, my nurse practitioner, Melissa, and I went upstairs to see MaryAnn.

As I stepped into the patient's room, I observed two very sharp and focused dark brown eyes in a halo of beautiful white, grey hair. I introduced Melissa and myself, and MaryAnn got right to the point.

"What's wrong with me?"

"You are obstructed," I explained. "Let me show you the anatomy." I went to the white board and began drawing.

"You have a standard gastric bypass, and judging from your medications, vital signs, and labs, it was very successful. But you also have a very unusual situation," I said, circling a section of my drawing of the gastrointestinal system. "You are obstructed in the disconnected part of your stomach. Something is blocking the duodenum, the part of the small intestine that drains the stomach. Food doesn't go there; it goes through your small gastric pouch and directly into another part of the intestine, bypassing a major part of the stomach. That 'stomach remnant' makes fluid that usually drains through the small intestine. That is where you are blocked. I looked at the CT scan, we need a biopsy of whatever is blocking this. It may not be a good thing. It may, in fact, be cancer."

She looked steadily at me. "Am I going to die from it?" she asked.

"Perhaps," I said. "Actually, it's likely."

"I need you to be absolutely straight with me. My husband and I are the guardians of my twelve-year-old granddaughter, Cassie. Her mother died of a drug overdose. My husband and I have been working for years to adopt her as our legal heir and have full custody until she reaches twenty-one in order to protect her from the man who may or may not be her father who's also a drug addict. We have our hearing with the judge in a week. No matter what, I have to be there."

"Let me go and talk with our gastroenterologist. He's a pretty special human being, as long as you don't have to talk to him for a long time, and a great technician. I have an idea. However, I have to talk to him about it first," I offered.

"Are you going to operate on me?" she asked.

"I hope not. I will try to figure this out without surgery, or you won't make your court date."

I went downstairs to talk to a talented gastroenterologist who specialized in interventions of a unique nature. I pulled up the CT and said, "My guess is pancreatic cancer or perhaps duodenal cancer. Either way, bad news," I said. "I have to call in hepatobiliary surgery, as that is their purview, but I don't think this is resectable, not that they won't try." He and I both smiled, a shared joke between doctors who were also "interventional."

"You remember when you did that procedure with the dumbbell shaped stent? I think I remember you placed it between two pieces of intestine and solved an obstruction?" I asked.

"Yeah, it was kind of brilliant, wasn't it? What are you thinking?"

"What if you bridged between the gastric remnant and the gastric pouch of the bypass? Left it in place? Wouldn't that decompress the remnant into the part of the intestine hooked up there?"

"Ohhhhh," he said. "Decompressing her through the bypass."

"Yeah, and maybe since you have access to the distal remnant, you can suck all that gastric juice out and get a biopsy. Just saying." He understood that doing this was a way to get a diagnosis without surgery so that MaryAnn could get to court for her custody case. We didn't need prior authorization because she had been admitted emergently. What we needed was a solution aligned with her immediate goals, within the context of her complex situation.

"If she consents, I will try to do it. Make sure and tell her it's a one-off. Make sure she talks to the hepatobiliary team. They can be testy if not consulted. I haven't done this particular thing before, although, as you know, I place stents all day long and am really good at it. I'll talk to her as well, but you know that's not what I am good at, the human part." he said.

"There is no try, there is only do." We both laughed, the kind of laugh you share when you know you are about to try something novel because the problem you are faced with demands it.

"I know, I know," he said.

Then I turned, and as I was leaving said, "Today please, or tomorrow early morning latest. There is urgency. So today. Please."

"Wow two pleases in one case; you must be serious."

"I am. By the way, thank you." He waved his hand, already focused on the task he had at hand. After I left, I called the hepatobiliary guys, and they reviewed the case and went to MaryAnn's room to talk to her about it. They offered her exploratory surgery with a Whipple procedure if they could do it. That's a complex operation for removing cancer from the pancreas, keeping it from spreading to other organs. The team was brilliant and courageous, exceptional in the art of surgery—qualities absolutely necessary in that specialty.

When I passed the chief of hepatobiliary surgery in the hall, he said, "She wants to talk to you."

"I'm on my way, just talked to GI."

"And?" he said.

"If the patient wants to take the risk, we will place a dumbbell-shaped stent across from the pouch to the remnant and then decompress the distal remnant of the stomach and get a biopsy. Leave the stent in place. If all goes well, she will decompress her through the stent into the bypass."

The chief surgeon said, "Innovative approach. I think it will do the job."

"Yes, I think so, if we can do it. A thousand things could go wrong, but we both know she is probably unresectable from traditional surgery. She has a particular goal."

"Oh, that's interesting that she didn't tell me about it." he said.

When I got to MaryAnn's room, she was sitting up and clearly upset.

"Their plan doesn't meet my goals. I feel trapped."

I went back to my white board.

"Here is an alternative." I drew out what I had asked the interventional GI guy to do, explaining it carefully, including the fact that it had likely never been done before. "Look, you have a unique situation, both culturally because of the adoption situation, but also because of this new problem. Frankly, I think you have cancer of the duodenum or pancreas, and it has blocked off the drainage of the distal gastric remnant. We can probably get a biopsy after we decompress the stomach remnant. That should give you all the information you need to make a good decision."

"I feel like I am pregnant," she said. "What should I do?"

"What is your question right now?" I replied.

"Am I going to die from this?"

I understood that MaryAnn was a straight shooter. She wanted facts so she could evaluate her decision carefully, weighing it against her immediate cultural needs.

"Yes," I said quietly. "Just like every other person on the planet, eventually, but for you it is likely to come sooner. With a stent decompression, you can eat and drink normally and it should work for a while."

"The other surgery, what do you think?" A tough question, but fair, as she had so much at stake.

"In order to determine if the cancer is resectable, the hepatobiliary team has to do a lot of damage. You may not ever leave the hospital; they may have to stop operating because of the extent of the cancer or something might happen that would put you in the ICU. There is a small chance, in my view, that they will be successful and you will have an uneventful recovery. However, doing this doesn't shut down the possibility of coming back for the attempt at the Whipple in a few weeks."

MaryAnn sat in silence for a while. "Stent and biopsy," she decided.

"We will do it today and, if it works, you should plan to go home in the next few days. Plenty of time to make it to court. Do you have anyone to come and get you?"

"If I can go home on Saturday, school is out, and my husband and granddaughter can come and get me."

"Ok. It's a plan."

The procedure went well. That GI guy is a magician, as he will tell you. Turns out, she did have pancreatic cancer blocking her duodenum. Before she left that Saturday, I came in to meet her family.

"What does it take to be a surgeon?" her granddaughter, Cassie, asked.

"You have to love people and want to help them," I explained. "You get up early and spend a lot of your time worrying about them. Even when you do your best, things don't always work out, and that is hard to live with sometimes. I guess it takes a whole lot of humanity."

"Is it worth it?"

"Absolutely," I assured her. "By the way, you have a very special grandmother."

Cassie looked up at me with big eyes and said, "My grandmother said she will be leaving us soon." So, MaryAnn had been straight up with her husband and granddaughter.

"How are you?" I asked.

"It will be a big loss for us, but we will be family. I will do good in school and be what I can. Maybe a surgeon."

"Anytime you wonder if you are good enough, I want you to close your eyes and hear my voice saying just two little words, *you are*. Cassie, you are absolutely good enough. Perhaps there will be even better things to be in the future than a surgeon. Take care." I shook her hand.

Three months later, I got a call from the head nurse, "There's a MaryAnn up here, she says she is your patient. She is refusing to go to the ICU or have any procedures. She just wants to talk with you. Hurry, Dr. Blackstone. She won't be here very long."

I was in the middle of a long case and didn't get out until around 8 p.m. I hurried up to the ward. MaryAnn's room was dark. She was barely there.

"Where are your husband and granddaughter?"

"I didn't want them here. I don't want this cancer to darken their door. Cassie is safe."

I sat down and held her hand.

"I am here."

We didn't speak again.

The Final Frontier of Uncertainty

The most profound experience in human life is death. It is the final frontier of uncertainty—the moment when everything we know dissolves into what we cannot know. What remains is the imprint of a life lived: the culture that shaped us, the choices we made, the echoes we leave in the minds and hearts of others. That invisible thread of connection.

Whether your journey never found you outside the borders of your hometown or it stretched across continents, you left that thread of connection behind. You mattered. And now, for the first time in history, that journey does not end with memory alone. It continues—with technology. With data. With a digital legacy. With a partnership between humanity and intelligence of our own design. Your children will know you by what they inherit from you in their own *Pulse*. That biological imprint will define all the generations for centuries to come. But the responsibility for its use, at least for now, remains ours.

Progress will not look like the past. It will challenge what we believe about identity, and what it means to be human. It will be fraught with uncertainty. And yet, it is ours to shape. The most powerful force we must create or recreate, is not a surgical robot, a quantum algorithm, or a cure for cancer. It is *trust*. Trust in one another regardless of origin. Trust in our systems that we build together. Trust in a shared future that belongs to everyone.

Health 4.0 is more than a reform—it is the beginning of this new era. A new infrastructure for life, and for what lies beyond it. Because to heal is to prepare for what comes next. And what comes next is vast: longevity, regeneration, space travel, and the birth of a new civilization, seeded by both memory and machine.

In the end, health care's biggest problem is humanity's biggest problem. But it is also our greatest opportunity.

Let this be our legacy: to build a system that deserves trust. To leave behind not just data, but the essence, the invisible thread of connection which says, I was here. To meet the future, not with fear, but with grit, ingenuity, and resolve. We are Americans. We are human.

We build this together.

Thank you for being part of the journey.
Robin Blackstone, New York City, 26 July 2025

Acknowledgments

Writing *Doctor AI: Reimagining Healthcare. Rebuilding Trust. Delivering Health 4.0* has been a journey made possible by the support, insights, and encouragement of many people. I am deeply grateful to the beta readers who gave their time to read early drafts, challenge my assumptions, and offer thoughtful feedback that made this book stronger. Thank you for sharing your insights: Eric Ahnfeldt, MD; Scott Bass, JD; Marni Blivice; Michael Bonventre; James Byerley, JD; Bonnie Cornell; Melissa Davis, DNP; Holly Hedegaard, MD, MSPH; Amy Holloway, PA; Divya Kewalramani, MD; Harris Kwaja, MD; Wendy Lyons, RN; Ruth Marten; Jordan McFarland; Victor Mirontschuk, FAIAI; Shreyas Mukund, PhD; Tom Obrien; Melanie Pflaum; Nico Pronk, PhD; Karl Ronn; Susan Schlenker; Carrie Withey, JD; and Mary Woolley, CEO.

I would like to acknowledge the creative team that brought this book to life. This process has been both gritty and rewarding, and I am grateful for each of your talents: Jen Singer, developmental editor; Debbie Abrams Kaplan, copy editor; Anastasia Vasilakis, cover and interior art designer; and the publishing team at Jenkins including Leah Nicholson, Yvonne Roehler, Jerrold Jenkins, and Olivia Haase.

To my friends and family—your unwavering belief in me provided the courage and determination to see this project through. Your patience, encouragement, and faith in my vision made all the difference. As this work moves from page to reality, I will continue to rely on your support to bring this idea to life, not only for the American people but for all nations seeking to shape their own cultural expression of future health.

What remains to be seen is whether America will rise to this moment—whether we will summon the grit, resolve, imagination, and expertise to build a future worthy of our republic. Whether the 28th Amendment to the Constitution will enshrine health as a fundamental right, and whether we will finally make health, not just health care, a pillar of our national strength. The H4 Alliance will begin this work, and if Congress finds the will to enable a universal system, so much the better. If not, we will already have moved forward to Health 4.0.

The test before us is not only political or economic, but moral: Can we design a system where every person is valued, every life has dignity, and our shared commitment to health becomes the foundation of the next great chapter of the American story? For if we succeed—if we dare to reimagine, architect Health 4.0, adopt Doctor AI, and believe in our own future—this generation will not only have healed a broken system but laid the cornerstone for a healthy, free, and just future for all humanity.

Robin Blackstone, MD

Notes

1. Himmelstein David U. Robert M. Lawless, Deborah Thorne, Pamela Foohey, and Steffie Woolhandler, "Medical Bankruptcy: Still Common Despite the Affordable Care Act." *Am J Public Health*, 2019 Mar;109(3):431-433. https://pmc.ncbi.nlm.nih.gov/articles/PMC6366487/.

2. Munira Z. Gunja, Evan D. Gumas, and Reginald D. Williams II, "U.S. Health Care from a Global Perspective, 2022: Accelerating Spending, Worsening Outcomes," Issue Brief. The Commonwealth Fund, January 31, 2023. https://doi.org/10.26099/8ejy-yc74.

3. "Augmented Intelligence in Medical Education: 2019 CME Report." American Medical Association, August 2019. https://www.ama-assn.org/system/files/2019-08/ai-2019-cme-report.pdf.

4. T. Christian Miller, Patrick Rucker, and David Armstrong, "'Not Medically Necessary': Inside the Company Helping America's Biggest Health Insurers Deny Coverage for Care" ProPublica, October 23, 2024. https://www.propublica.org/article/evicore-health-insurance-denials-cigna-unitedhealthcare-aetna-prior-authorizations.

5. "Luigi Mangione Official Legal Fund for all 3 Cases." GiveSendGo, accessed July 15, 2025, https://www.givesendgo.com/legalfund-ceo-shooting-suspect.

6. Paul S, Shradha Salunkhe, Kasireddy Sravanthi, Shailaja V. Mane, "Pioneering Hand Hygiene: Ignaz Semmelweis and the Fight Against Puerperal Fever." Cureus. 2024 Oct 17;16(10): e71689. https://pmc.ncbi.nlm.nih.gov/articles/PMC11568873/.

7. "Medicare and Medicaid Act (1965)." National Archives. Accessed July 22, 2025. https://www.archives.gov/milestone-documents/medicare-and-medicaid-act.

8. Moses, H. et al., "The Anatomy of Health Care in the United States." JAMA, November 13, 2013, 10;(18):1947-1964. https://jamanetwork.com/journals/jama/article-abstract/1769890.

9. Stuart Guterman, "Wielding the Carrot and the Stick: How to Move the U.S. Health Care System Away from Fee-for-Service Payment." The Commonwealth Fund, August 27, 2013. http://bit.ly/451gBdg.

10. Thomas Bodenheimer and Kevin Grumbach, *Understanding Health Policy: A Clinical Approach, Seventh Edition, 7th Edition.* (McGraw Hill, 2016).

11. "Implementation of the Health Maintenance Organization Act of 1973, as Amended." U.S. Government Accountability Office, March 3, 1978. https://www.gao.gov/products/105122.

12. Blumenthal, David, "Stimulating the Adoption of Health Information Technology." NEJM, April 9, 2009, 360:1477-1479. https://www.nejm.org/doi/abs/10.1056/NEJMp0901592.

13. Shanafelt, T. et al, "Relationship Between Clerical Burden and Characteristics of the Electronic Environment With Physician Burnout and Professional Satisfaction." Mayo Clinical Proceedings, July 2016, Vol. 91, Issue 7, p836-848. https://www.mayoclinicproceedings.org/article/S0025-6196(16)30215-4/abstract.

14. "Peer-to-peer Health Care." Pew Research Center, February 28, 2011. https://www.pewresearch.org/internet/2011/02/28/peer-to-peer-health-care-2/.

15. Van Zee, A. "The Promotion and Marketing of OxyContin: Commercial Triumph, Public Health Tragedy." *Am J Public Health*, Feb. 2009, 99(2):221–227. https://pmc.ncbi.nlm.nih.gov/articles/PMC2622774/.

16. Allana Akhtar, "An FDA official who led the approval of OxyContin got a $400,000 gig at Purdue Pharma a year later, a new book reveals." *Business Insider*, May 2, 2021. https://www.businessinsider.com/fda-chief-approved-oxycontin-six-figure-gig-at-purdue-pharma-2021-5.

17. Scher, C. et al., "Moving Beyond Pain as the Fifth Vital Sign and Patient Satisfaction Scores to Improve Pain Care in the 21st Century." Pain Manag Nursing, Dec. 15, 2017. 19(2):125–129. https://pmc.ncbi.nlm.nih.gov/articles/PMC5878703/#R1.

18. Kerns, RD. et al., "Implementation of the veterans health administration national pain management strategy." Transl Behav Med., Dec. 2011, 1(4):635-43. https://pubmed.ncbi.nlm.nih.gov/24073088/.

19. Berry, PH et al., "The new JCAHO pain standards: implications for pain management nurses." March 2000, 1(1):3-12, https://pubmed.ncbi.nlm.nih.gov/11706454/.

20. Van Zee, A. "The Promotion and Marketing of OxyContin: Commercial Triumph, Public Health Tragedy." *Am J Public Health*, Feb. 2009, 99(2):221–227. https://pmc.ncbi.nlm.nih.gov/articles/PMC2622774/.

21. Jane Porter and Hershel Jick, "Addiction Rare in Patients Treated with Narcotics." *NEJM*, Jan 10, 1980, 302:123. https://www.nejm.org/doi/full/10.1056/NEJM198001103020221.

22. "PRESCRIPTION DRUGS: OxyContin Abuse and Diversion and Efforts to Address the Problem." United States General Accounting Office, Report to Congressional Requesters, December 2003. https://www.gao.gov/assets/gao-04-110.pdf.

23 "Understanding the Opioid Overdose Epidemic." CDC Overdose Prevention, June 9, 2025. https://www.cdc.gov/overdose-prevention/about/understanding-the-opioid-overdose-epidemic.html.

24. Holly Hedegaard, Arialdi M. Miniño, Merianne R. Spencer, and Margaret Warner, "*Drug Overdose Deaths in the United States, 1999–2020*," NCHS Data Brief no. 428 (Hyattsville, MD: National Center for Health Statistics, December 2021), https://doi.org/10.15620/cdc:112340.

25. Matteson, CL et al, "Trends and Geographic Patterns in Drug and Synthetic Opioid Overdose Deaths—United States, 2013–2019." *Morbidity and Mortality Weekly Report*, February 12, 201. Vol. 70, No. 6. https://www.cdc.gov/mmwr/volumes/70/wr/pdfs/mm7006a4-H.pdf.

NOTES

26. Ashton M. Verdery et al., "Deaths of Despair and the Long Reach of Grief in the United States," *Proceedings of the National Academy of Sciences of the United States of America* 115, no. 28 (July 10, 2018): E6291–E6300, https://doi.org/10.1073/pnas.1801663115.

27. Romanowicz, M., et al., "The effects of parental opioid use on the parent–child relationship and children's developmental and behavioral outcomes: a systematic review of published reports." *Child and Adolescent Psychiatry and Mental Health. January 12, 2019. https://capmh.biomedcentral.com/articles/10.1186/s13034-019-0266-3.*

28. Mardani M, Alipour F, Rafiey H, Fallahi-Khoshknab M, Arshi M. Challenges in addiction-affected families: a systematic review of qualitative studies. BMC Psychiatry. 2023 Jun 16;23(1):439. doi: 10.1186/s12888-023-04927-1. PMID: 37328763; PMCID: PMC10273571.

29. "Affordable Care Act." Ballotpedia, accessed July 22, 2025. https://ballotpedia.org/Affordable_Care_Act.

30. "Park III: Administrative, Procedural, and Miscellaneous." IRS. 26 CFR 601.602: Tax forms and instructions, Rev. Proc. 2023-23, accessed July 22, 2025. https://www.irs.gov/pub/irs-drop/rp-23-23.pdf.

31. Alnijadi AA, Li M, Wu J, Xiong X, Lu ZK. Trend and effects of high-deductible health insurance plans in the health care system: financial access problems in management of cognitive impairment. J Manag Care Spec Pharm. 2022 Jan;28(1):7-15. doi: 10.18553/jmcp.2022.28.1.07. PMID: 34949113; PMCID: PMC10372991.

32. "Understanding consumer preferences can help capture value in the individual market." McKinsey & Company, October 1, 2016. https://www.mckinsey.com/industries/healthcare/our-insights/understanding-consumer-preferences-can-help-capture-value-in-the-individual-market.

33. Cooper, Z. et al., "Out-Of-Network Billing And Negotiated Payments For Hospital-Based Physicians. Health Affairs, December 16, 2019, Vol. 39, No. 1., https://www.healthaffairs.org/doi/10.1377/hlthaff.2019.00507.

34. Bernstein, DN, Jonathan R. Crowe, "Price Transparency in United States' Health Care: A Narrative Policy Review of the Current State and Way Forward." *Inquiry*, May 26, 2024, 61:00469580241255823. https://pmc.ncbi.nlm.nih.gov/articles/PMC11129567/.

35. Watson, KB., et al., "Trends in Multiple Chronic Conditions Among US Adults, By Life Stage, Behavioral Risk Factor Surveillance System, 2013–2023." CDC, Preventing Chronic Disease, April 176, 2025. Volume 22. https://www.cdc.gov/pcd/issues/2025/24_0539.htm.

36. Watson, KB., et al., "Trends in Multiple Chronic Conditions Among US Adults, By Life Stage, Behavioral Risk Factor Surveillance System, 2013–2023." CDC, Preventing Chronic Disease, April 176, 2025. Volume 22. https://www.cdc.gov/pcd/issues/2025/24_0539.htm.

37. Erdem, E. et al., "Medicare Payments: How Much Do Chronic Conditions Matter?" Medicare Medicaid Res Rev., June 18, 2013, 3(2):mmrr.003.02.b02. https://pmc.ncbi.nlm.nih.gov/articles/PMC3983726/.

38. "Fast Facts: Health and Economic Costs of Chronic Conditions." CDC Chronic Disease, July 12, 2014. https://www.cdc.gov/chronic-disease/data-research/facts-stats/index.html.

39. Gollust, SE., et al., "The Emergence of COVID-19 COVI-19-19 in the US: A Public Health and Political Communication Crisis." *J Health Polit Policy Law*, Dec. 1, 2020, 45(6):967-981. https://pubmed.ncbi.nlm.nih.gov/32464658/.

40. Kamran Abbasi, "COVID-19 COVI-19-19: politicisation, "corruption," and suppression of science." *BMJ*, November 13, 2020. 2020;371:m4425. https://www.bmj.com/content/371/bmj.m4425.

41. "Health Disparities: Provisional Death Counts for COVID-19 COVI-19-19." CDC. Accessed July 22, 2025. https://www.cdc.gov/nchs/nvss/vsrr/COVID-19 COVI-1919/health_disparities.htm.

42. Gollwitzer, A. et al., "Partisan differences in physical distancing are linked to health outcomes during the COVID-19 COVI-19-19 pandemic." *Nat Hum Behav.*, Nov. 4, 2020, (11):1186-1197. https://pubmed.ncbi.nlm.nih.gov/33139897/.

43. Casey Ross and Bob Herman. "UnitedHealth pushed employees to follow an algorithm to cut off Medicare patients' rehab care." *STAT News*, Nov. 14, 2023. https://www.statnews.com/2023/11/14/unitedhealth-algorithm-medicare-advantage-investigation/.

44. Ratwani RM, Sutton K, Galarraga JE. Addressing AI Algorithmic Bias in Health Care. *JAMA*.2024;332(13):1051–1052. doi:10.1001/jama.2024.13486.

45. "The Big Tech in Healthcare Report: How Amazon, Google, Microsoft, Apple & Oracle are fighting for the $11T Market." CBInsights, accessed July 22, 2025. https://runwise.co/wp-content/uploads/2023/08/CB-Insights_Big-Tech-In-Healthcare-2022-1.pdf.

46. Obermeyer, Z., et al., "Dissecting racial bias in an algorithm used to manage the health of populations." *Science*, Oct. 25, 2019. Vol 366, Issue 6464. https://www.science.org/doi/10.1126/science.aax2342.

47. Garrett Hardin, "The Tragedy of the Commons," Science 162, no. 3859 (1968): 1243-1248. DOI: 10.1126/science.162.3859.124.

48. Elinor Ostrom, Governing the Commons: The Evolution of Institutions for Collective Action (Cambridge: Cambridge University Press, 1990.

49. Elinor Ostrom, "Beyond Markets and States: Polycentric Governance of Complex Economic Systems,: American Economic Review 100, no 3. (2010):641-672.

50. French, Eric B., et al, "End-of-Life Medical Spending in Last Twelve Months of Life Is Lower Than Previously Reported," *Health Affairs,* July 2017, Vol. 36, No.7:1211-1217. https://www.healthaffairs.org/doi/10.1377/hlthaff.2017.0174.

51. "Physicians Spend About 16 Minutes on EHRs Per Patient Visit." *ASH Clinical News*, 2020. https://ashpublications.org/ashclinicalnews/news/4924/Physicians-Spend-About-16-Minutes-on-EHRs-Per.

52. "Some Medicare Advantage Organization Denials of Prior Authorization Requests Raise Concerns About Beneficiary Access to Medically Necessary Care," OEI-09-18-00260. U.S. Department of Health and Human Services, Office of Inspector General, April 27, 2022. https://oig.hhs.gov/reports/all/2022/some-medicare-advantage-organization-denials-of-prior-authorization-requests-raise-concerns-about-beneficiary-access-to-medically-necessary-care/.

53. Himmelstein David U. Robert M. Lawless, Deborah Thorne, Pamela Foohey, and Steffie Woolhandler, "Medical Bankruptcy: Still Common Despite the Affordable Care Act." *Am J Public Health*, 2019 Mar;109(3):431-433. https://pmc.ncbi.nlm.nih.gov/articles/PMC6366487/. https://files.consumerfinance.gov/f/201412_cfpb_reports_consumer-credit-medical-and-non-medical-collections.pdf.

54. Liz Hamel, Mira Norton, Karen Pollitz, Larry Levitt, Gary Claxton, and Mollyann Brodie, "The Burden of Medical Debt: Results from the Kaiser Family Foundation/New York Times Medical Bills Survey." Kaiser Family Foundation, January 5, 2016. https://www.kff.org/health-costs/report/the-burden-of-medical-debt-results-from-the-kaiser-family-foundationnew-york-times-medical-bills-survey/view/print/.

55. "Private Health Plans: Comparison of Employer-Sponsored Plans to Healthcare.gov Marketplace Plans." GAO-25-106798, U.S. Government Accountability Office, November 27, 2024. https://www.gao.gov/products/gao-25-106798.

56. Michael Chernew, Harrison Mintz, "Administrative Expenses in the US Health Care System: Why So High?" *JAMA* 326, no. 17 (November 2, 2021): 1701–1702, https://jamanetwork.com/journals/jama/fullarticle/2785479.

57. Woolhandler, Steffie, Terry Campbell, and David U. Himmelstein. "Costs of Health Care Administration in the United States and Canada." *New England Journal of Medicine* 349, no. 8 (August 21, 2003): 768–775. https://doi.org/10.1056/NEJMsa022033.

58. Himmelstein, David U., Miraya Jun, Reinhard Busse, et. al. "A Comparison of Hospital Administrative Costs in Eight Nations: US Costs Exceed All Others by Far." *Health Affairs* 33, no. 9 (September 2014): 1586–1594. https://doi.org/10.1377/hlthaff.2013.1327.

59. Kaiser Family Foundation 2023 Employer Health Benefits Survey. https://www.kff.org/health-costs/2023-employer-health-benefits-survey/?utm_source=chatgpt.com.

60. Trinh, Hahn Q, James W. Begun, Roice D. Luke, "Hospital service duplication: evidence on the medical arms race." *Health Care Manage Rev*. 2008 Jul-Sep;33(3):192-202. doi: 10.1097/01.HMR.0000324903.19272.0c. PMID: 18580299. https://pubmed.ncbi.nlm.nih.gov/18580299/.

61. "The Role Of Clinical Waste In Excess US Health Spending." *Health Affairs Research Brief*, June 9, 2022. 10.1377/hpb20220506.432025. https://www.healthaffairs.org/content/briefs/role-clinical-waste-excess-us-health-spending.

62. Kozhimannil KB, Hung P, Henning-Smith C, Casey MM, Prasad S. Association Between Loss of Hospital-Based Obstetric Services and Birth Outcomes in Rural Counties in the United States. JAMA. 2018 Mar 27;319(12):1239-1247. doi: 10.1001/jama.2018.1830. PMID: 29522161; PMCID: PMC5885848.

63. Hailey Waldman, Alexandra Zimmerman, "Maternal health in rural America." National Rural Health Association White Paper, February 2024. https://www.ruralhealth.us/nationalruralhealth/media/documents/maternal-health-in-rural-america-white-paper-final-%281%29.pdf.

64. "2025 rural health state of the state." Chartis. Accessed July 18, 2025. https://www.chartis.com/sites/default/files/documents/CCRH%20WP%20-%202025%20Rural%20health%20state%20of%20the%20state_021125.pdf.

65. Eileen Appelbaum and Rosemary Batt, "Private Equity Buyouts in Healthcare: Who Wins, Who Loses?" Working Paper No. 118, Institute for New Economic Thinking, March 15, 2020. https://www.ineteconomics.org/research/research-papers/private-equity-buyouts-in-healthcare-who-wins-who-loses.

66. Barber MJ, Gotham D, Khwairakpam G, Hill A. Price of a hepatitis C cure: Cost of production and current prices for direct-acting antivirals in 50 countries. J Virus Erad. 2020 Jun 18;6(3):100001. doi: 10.1016/j.jve.2020.06.001. PMID: 33251019; PMCID: PMC7646676.

67. Elizabeth Seeley, "The Impact of Pharmaceutical Wholesalers on U.S. Drug Spending." The Commonwealth Fund, July 20, 2022. https://www.commonwealthfund.org/publications/issue-briefs/2022/jul/impact-pharmaceutical-wholesalers-drug-spending.

68. Schpero, W., Thomas Wiener, Samuel Carter, Paula Chatterjee, "Lobbying Expenditures in the US Health Care Sector, 2000-2020." JAMA Health Forum. October 7, 2022. 3(10):e223801. https://pubmed.ncbi.nlm.nih.gov/36306120/.

69. "Debt Collection Practices (Regulation F); Deceptive and Unfair Collection of Medical Debt," Consumer Financial Protection Bureau FR Document No. 2024-22962, 89 FR 80715–24, October 4, 2024. https://www.federalregister.gov/documents/2024/10/04/2024-22962/debt-collection-practices-regulation-f-deceptive-and-unfair-collection-of-medical-debt.

70. Crespin, Daniel, Michael Dworsky, Jonathan Levin, Teague Ruder, and Christopher M Whaley, "Upcoding Linked To Up To Two-Thirds Of Growth In Highest-Intensity Hospital Discharges in 5 States, 2011-19," *Health Affairs*, December 2024. https://www.healthaffairs.org/doi/10.1377/hlthaff.2024.00596.

71. Steve Straub, "The American Medical Association Has a Dirty Little Government Mandated Secret." TFPP Wire, April 17, 2025. https://tfppwire.com/ama-dirty-little-secret/.

72. Roger Collier, "American Medical Association membership woes continue." *CMAJ*, Aug. 9, 2011. 83(11): E713–E714. https://pmc.ncbi.nlm.nih.gov/articles/PMC3153537/.

73. "Billing and Coding Guide." NASTAD, October 2023. https://nastad.org/sites/default/files/2023-10/PDF-HIV-Prevention-BillingAndCoding-101223.pdf.

74. Wendy Warring. "Integrating Behavioral Health in Primary Care: Overcoming Decades of Challenges." *Health Affairs* May 17, 2021. https://www.healthaffairs.org/content/forefront/integrating-behavioral-health-primary-care-overcoming-decades-challenges.

75. National Academies of Sciences, Engineering, and Medicine, *Pain Management and the Opioid Epidemic: Balancing Societal and Individual Benefits and Risks of Prescription Opioid Use.* (National Academies Press, 2017), page 13. https://nap.nationalacademies.org/catalog/24781/pain-management-and-the-opioid-epidemic-balancing-societal-and-individual, page 12.

76. Lee MJ, "On Patient Safety: How Well Do We Police Ourselves?" Clin Orthop Relat Res. 2015 May;473(5):1552-4. https://pmc.ncbi.nlm.nih.gov/articles/PMC4385382/.

77. Roy V, Victor Amana, Joseph S. Ross, Cary P. Gross, "Shareholder Payouts Among Large Publicly Traded Health Care Companies." *JAMA Intern Med.* April 1, 2025;185(4):466-468. doi: 10.1001/jamainternmed.2024.7687. PMID: 39928316; PMCID: PMC11811864. https://pubmed.ncbi.nlm.nih.gov/39928316/.

78. Marshall, B. and Paul Adams, "*Helicobacter pylori*: A Nobel pursuit?" *Can J Gastroenterol.* Nov 2008. 22(11):895–896. https://pmc.ncbi.nlm.nih.gov/articles/PMC2661189/.

79. https://compliance.ama-assn.org/hc/en-us/articles/16197630737431-Internal-End-User-License-Agreement-Royalty-Rates-for-2026-and-2027.

80. Anderson, J. and Kathleen Abrahamson, "Your Health Care May Kill You: Medical Errors." *Stud Health Technol Inform*, 2017:234:13-17. https://pubmed.ncbi.nlm.nih.gov/28186008/.

81. Wu, Dekai. *Raising AI: An Essential Guide to Parenting Our Future* (The MIT Press, 2025). https://mitpress.mit.edu/9780262049764/raising-ai/.

82. Wallis, K., "No-fault, no difference: no-fault compensation for medical injury and healthcare ethics and practice." Br J Gen Pract, Jan 2017, 67(654):38–39. https://pmc.ncbi.nlm.nih.gov/articles/PMC5198606/.

83. Welling, M, Annika Takala, "Patterns of malpractice claims and compensation after surgical procedures: a retrospective analysis of 8,901 claims from the Finnish patient insurance registry." *Patient Safety in Surgery*, February 10, 2023. https://pssjournal.biomedcentral.com/articles/10.1186/s13037-023-00353-0.

84. "Milestones in U.S. Food and Drug Law." FDA, January 30, 2023. https://www.fda.gov/about-fda/fda-history/milestones-us-food-and-drug-law.

85. https://www.cdc.gov/nchs/data/databriefs/db508.pdf.

86. Laurie Ricciuto et al. Sources of added Sugars Intake Among the US Population: Analysis of Selected Sociodemographic Factors Using the National Health and Nutrition Examination Survey 2011-2018.Front. Nutr.,16 June 2021 Https://doi.org/10.3389/fnut.2021.687643.

87. https://www.who.int/docs/default-source/documents/replace-transfats/replace-action-package.pdf.

88. https://www.ams.usda.gov/press-release/usda-releases-2023-pesticide-data-program-annual-summary.

89. Emmerich, S., et al., CDC National Center for Health Statistics, NCHS Data Brief No. 508, September 2024. "Obesity and Severe Obesity Prevalence in Adults: United States, August 2021–August 2023."

90. Monteiro et al. MBJ, 2023; Martinez Steele et al. BMI Open, 2016.

91. Boyd A. Swinburn et al. The global obesity pandemic: shaped by global drivers and local environments. Obesity. Volume 378, Issue 9793P804-814, 2011.

92. Theilade S, Christensen MB, Vilsbøll T, Knop FK. An overview of obesity mechanisms in humans: Endocrine regulation of food intake, eating behaviour and common determinants of body weight. Diabetes Obes Metab. 2021 Feb;23 Suppl 1:17-35. doi: 10.1111/dom.14270. PMID: 33621414.

93. Yao Z, Tchang BG, Chae K, Albert M, Clark JM, Blaha MJ. Adverse effects of obesity on overall health, quality of life, and related physical health metrics: A cross-sectional and longitudinal study from the All of Us Research Program. J Intern Med. 2025 Jun;297(6):657-671. doi: 10.1111/joim.20083. Epub 2025 May 5. PMID: 40325914.

94. Pories WJ, Swanson MS, MacDonald KG, Long SB, Morris PG, Brown BM, Barakat HA, deRamon RA, Israel G, Dolezal JM, et al. Who would have thought it? An operation proves to be the most effective therapy for adult-onset diabetes mellitus. Ann Surg. 1995 Sep;222(3):339-50; discussion 350-2. doi: 10.1097/00000658-199509000-00011. PMID: 7677463; PMCID: PMC1234815.

95. Gasoyan, H. et al., "Reasons for Underutilization of Bariatric Surgery: The Role of Insurance Benefit Design." *Surg Obes Relat Dis.*, October 13, 2018, 15(1):146–151. https://pmc.ncbi.nlm.nih.gov/articles/PMC6441615/.

96. Nauck MA, Quast DR, Wefers J, Meier JJ. GLP-1 receptor agonists in the treatment of type 2 diabetes - state-of-the-art. Mol Metab. 2021 Apr; 46:101102. doi: 10.1016/j.molmet.2020.101102. Epub 2020 Oct 14. PMID: 33068776; PMCID: PMC8085572.

97. https://www.kff.org/health-costs/poll-finding/kff-health-tracking-poll-may-2024-the-publics-use-and-views-of-glp-1-drugs/.

98. https://icer.org/wp-content/uploads/2025/04/Affordable-Access-to-GLP-1-Obesity-Medications-_-ICER-White-Paper-_-04.09.2025.pdf.

99. https://www.goodrx.com/classes/glp-1-agonists/glp-1-drugs-cost-and-savings.

100. "Shifting the Paradigm for Health Care—Bending the Cost Curve: Understand the GLP-1 ERA." The Milken Institute 2025 Global Conference—Toward a Flourishing Future. Accessed July 22, 2025. https://milkeninstitute.org/sites/default/files/2025-05/shifting-paradigm-health-care-bending-cost-curve-glp-1-era_Transcript_GC25.pdf.

101. Anne B Martin et al. Health Affairs 44, No. 1 (2020):12-22 DO.

102. "Trends in health care spending." AMA, April 17, 2025. https://www.ama-assn.org/about/ama-research/trends-health-care-spending.

103. https://www.healthsystemtracker.org/chart-collection/health-spending-u-s-compare-countries.

104. "Guidance for Industry: Notification of a Health Claim or Nutrient Content Claim Based on an Authoritative Statement of a Scientific Body." U.S. Food and Drug Administration, FDA-1998-D-0102, June 1998. https://www.fda.gov/regulatory-information/search-fda-guidance-documents/guidance-industry-notification-health-claim-or-nutrient-content-claim-based-authoritative-statement.

105. Turing, AM, "Computing Machinery And Intelligence." *Mind,* 1950, 49: 433-460, https://courses.cs.umbc.edu/471/papers/turing.pdf.

106. Nillson, N. "Shakey The Robot." Technical Note 323, SRI International, April 1984. https://www.sri.com/wp-content/uploads/2021/12/629.pdf.

107. Hendler, J. "Avoiding Another AI Winter." IEEE Intelligent Systems, March 1, 2008, Vol. 23 Issue 2. https://dl.acm.org/doi/10.1109/MIS.2008.20.

108. Campbell, M. et al, "Deep Blue." Artificial Intelligence, January 2002, Vol. 134, Issues 1-2. https://www.sciencedirect.com/science/article/pii/S0004370201001291.

109. Silver, D. et al., "Mastering the game of Go without human knowledge." Nature, October 19, 2017, 550, pages354–359. https://www.nature.com/articles/nature24270.

110. Stiff, A., Maarten Fornerod, Bailee N. Kain, et. al. "Multiomic profiling identifies predictors of survival in African American patients with acute myeloid leukemia." *Nat Genet* 56, 2434–2446 (2024). https://doi.org/10.1038/s41588-024-01929-x.

111. "Physicians Spend About 16 Minutes on EHRs Per Patient Visit." *ASH Clinical News*, 2020. https://ashpublications.org/ashclinicalnews/news/4924/Physicians-Spend-About-16-Minutes-on-EHRs-Per.

112. Anindya Ghose, Xitong Guo, Beibei Li, and Yuanyuan Dang, "Empowering Patients Using Smart Mobile Health Platforms: Evidence from a Randomized Field Experiment." *arXiv*, February 17, 2021. https://arxiv.org/abs/2102.05506.

113. Makery, M. et al., "Medical error—the third leading cause of death in the US." *BMJ*, May 3, 2016, 353:i2139. https://www.bmj.com/content/353/bmj.i2139.full.

114 James, John T. "A New, Evidence-based Estimate of Patient Harms Associated with Hospital Care." *Journal of Patient Safety* 9, no. 3 (September 2013): 122–28. https://doi.org/10.1097/PTS.0b013e3182948a69.

115. https://www.cdc.gov/medication-safety/data-research/facts-stats/index.html.

116. Watanabe, Jonathan H., Terry McInnis, and Jan D. Hirsch. "Cost of Prescription Drug-Related Morbidity and Mortality." *The Annals of Pharmacotherapy* 2018 Sep;52(9):829-837. https://pubmed.ncbi.nlm.nih.gov/29577766/.

117. Dunnenberger, Henry M., et al. "Preemptive Clinical Pharmacogenetics Implementation: Current Programs in Five US Medical Centers." *Annual Review of Pharmacology and Toxicology* 55 (2015): 89–106. https://doi.org/10.1146/annurev-pharmtox-010814-124835. https://www.nature.com/articles/s41397-024-00326-1.

118 Chenchula, S., Atal, S. Uppugunduri, C.R.S. "A review of real-world evidence on preemptive pharmacogenomic testing for preventing adverse drug reactions: a reality for future health care." *Pharmacogenomics J* 24,9(2024). https://doi.org/10.1038/s41397-024-00326-1.

119. Mary Beth Nierengarten, "Cancer Statistics, 2024, Deaths drop, incidences increase, prevention needed." *Cancer*, May 17, 2024, https://acsjournals.onlinelibrary.wiley.com/doi/full/10.1002/cncr.35347.

120. "Cancer Stat Facts: Cancer of Any Site." National Cancer Institute, accessed July 15, 2025, https://seer.cancer.gov/statfacts/html/all.html.

121. Yana Puckett and Karen Garfield, *Pancreatic Cancer*. (STATPearls, September 10, 2024). https://www.ncbi.nlm.nih.gov/books/NBK518996/.

122. "Cancer Stat Facts: Ovarian Cancer." National Cancer Institute, accessed July 15, 2025, https://seer.cancer.gov/statfacts/html/ovary.html.

123. "Breast Cancer Facts & Figures 2019-2020." American Cancer Society, 2019. https://www.cancer.org/content/dam/cancer-org/research/cancer-facts-and-statistics/breast-cancer-facts-and-figures/breast-cancer-facts-and-figures-2019-2020.pdf.

124. "Cancer Stat Facts: Lung and Bronchus Cancer." National Cancer Institute, accessed July 15, 2025, https://seer.cancer.gov/statfacts/html/lungb.html.

125. "Cancer Stat Facts: Cervical Cancer." National Cancer Institute, accessed July 15, 2025, https://seer.cancer.gov/statfacts/html/cervix.html.

126. "Cancer Stat Facts: Cervical Cancer." National Cancer Institute, accessed July 15, 2025, https://seer.cancer.gov/statfacts/html/cervix.html.

127. "Cancer Stat Facts: Lung and Bronchus Cancer." National Cancer Institute, accessed July 15, 2025, https://seer.cancer.gov/statfacts/html/lungb.html.

128. "Cancer Stat Facts: Colorectal Cancer." National Cancer Institute, accessed July 21, 2025, https://seer.cancer.gov/statfacts/html/colorect.html.

129. "Colorectal Cancer Statistics." Centers for Disease Control and Prevention, accessed July 15, 2025, https://www.cdc.gov/colorectal-cancer/statistics/index.html.

130. Bussetty, Arvind, Jing Shen and Petros Benias, "Incidence of Pancreas and Colorectal Adenocarcinoma in the US." *JAMA Network Open*, April 2025. https://jamanetwork.com/journals/jamanetworkopen/fullarticle/2832755.

131. Arana-Aari, E. et al, "Screening colonoscopy and risk of adverse events among individuals undergoing fecal immunochemical testing in a population-based program: A nested case-control study." United European Gastroenterol J, 2018 Jan 24;6(5):755–764. doi: 10.1177/205064061875610. https://pmc.ncbi.nlm.nih.gov/articles/PMC6068784/.

132. Sana Khan and Patricia Pinto-Garcia, "How Much Does a Colonoscopy Cost?" GoodRx, September 27, 2023. https://www.goodrx.com/conditions/colon-cancer/colonoscopy-cost.

133. Than, M. et al., "Diagnostic miss rate for colorectal cancer: an audit." *Ann Gastroenterol*, Jan-Mar 201, 28(1):94–98. https://pmc.ncbi.nlm.nih.gov/articles/PMC4290010/.

134. Chung, DC, et al, "A Cell-free DNA Blood-Based Test for Colorectal Cancer Screening," N Engl J Med 2024;390:973-983, DOI: 10.1056/NEJMoa2304714. https://www.nejm.org/doi/10.1056/NEJMoa230471.

135. "National Comprehensive Cancer Network (NCCN) Updates Colorectal Cancer Screening Guidelines to Include Shield Blood-Based Screening," Guardant, June 2, 2025. https://investors.guardanthealth.com/press-releases/press-releases/2025/National-Comprehensive-Cancer-Network-NCCN-Updates-Colorectal-Cancer-Screening-Guidelines-to-Include-Shield-Blood-Based-Screening/default.aspx.

136. "Screening for Colorectal Cancer - Blood-Based Biomarker Tests," CMS, accessed July 21, 2025, CAG-00454N.

137. Tang, W. et al "The promise of mRNA vaccines in cancer treatment: Technology, innovations, applications, and future directions." *Critical Reviews in Oncology/ Hematology*, August 2025, https://doi.org/10.1016/j.critrevonc.2025.104772.

138. Rojas, LA et al. "Personalized RNA neoantigen vaccines stimulate T cells in pancreatic cancer." *Nature*, May 10, 2023, 618, pages144–150 (2023). https://www.nature.com/articles/s41586-023-06063-y.

139. National Breast Cancer Foundation, "Breast Cancer Facts & Stats," June 21, 2025, https://www.nationalbreastcancer.org/breast-cancer-facts/.

140. National Breast Cancer Foundation, *Breast Cancer Facts & Stats*. https://www.nationalbreastcancer.org/breast-cancer-facts/.

141. Nancy Lapid, "Health Rounds: Roche/BioNTech experimental vaccine shows early promise in pancreatic cancer." *Reuters*, March 5, 2025. https://www.reuters.com/business/healthcare-pharmaceuticals/health-rounds-rochebiontech-experimental-vaccine-shows-early-promise-pancreatic-2025-03-05/.

142. Rojas, LA et al. "Personalized RNA neoantigen vaccines stimulate T cells in pancreatic cancer." *Nature*, May 10, 2023, 618, pages144–150 (2023). https://www.nature.com/articles/s41586-023-06063-y.

143. Kantoff, Philip W., et al. "Sipuleucel-T Immunotherapy for Castration-Resistant Prostate Cancer." *New England Journal of Medicine* 363, no. 5 (2010): 411–422. https://doi.org/10.1056/NEJMoa1001294.

144. Lassoued, W., et al. "Programmed death-1 inhibition increases vaccine-induced T-cell infiltration in patients with prostate cancer." *J Immunother Cancer*, June 22, 2025, 13(6):e010851. https://pmc.ncbi.nlm.nih.gov/articles/PMC12184344/.

145. Parsons, JK et al, "A Randomized, Double-blind, Phase II Trial of PSA-TRICOM (PROSTVAC) in Patients with Localized Prostate Cancer: The Immunotherapy to Prevent Progression on Active Surveillance Study." *Eur Urol Focus*, 2018 Sep;4(5):636-638. doi: 10.1016/j.euf.2018.08.016. https://pubmed.ncbi.nlm.nih.gov/30197041/.

146. Melissa Rohman, "Active Surveillance of Prostate Cancer On the Rise." *Feinberg School of Medicine News Center*, December 20, 2024, https://news.feinberg.northwestern.edu/2024/12/20/active-surveillance-of-prostate-cancer-on-the-rise/.

147. Carmen Phillips, "Active Surveillance for Low-Risk Prostate Cancer Continues to Rise." *Cancer Currents Blog*, National Cancer Institute, June 23, 2022, https://www.cancer.gov/news-events/cancer-currents-blog/2022/prostate-cancer-active-surveillance-increasing.

148. Muaddi H. et al, "The evolving use of robotic surgery: a population-based analysis." Surgical Endoscopy, October 17, 2022, Volume 37, pages 1870–1877, (2023). https://link.springer.com/article/10.1007/s00464-022-09643-7.

149. Woodard, Colin. *American Nations: A History of the Eleven Rival Regional Cultures of North America* Viking, 2011.

150. Bohn, Sarah and Jenny Duan, "California's Economy." Public Policy Institute of California, accessed July 21, 2025. https://www.ppic.org/publication/californias-economy/.

151. "Bachelor's Degree or Higher by State." Federal Reserve Bank of St. Louis, 2023 data. Accessed July 23, 2025. https://fred.stlouisfed.org/series/GCT1502MA.

152. "Which states are the most educated?" USA Facts, May 14, 2023. https://usafacts.org/articles/which-states-are-the-most-educated/.

153. "Where are the largest immigrant communities in the US?" USA Facts, January 4, 2025. https://usafacts.org/articles/where-are-the-largest-immigrant-communities-in-the-us/.

154. "Which states have the highest and lowest life expectancy?" USA Facts, March 27, 2025. https://usafacts.org/articles/which-states-have-highest-and-lowest-life-expectancy/.

155. "Hospital telehealth adoption by state." Definitive Healthcare, February 12, 2024. https://www.definitivehc.com/resources/healthcare-insights/hospital-telehealth-adoption-by-state.

156. "GDP by State." Bureau of Economic Analysis, accessed July 23, 2025. https://www.bea.gov/data/gdp/gdp-state.

157. "Bachelor's Degree or Higher by State." Federal Reserve Bank of St. Louis, 2023 data. Accessed July 23, 2025. https://fred.stlouisfed.org/series/GCT1502IL.

158. "Bachelor's Degree or Higher by State." Federal Reserve Bank of St. Louis, 2023 data. Accessed July 23, 2025. https://fred.stlouisfed.org/series/GCT1502PA.

159. "Where are the largest immigrant communities in the US?" USA Facts, January 4, 2025. https://usafacts.org/articles/where-are-the-largest-immigrant-communities-in-the-us/.

160. "Which states have the highest and lowest life expectancy?" USA Facts, March 27, 2025. https://usafacts.org/articles/which-states-have-highest-and-lowest-life-expectancy/.

161. "Hospital telehealth adoption by state." Definitive Healthcare, February 12, 2024. https://www.definitivehc.com/resources/healthcare-insights/hospital-telehealth-adoption-by-state.

162. "Per person state public health funding." State Health Compare. Data from 2023. Accessed July 23, 2025. https://bit.ly/3IYej7f.

163. https://statehealthcompare.shadac.org/rank/117/per-person-state-public-health-funding#2,3,4,5,6,7,8,9,10,11,12,13,14,15,16,17,18,19,20,21,22,23,24,25,26,27,28,29,30,31,32,33,34,35,36,37,38,39,40,41,42,43,44,45,46,47,48,49,50,51,52/a/76/154/false/location.

164. "Nebraska, Key Health Indicators," CDC, accessed July 21, 2025. https://www.cdc.gov/nchs/pressroom/states/nebraska/ne.htm.

165. "North Dakota, Key Health Indicators," CDC, accessed July 21, 2025. https://www.cdc.gov/nchs/pressroom/states/northdakota/nd.htm.

166. Shabnam Shenasi Azari, Virginia Jenkins, Joyce Hahn, and Lauren Medina, "The Foreign-Born Population in the United States: 2022." United States Census Bureau, April 2024, ACSBR-019. https://www2.census.gov/library/publications/2024/demo/acsbr-019.pdf.

167. "Hospital telehealth adoption by state." Definitive Healthcare, February 12, 2024. https://www.definitivehc.com/resources/healthcare-insights/hospital-telehealth-adoption-by-state.

168. "Texas Leads Nation With Fastest Economic Expansion." Office of the Texas Governor, March 31, 2023. https://gov.texas.gov/news/post/texas-leads-nation-with-fastest-economic-expansion.

169. "County Population Totals and Components of Change: 2020-2024—Annual Estimates of the Resident Population for Counties: April 1, 2020, to July 1, 2024 (CO-EST2024-POP)," United States Census Bureau, March 2025. https://www.census.gov/data/tables/time-series/demo/popest/2020s-counties-total.html.

170. "Which states have the highest and lowest life expectancy?" USA Facts, March 27, 2025. https://usafacts.org/articles/which-states-have-highest-and-lowest-life-expectancy/.

171. "Hospital telehealth adoption by state." Definitive Healthcare, February 12, 2024. https://www.definitivehc.com/resources/healthcare-insights/hospital-telehealth-adoption-by-state.

172. "Per person state public health funding." State Health Compare. Data from 2023. Accessed July 23, 2025. https://bit.ly/3IYej7f.

173. Hollie Silverman, "Navajo Nation vaccinates more than half of its adult population, outpacing US national rate." *CNN*, April 26, 2021. https://www.cnn.com/2021/04/26/us/navajo-nation-vaccination-rate.

174 Natalie Gubbay and H. Trostle, "The geographic divide in Native incomes and earnings." Federal Reserve Bank of Minneapolis, November 13, 2023. https://www.minneapolisfed.org/article/2023/the-geographic-divide-in-native-incomes-and-earnings.

175. "Reports to Congress on the Social and Economic Conditions of Native Americans FY 2020"Impact of COVID-19 COVI-19-19 on Native Americans with Selected HHS Programs Response' https://www.govinfo.gov/content/pkg/CMR-HE25-00190785/pdf/CMR-HE25-00190785.pdf.

176. Joseph Friedman, Helena Hansen, Joseph P Gone, Deaths of despair and Indigenous data genocide, The Lancet, Volume 401, Issue 10379,2023, Pages 874-876, ISSN 0140-6736, https://doi.org/10.1016/S0140-6736(22)02404-7.

177. Davis, J. A., & Otterstrom, S. M. (1996). Constraints to the Growth of Native American Gaming. *UNLV Gaming Research & Review Journal, 3*(2). Retrieved from https://oasis.library.unlv.edu/grrj/vol3/iss2/5 DOI: https://doi.org/10.9741/2327-8455.1222.

178. Shaina Elizabeth Philpot, "American Indian Students' Sense of Belonging at Predominantly White Institutions and Tribal Colleges and Universities." *Journal of American Indian Higher Education*, April 25, 2024. https://tribalcollegejournal.org/american-indian-students-sense-of-belonging-at-predominantly-white-institutions-and-tribal-colleges-and-universities/.

179. "How many immigrants are in the United States?" USA Facts, accessed July 23, 2025. https://usafacts.org/answers/how-many-immigrants-are-in-the-us/country/united-states/.

180. Camille Padilla Dalmau, "Universal health care may drive the vote in Puerto Rico." Harvard Public Health, October 23, 2024. https://harvardpublichealth.org/policy-practice/universal-healthcare-may-drive-vote-puerto-rico/.

181. "Alaska." United States Census Bureau, 2023 data. Accessed July 23, 2025. https://data.census.gov/profile/Alaska?g=040XX00US02.

182. "Hawaii." United States Census Bureau, 2023 data. Accessed July 23, 2025. https://data.census.gov/profile/Hawaii?g=040XX00US15.

183. "Hospital telehealth adoption by state." Definitive Healthcare, February 12, 2024. https://www.definitivehc.com/resources/healthcare-insights/hospital-telehealth-adoption-by-state.

184. "Puerto Rico." United States Census Bureau, 2023 data. Accessed July 23, 2025. https://data.census.gov/profile/Puerto_Rico?g=040XX00US72.

185 https://people.duke.edu/~rcd2/Dissertation/References/Tobacco%20Specific/Master%20Settlement%20Agreement/CRSTobMasSetAgrRL30058.pdf.

186 Eric C. Schneider et al, "Mirror, Mirror 2021: Reflecting Poorly—Health Care in the U.S. Compared to Other High-Income Countries." The Commonwealth Fund, August 4, 2021. https://www.commonwealthfund.org/publications/fund-reports/2021/aug/mirror-mirror-2021-reflecting-poorly.

187. "Healthy People 2030: Social Determinants of Health." U.S. Department of Health and Human Services, Office of Disease Prevention and Health Promotion, accessed July 15, 2025, https://odphp.health.gov/healthypeople/priority-areas/social-determinants-health.

188. "Fast Facts: Vision Loss." Centers for Disease Control and Prevention (CDC), May 15, 2024. https://www.cdc.gov/visionhealth/basics/index.html.

189. Chern, A. et al. "The Longitudinal Association of Subclinical Hearing Loss With Cognition in the Health, Aging and Body Composition Study." *Front Aging Neurosci*, March 1, 2022, 13:789515. https://pmc.ncbi.nlm.nih.gov/articles/PMC8923153/.

190. Jilla AM, Carole E. Johnson, Nick Huntington-Klein, "Hearing aid affordability in the United States." *Disabil Rehabil Assist Tech*, April 18, 2023. (3):246-252, https://pubmed.ncbi.nlm.nih.gov/33112178/.

191. U.S. Department of Health and Human Services. *Oral Health in America: Advances and Challenges*. National Institutes of Health, 2021. https://www.nidcr.nih.gov/oralhealthinamerica.

192. Anne K. Driscoll and Brady E. Hamilton, "Effects of Age-specific Fertility Trends on Overall Fertility Trends: United States, 1990–2023." National Vital Statistics Reports. March 6, 2025, Volume 74, Number 3. https://www.cdc.gov/nchs/data/nvsr/nvsr74/nvsr74-3.pdf.

193. Mike Stobbe, "The US infant mortality rate rose last year. The CDC says it's the largest increase in two decades." Associated Press, November 1, 2023. https://apnews.com/article/infant-deaths-us-cdc-mortality-c808796da0415b6ecc0629938421e1b5.

194. "Working Together to Reduce Black Maternal Mortality." CDC Women's Health. April 8, 2024. https://www.cdc.gov/womens-health/features/maternal-mortality.html.

195. "Infant Mortality in Mississippi." America's Health Rankings. Accessed July 22, 2025. https://www.americashealthrankings.org/explore/measures/IMR_MCH/MS.

196. "Infant Mortality in Massachusetts." America's Health Rankings. Accessed July 22, 2025. https://www.americashealthrankings.org/explore/measures/IMR_MCH/MA.

ADDITIONAL WORKS CONSULTED

1. Government & Commission Reports

Gamble, Cindy, JanMarie Ward, and Ashley Olmstead, "Washington State American Indian Health Commission: Maternal Mortality Listening Sessions and Recommendations." Olympia: Washington State Department of Health and American Indian Health Commission, 2023. waportal.org+1doh.wa.gov+1.

Bat-Sheva Stein, et. al., "Maternal Mortality Review Panel Report: Maternal Deaths 2017–2020." Olympia: Washington State Department of Health, 2023. doh.wa.gov+1waportal.org+1.

Northwest Portland Area Indian Health Board. *American Indian & Alaska Native Community Health Profile for Washington State*. Portland: NPAIHB, 2014. washingtonstatestandard.com+10npaihb.org+10old.npaihb.org+10.

2. Scholarly Studies on Tribal & AI/AN Maternal Health

Burns, Ailish, Teresa DeAntley, Susan E. Short, "The maternal health of American Indian and Alaska Native People: a scoping review." *Social Science and Medicine* 27, Soc Sci Med. 2023 Jan;317:115584. doi: 10.1016/j.socscimed.2022.115584. https://pmc.ncbi.nlm.nih.gov/articles/PMC9875554/.

Walkup, John T., et al. "Social Determinants of Health Among American Indians and Alaska Native People: A Community-Based Analysis." *American Journal of Public Health* 112, no. 3 (March 2022): 456–62. DOI:10.2105/AJPH.2021.306402. https://pmc.ncbi.nlm.nih.gov/articles/PMC9875554/.

Carroll, Lauren J., et al. "Pregnancy-Related Deaths Among American Indian or Alaska Native Women in 2020: Data From the CDC Maternal Mortality Review Committee." *JAMA Network Open* 6, no. 5 (May 2024): e243759. DOI:10.1001/jamanetworkopen.2024.3759.

Johnson, Rose M., and Marissa K. Barnett. "Addressing Disparities in the Health of American Indian and Alaska Native Populations." *BMC Health Services Research* 18 (January 2019): 125. DOI:10.1186/s12913-018-3830-3.

3. Tribal & Community-Focused Data Sources

"Resource: Data on Infant and Maternal Health Disparities in Native Communities." National Council of Urban Indian Health, October 13, 2022. https://ncuih.org/2022/10/13/resource-data-on-infant-and-maternal-health-disparities-in-native-communities/.

"Overview: American Indian and Alaska Native Maternal Health." National Council of Urban Indian Health, accessed July 15, 2025. http://ncuih.org/maternal-health/.

"DOH awards funding to strengthen maternal health in Tribal and rural communities." Washington State Department of Health, May 12, 2025. https://doh.wa.gov/newsroom/doh-awards-funding-strengthen-maternal-health-tribal-and-rural-communities.

4. Health Outcomes & Mortality

Patel, Sandeep S., et al. "Official U.S. Records Underestimate Native Americans' Deaths and Life Expectancy: Implications for Health Surveillance." *American Journal of Public Health* 115, no. 1 (January 2025): 103–10. DOI:10.2105/AJPH.2024.307105.

Garcia, Elena R., and Daniel M. Williams. "Addressing Racial Misclassification in American Indian and Alaska Native Mortality Data." *JAMA* 333, no. 23 (June 16, 2025): 1223–25. DOI:10.1001/jama.2025.0823.

Deng, Grace. "Maternal Mortality Rates Rise in WA, Especially for Indigenous Communities." *Washington State Standard*, July 6, 2023. https://washingtonstatestandard.com/briefs/maternal-mortality-rates-rise-in-wa-especially-for-indigenous-communities/.

Branch, Washington State Department of Health. "Transparency in Statewide Maternal Deaths: Pregnancy-Associated Deaths—American Indian/Alaska Native Rate 8.5× Non-Hispanic White." *DOH Maternal Mortality Review Panel*, 2023.

5. Behavioral & Mental Health

Indian Health Service. "Behavioral Health Fact Sheets." Accessed July 16, 2025. https://www.ihs.gov/newsroom/factsheets/behavioralhealth/.

Friedman, Joseph, and Helena Hansen, "Trends in Deaths of Despair by Race and Ethnicity, 1999–2022." *JAMA Psychiatry* 2024;81(7):731–732. doi:10.1001/jamapsychiatry.2024.0303, https://jamanetwork.com/journals/jamapsychiatry/fullarticle/2817597.

6. Policy Context & Historical-Structural Factors

Bose, Devna, Graham Lee Brewer, and Becky Bohrer, "RFK Jr. wants to target chronic disease in US tribes. A key program to do that was gutted." *Associated Press*, April 12, 2025. https://apnews.com/article/healthy-tribes-rfk-chronic-disease-native-american-1b7f0a2da601fb54cd8cfa0a7a3c4b0c.

Theobald, Brianna. "A 1970 Law Led to the Mass Sterilization of Native American Women. That History Still Matters." *Time*, November 27, 2019. Https://time.com/5737080/native-american-sterilization-history/.

About the Author

ROBIN BLACKSTONE, MD, is a physician, innovator, and systems thinker whose career has been defined by leadership and transformation in healthcare. Trained as a surgeon and recognized nationally for her contributions to patient care, she has worked for decades at the intersection of medicine, education, and policy. These experiences gave her an unfiltered view of healthcare systems—their extraordinary capabilities, their entrenched failures, and the crisis of trust now facing both patients and professionals.

Her leadership has spanned clinical, organizational, and policy levels. She has directed surgical programs, chaired professional societies, and contributed to reforms that shaped how care is delivered across the United States. In every role, she has pushed beyond short-term fixes to confront structural forces that undermine healthcare: fragmentation, inequity, weak governance, and corporate capture. Blackstone's perspective is shaped not only by her years in operating rooms and boardrooms but also by her conviction that culture and trust are inseparable from health. She argues that

AI and digital health innovation must be harnessed as tools for equity and empowerment, not as replacements for human judgment.

For her, governance is the hinge between aspiration and reality: technology can empower only if guided by transparent oversight; trust can be rebuilt only if leaders are held accountable. Her debut book, *Doctor AI: Reimagining Healthcare. Rebuilding Trust. Delivering Health 4.0* reflects both the urgency of reform and the depth of her expertise. It distills decades of experience into a bold call for healthcare systems redesign—anchored in culture, guided by trust, and enabled by Health 4.0.

Through her writing, speaking, and leadership, Blackstone continues to champion a future in which healthcare equity, autonomy, and innovation converge—not only in the United States but across the globe—to fulfill the true promise of medicine: comprehensive, trustworthy, and designed for people first.